Non-Suicidal Self-Injury

Grounded in a wellness, strengths-based, and developmental perspective, *Non-Suicidal Self-Injury* is the ideal guide for counselors and other clinicians seeking to understand self-injurious behaviors without pathologizing them. The book covers topics not previously discussed in other works, including working with families, supervising counselors working with clients who self-injure, DSM-5 criteria regarding the NSSI diagnosis, NSSI as a protective factor for preventing suicidal behavior, and advocacy efforts around NSSI. In each chapter clinicians will also find concrete tools, including questions to ask, psychoeducational handouts for clients and their families, treatment handouts or treatment plans for counselors, and more. *Non-Suicidal Self-Injury* also includes real-life voices of individuals who self-injure as well as case vignettes to provide examples of how theoretical models or treatments discussed in this book immediately apply to practice.

Kelly L. Wester, PhD, is a professor of counselor education at the University of North Carolina at Greensboro and a licensed professional counselor with Family Solutions, an outpatient mental health agency. Her counseling and research experience with youth and self-injury includes settings such as residential treatment facilities, correctional facilities, college settings, and community counseling agencies.

Heather C. Trepal, PhD, is a faculty member in the department of counseling at the University of Texas at San Antonio, a licensed professional counselor, and board-approved supervisor. She has served as the president of the Association for Creativity in Counseling, chair of the ACA Graduate Student Committee, and president of both the national and southern regions of the Association for Counselor Education and Supervision.

Non-Suicidal Self-Injury

Wellness Perspectives on Behaviors, Symptoms, and Diagnosis

KELLY L. WESTER AND HEATHER C. TREPAL

Routledge
Taylor & Francis Group
NEW YORK AND LONDON

First published 2017
by Routledge
711 Third Avenue, New York, NY 10017

and by Routledge
2 Park Square, Milton Park, Abingdon, Oxon, OX14 4RN

Routledge is an imprint of the Taylor & Francis Group, an informa business

Library of Congress Cataloging in Publication Data
Names: Wester, Kelly L., author. | Trepal, Heather C., author.
Title: Non-suicidal self-injury : wellness perspectives on behaviors, symptoms, and diagnosis / Kelly L. Wester, Heather C. Trepal.
Description: New York, NY : Routledge, 2017. | Includes bibliographical references and index.
Identifiers: LCCN 2016017190 | ISBN 9781138780354 (hardback : alk. paper) | ISBN 9781138780361 (pbk. : alk. paper) | ISBN 9781315770819 (ebook)
Subjects: MESH: Self-Injurious Behavior | Psychotherapy—methods
Classification: LCC RC480.5 | NLM WM 165 | DDC 616.89/14—dc23
LC record available at https://lccn.loc.gov/2016017190

ISBN: 978-1-138-78035-4 (hbk)
ISBN: 978-1-138-78036-1 (pbk)
ISBN: 978-1-315-77081-9 (ebk)

Typeset in Minion
by Apex CoVantage, LLC

I dedicate this book to my parents, who have always inspired me to go as far as I can go and to follow my dreams; to my husband Nathaniel, who provides support in so many ways; and of course to my clients, who have shown me what it is to be strong and resilient.

—Kelly Wester

To all of my clients and supervisors who shared your experiences with and knowledge of self-injury, this book would not be possible without you. This book is dedicated to Todd. You are loved and missed every day.

—Heather Trepal

Contents

Introduction

Brief Introduction to NSSI

Non-suicidal self-injury (NSSI) is becoming more prevalent and has become a global concern (Lewis & Plener, 2015). NSSI is being engaged in more frequently by youth in primary and secondary school settings, at earlier and earlier ages; it is occurring more frequently in college settings; as well as has been more prevalent in outpatient counseling settings. This is causing an increase in the number of mental health professionals that are requesting and seeking training on NSSI behaviors and interventions, teachers and school staff who seek additional information to implement strategies and policies in their schools, as well as parents who want to know more in order to help their children. As the director of a mental health facility, Barent Walsh (2012) stated that while originally NSSI was primarily a behavior engaged in by individuals who felt negatively toward their bodies, a "newer" group has emerged that self-injures based on the inability to manage stress, cope with aversive emotions, communicate with others, or reconnect to or ground one's physical body. NSSI has been found across all demographics, including males and females, various ethnic and racial groups, and across a wide range of ages and socioeconomic factors. No one individual or demographic is necessarily sheltered from engaging in or being connected to someone who engages in NSSI.

When talking about these behaviors, or seeking consultation, most mental health practitioners, teachers, and parents will refer to "cutting"; however, as you will read in this book, NSSI is so much more than simply cutting behaviors. And there are many inter- and intrapersonal factors to consider when assessing or working with individuals who self-injure. Mental health professionals in various settings have consistently indicated that they feel inadequately prepared to work with clients who engage in NSSI (Trepal & Wester, 2006; 2007). The existence and discussion of NSSI in the media has drastically increased, as well. With instances of NSSI in the media prior to 1990 being rare to non-existent, Whitlock, Purington, and Gershkovich (2009) in a 5-year period during the early 2000s found over 1,700 news stories related to self-injury, and a search on YouTube in 2016 revealed over 136,000 videos on self-injury (which is an increase of 11,000 videos in one year following a similar search conducted in 2015). These findings do not even include what can be found in music or on the Internet in regards to online organizations, social media groups, blogs, and chat rooms. Celebrities such as Angelina Jolie, Demi Lovato, Lindsay Lohan, Colin Farrell, Fiona Apple, and Johnny Depp have talked about their use of self-harm. These behaviors can cause social contagion, which ultimately can increase NSSI engagement. Individuals have indicated that they socially learned about NSSI through peers, social media, movies, and even in health education classes.

Given the continued increase in the behaviors, NSSI was proposed as a distinct diagnosis in the Diagnostic and Statistical Manual 5 (which will be discussed in further detail in Chapter 5). Due to the continued need of mental health practitioners for more information on NSSI, this book was written to provide basic information, as well as clinical interventions, and methods of considering and working with individuals who self-injure on multiple levels (e.g., individual services, family needs, organizational policies and procedures).

Mental health practitioners come in many forms and are members of many professions. What they have in common is that they all work with clients whom they hope to help gain increased functioning in their daily lives. These clients, more than likely, include clients who self-injure. Therefore, self-injury spans across all mental health disciplines, with practitioners treating clients who self-injure in a variety of settings. Mental health professionals include psychiatrists, psychologists, counselors, social workers, and marriage and family therapists, among others. This book will use the terms "mental health practitioner" and "clinician" interchangeably. Additionally, if you are a mental health practitioner who does not refer to individuals you work with as "clients," but instead refer to them as patients or students, or even guests, please know that "clients" is used interchangeably and can refer to any individual whom a clinician is working with who self-injures.

This book is laid out in four major sections: Section I: Non-Suicidal Self-Injury: Basic Information and Considerations illustrates what NSSI is, and what it is not. The first chapter provides definitions, example behaviors and methods, and prevalence and population considerations. The second chapter focuses on various models and theoretical frameworks that have been created to understand the development and maintenance of NSSI behaviors. The final chapter in this section discusses the complicated relationship with, yet difference between, NSSI and suicidal behaviors. Section II: Assessment and Diagnostic Considerations provides information related to gathering information about NSSI behaviors, and diagnosis that may be needed for further treatment considerations. Specifically, this section includes questions to consider when conducting intakes and assessments, gathering information about NSSI behaviors, and becoming more self-aware of one's own reactions and judgments to self-injury. Additionally, a chapter specifically devoted to diagnosis is included, including the NSSI proposal to the DSM-5, information about comorbidity with other diagnoses, and thinking through NSSI using an addictions framework. This section ends with ethical considerations in treatment.

Section III: Treatment Considerations provides practical hands-on information for mental health clinicians in various settings. This section includes a chapter providing treatment methods and interventions that are supported by research, and a chapter providing a variety of interventions that have been supported by research, suggested by others, or used by the authors in working with clients who self-injure. Section IV: Education and Advocacy comprises information that focuses on the needs of working with individuals who engage in NSSI in various contexts. More specifically, information is provided about postvention for families, supervising mental health practitioners working with clients who self-injure, and other ways for practitioners to provide advocacy and prevention efforts around NSSI.

Introduction of Strength-Based, Wellness Orientation

While this book is directed toward mental health professionals and is designed in a way that provides basic overarching information about NSSI and considerations within different settings; it is also designed with ready-to-use information. Specifically, some chapters about assessment, family education, and treatment will have ready-to-use handouts and tables that can be copied and provided to others or used in intake assessments. Additionally, this book differs from other books on NSSI in that it is written from a strength-based, wellness approach in looking at the behavior.

The World Health Organization (WHO) defined health as "A state of complete physical, mental and social well-being, and not merely the absence of disease." Therefore, when thinking about NSSI, it is not solely about decreasing or extinguishing the behavior, but also understanding and working with the whole person and his or her context. Additionally, a wellness approach signifies the need to strive for optimal functioning and prevention, rather than solely focusing on the disease in a reductionist fashion (in this case, NSSI would be considered a "disease"). Paul Granello best summarized wellness counseling by saying, "Wellness counseling is an approach to helping based upon the belief in human potential and client strengths" (p. 29).

Multiple models of wellness exist. While going into each model specifically is not within the context of this book, highlights will be provided to gain a better

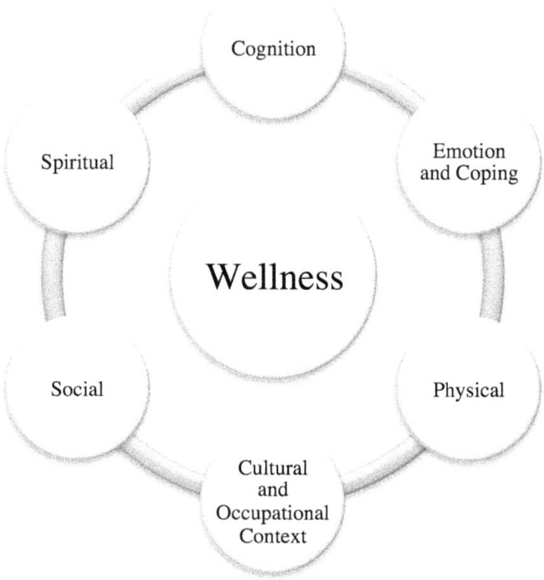

FIGURE 0.1. Integration of multiple wellness models

understanding of how we will be discussing NSSI behaviors throughout. Summarizing and integrating the main wellness models of Hettler's (1980) Hexagonal Model of Wellness, Witmer and Sweeney's (1991) Wheel of Wellness, Myers and Sweeney's (2005) Indivisible Self, and Granello's (2012) Clinical and Educational Model of Wellness, it was found that six domains should be considered when assessing wellness (Figure 0.1). These six domains exist across the multiple wellness models listed above. These include Cognition, Emotion and Coping, Physical, Social, Cultural and Occupational Context, and Spiritual. Each of these is highlighted briefly in Table 0.1.

As in each wellness model, mental health is interwoven within and across all of these domains. If an individual were lacking in one domain, they would not be optimally functioning. All domains interact, and have empirically been shown to do so (Myers & Sweeney, 2008). Throughout the chapters in this book, you will find that individuals who engage in NSSI are not functioning optimally. For example, most have difficulties in identification of emotions, experience intense levels of aversive emotions, and lack in coping with and regulation of emotions. Therefore, in this example, the emotion and coping domain is not functioning at ideal levels for optimal mental health. Additionally, cultural identity, self-worth, stress management, and interpersonal supports have been found to be below optimal levels among individuals who engage in NSSI. And as the WHO indicated, mental health is not solely about the absence of problems or disorders but about

TABLE 0.1. Integrated Domains of Wellness

Cognition	All mental activities such as thinking, perception, memory, attribution, and appraisal. An example may be how one attributes blame in a particular situation; or the perception of control. This also includes self-perception and efficacy.
Emotion and Coping	Emotions, the perception of these emotions (e.g., positive, negative), and the ability to identify and label emotions. The management or regulation of emotions, and the ability to cope with emotions and stressors. The ability to engage in problem solving behaviors.
Physical	The positive use of exercise, and understanding and engagement in nutrition.
Cultural and Occupational Context	Considerations of diverse backgrounds, influence of time and place on the individual, and guidance of beliefs and values. This would include familial and cultural beliefs, as well as occupational (e.g., work, school) and family settings, and gender and/or cultural identity.
Spiritual	The beliefs and values that provide meaning and purpose in one's life, the ability to transcend one's self.
Social	Interpersonal relationships, perceived and actual support, the influence of others.

preventing illnesses from occurring. Therefore, according to the wellness perspective, mental health professionals need to consider how to prevent engagement in NSSI using the six domains above rather than solely working with individuals reactively. The importance of advocating and preventing NSSI is imperative.

What you will read throughout this book is the idea that NSSI is used as a method of coping, a way to connect to one's body, regulate intense aversive emotions, or to gain social interaction. At times NSSI is used to protect one from the engagement in or attempt of suicide. Therefore, on one hand, individuals who self-injure have found a creative, temporarily successful way to cope and manage stress; yet this method is not adaptive and in the long run can cause more stress, hopelessness, and problems due to the inability to maintain overall and optimal functioning in all areas of wellness.

References

Granello, P. F. (2012). *Wellness counseling*. Upper Saddle River, NJ: Pearson.

Hettler, B. (1980). Wellness promotion on a university campus. *Family and Community Health, 3*(1), 77–79.

Lewis, S. P., & Plener, P. L. (2015). Nonsuicidal self-injury: A rapidly evolving global field. *Child & Adolescent Psychiatry & Mental Health, 49*(9). doi: 10.1186/s13034-015-0081-4

Myers, J. E., & Sweeney, T. J. (2005). The indivisible self: An evidence-based model of wellness (reprint). *Journal of Individual Psychology, 61*, 269–279.

Myers, J. E., & Sweeney, T. J. (2008). Wellness counseling: The evidence base for practice. *Journal of Counseling & Development, 86*(4), 482–493.

Trepal, H. C., & Wester, K. L. (2006). School counselors and self-injurious behaviors: Assessing perceptions, prevalence and training issues. *Journal of School Counseling, 4*(18). Retrieved from http://www.jsc.montana.edu/pages/articles.html

Trepal, H. C., & Wester, K. L. (2007). Self-injurious behaviors, diagnoses, and treatment methods: What mental health professionals are reporting. *Journal of Mental Health Counseling, 29*(4), 363–375.

Walsh, B. (2012). *Treating self-injury* (2nd edition). New York, NY: Guilford Publications.

Whitlock, J. L., Purington, A., & Gershkovich, M. (2009). Media and the internet and non-suicidal self-injury. In M. K. Nock (Ed.), *Understanding nonsuicidal self-injury: Origins, assessment, and treatments* (pp. 139–156). Washington, DC: American Psychological Association Press.

Witmer, M. J., & Sweeney, T. J. (1991). A holistic model for wellness and prevention over the lifespan. *Journal of Counseling & Development, 71*, 140–148.

World Health Organization. (2014, n.d.). *Mental health*. Retrieved from http://www.who.int/topics/mental_health/en

Section I

Non-Suicidal Self-Injury: Basic Information and Considerations

one
Non-Suicidal Self-Injury: What It Is, and What It Is Not

As a mental health professional, there are many things we see each day. Imagine any of the following:

- Sitting in your counseling office and having a parent telling you in a shaky, fearful voice that her daughter is engaging in "cutting," and she doesn't know what to do
- Walking into a home visit, you see one of the youth in short sleeves with many burn marks up and down his arm
- Receiving a late-night phone call from a parent because her son is in the emergency room with cuts up and down his arms and she is fearful that he attempted suicide
- A youth coming into your office to inform you that her friend is harming herself and she is unsure what to do
- A group of students in your school engaging in self-injury in order to fit in
- A student on your campus who got caught cutting by her dorm hall resident advisor, and in her appointment with you she pleads that she was not trying to kill herself but instead was just engaging in self-injury—something she always does

Any of these cases, or others, may have happened to you. You may have been aware of what to do, next steps, questions to ask, and treatment to implement. However, at times discerning what these cuts or marks are, distinguishing between non-suicidal self-injury and suicide, as well as understanding how to respond to parents, administrators, or friends can be confusing. Discussing non-suicidal self-injury (NSSI) can be puzzling and tricky. One of the many reasons for this is that NSSI has been referred to by a variety of different names, has multiple different assessment measures, and tends to be referred to alongside or in combination with other self-harm behaviors such as eating disorders, substance abuse, and suicide. Therefore, with all of these nuances in definitions and assessments, it makes the comparison and exploration of prevalence rates difficult. In this chapter, we will begin to pick apart the idea of NSSI through exploring the usage of names and titles, as well as definitions, leading up to a discussion of prevalence rates and how NSSI plays out in various populations and demographics.

Across the past few decades, before reaching the title of non-suicidal self-injury, NSSI was referred to by many different names, including, but not limited to, self-injury, self-mutilation, parasuicide, self-harm, deliberate self-harm, self-injurious behaviors, and cutting, specifically. Today, some of these names are still used in various settings to refer to NSSI behaviors. However, some of the names for NSSI, such as parasuicide, entailed suicidal behaviors—specifically ideations and attempts, thus complicating differentiation of these behaviors. Other titles for NSSI, such as self-injurious behaviors, also made it difficult to separate out NSSI behaviors from other self-harming behaviors such as eating disorders, substance abuse, or even excessive exercising. These multiple definitions led to confusion, with both researchers and mental health professionals being unsure how to classify NSSI behaviors. Common definitions and understandings of the behavior are needed to truly work with and be effective in the treatment of NSSI.

Definitions

Self-injury is not a new concept. It has been present and documented since biblical times. Clinicians were reporting increases in self-cutting behaviors by clients with no intent to die as early as the 1960s (Graff & Mallin, 1967). Since the initial publications, common definitions have been decided upon, which led to the title of non-suicidal self-injury, or NSSI. NSSI is defined as the intentional, self-inflicted immediate damage to body tissue, without suicidal intent (Favazza, 1998; Glenn & Klonsky, 2009). Additionally, the idea that this behavior is not socially sanctioned has been added at times to the definition, but typically is not a main descriptor of NSSI. The idea that the behaviors may not be socially sanctioned can be complex, given the suggestion that NSSI has actually reached mainstream culture and has been considered a form of normed social deviance (see Chapter 2 for more information on sociological theories of NSSI).

Box 1.1 Non-Suicidal Self-injury (NSSI)

Intentional, self-inflicted harm that causes immediate damage to body tissue with no suicidal intent.

The NSSI definition is widely accepted and best represents the description of NSSI as a condition for future study in the Diagnostic and Statistical Manual 5 (Chapter 5); however, this is not the definition used by everyone. More specifically, this definition of NSSI is the primary definition used in the United States and Canada; European countries and Australia label NSSI under a larger header of Deliberate Self-Harm (DSH). In the United States, the Centers for Disease Control and Prevention (CDC) titles DSH as Self-Directed Violence (SDV). SDV includes NSSI along with behaviors that have suicidal intent such as parasuicide, self-poisoning, and at times substance abuse and eating-disordered behavior. While NSSI is embraced under CDC's SDV umbrella, it is maintained as its own behavior and, thus, separate from other forms of self-harm. Interestingly, although definitions differ based on country or geographical location, prevalence rates have been found to be similar (Muehlenkamp, Claes, Havertape, & Plener, 2012). For the purpose of this book, the United States and Canadian definitions of self-injury will be used. Therefore, throughout this book, unless otherwise stated, we will be referring to non-suicidal self-injury (NSSI), which is defined as intentional, self-inflicted harm that causes immediate damage to body tissue, with no intent to die or kill oneself as a result of the behavior.

While NSSI is clearly different from other self-harming behaviors, it is helpful to see it under a larger self-directed violence umbrella (see Figure 1.1). Understanding NSSI in this context can help clinicians and others better understand why individuals may choose NSSI in combination with, or as an alternative to, other problematic behaviors. In fact, NSSI has been found to be related to other maladaptive and avoidant coping methods, such as substance abuse, denial, or self-blame (Trepal, Wester, & Merchant, 2015; Wester & Trepal, 2010).

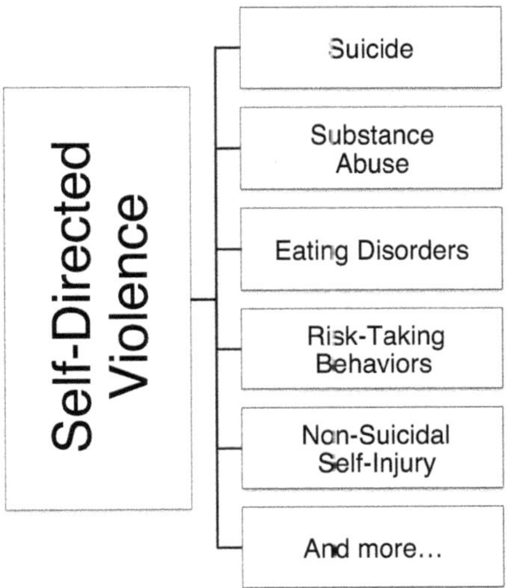

FIGURE 1.1. Self-directed violence

Methods

Now that we are working from a clear definition, what behaviors comprise NSSI? Having knowledge of the different methods individuals use to self-injure are important. The number of methods an individual engages in is important, as it positively relates to suicidal behaviors (Andover & Gibb, 2010; Brunner et al., 2007; Darke, Torok, Kaye, & Ross, 2010; Wester, Ivers, Villalba, & Trepal, 2016). Specifically, as the number of NSSI methods increase, the amount of suicidal ideation and risk of suicide attempts also increases. So assessment of the number and type of NSSI methods is important to consider.

The most common form of NSSI is cutting, but other methods include burning, hitting or punching oneself, banging one's head or other body part against something, erasing or carving into one's skin, rubbing objects into skin, pulling out hair, scratching oneself, preventing wounds from healing, sticking needles in one's skin, biting one's self, and breaking one's own bones. While less prevalent, breaking one's own bones has been present in about 1% of the general or college populations (Wester & McKibben, 2016). One individual who did break her bones commented, "I started self-injuring at age 4, though at the time, I didn't realize that's what it was. In the beginning, it was innocuous things like picking my lips until they bled, picking at mosquito bites, and chewing my nails into the quick. When I was in fifth grade, I started hitting myself in the head until I passed out. In high school I started removing my toenails and using blunt force trauma to try to break bones. In college I started using scissors and razor blades to cut. By the time I was in graduate school, I was self-injuring multiple times per day and had several broken bones." This quote comes from a study conducted by the first author and a colleague (Wester & McKibben, 2016). They conducted a study through social media asking individuals to provide their experiences and stories of NSSI. These individuals were all 18 years old and older. While most resided in the United States, a few respondents from other countries replied as well, with a total of 89 respondents. Quotes and statements from their stories will be provided throughout this book.

On average, individuals have been found to use two methods to self-injure, with little fluctuation between males and females or across race (Wester & Trepal, 2015). However, some individuals report using up to as many as eleven methods to self-harm. Individuals may begin self-injuring by using only one method, but can develop a tolerance to that method and either need to continually increase the severity of the method or begin using additional methods. This can be seen in the quote provided by the individual above who began self-injuring at a young age by engaging in behaviors that appeared more obsessive-compulsive or anxiety related, behaviors that might be considered normal for some 4- or 5-year-olds. However, she continued to increase the severity and frequency of her NSSI behaviors, from nail biting to self-hitting, to cutting herself with razor blades, to bone breaking. The increase in tolerance leads to a need to increase the depth in which one cuts, tries with various and more severe methods, or increases in the number of times they engage in NSSI to get the same effect or emotional relief they may seek (see Chapter 2 for more information on reasons for self-injury). Once a tolerance is built up to one method, the individual may switch methods or combine methods. Across time, NSSI behavior can increase in frequency or severity of tissue damage, in addition to the number of methods, due to a buildup in tolerance.

Taking into consideration that NSSI is behavior that is not socially sanctioned, some behaviors that have the potential to be NSSI based on definition (i.e., self-inflicted, intentional immediate tissue damage, no intent to die) are not typically considered NSSI. For example, consider tattoos and piercings. For the most part, in the United States and most other countries these behaviors are considered for decorative, self-expressive purposes, or even contain some cultural significance or meaning. While these behaviors are self-inflicted and cause immediate tissue damage, tattooing and piercing are not typically considered to be NSSI. However, to rule out piercing and tattoos completely from NSSI behavior simply because they are socially sanctioned is irrational.

One reason a person might engage in NSSI is emotion regulation, or to relieve intense, aversive emotions. Therefore, even when an individual is engaging in tattooing or piercing, a clinician needs to understand the purpose of those behaviors. Are the tattoos or piercings for self-expression or are they done to alleviate emotions? Do the tattoos help to socially connect one to others? If an individual goes to get piercings or tattoos every time she is angry, more than likely the individual is using these socially sanctioned behaviors to engage in self-injury rather than artistic self-expression or cultural rituals. For example, the first author worked with an adolescent client who self-tattooed with a pen and a needle every time he was angry. He reported self-tattooing and feeling the needle go into his skin was the only thing that alleviated his anger. This was a form of NSSI, where the adolescent used tattooing as a method to alleviate an aversive emotion (i.e., anger) by self-inflicting tissue damage. Thus, while definitions and descriptions of NSSI are important, it is also important to understand the reasons behind why individuals engage in specific sanctioned or unsanctioned behaviors to understand the possible connection to NSSI.

While the number and type of NSSI methods are important to consider, it is also important to explore the frequency of engagement. Very few individuals have been found to only engage in one incident of self-injury (23%, Glenn & Klonsky, 2009), while the majority of individuals have reported multiple incidents of NSSI. For those who engage in only one incident, they may have simply experimented with NSSI and found it not to be beneficial, or they may be at the beginning stages of engaging in these behaviors. A client who only engages in NSSI one time is not the typical one that will be seen in a counseling office. More often, clinician's will work with clients who have engaged in NSSI multiple times, across a longer span of time. As an example of time span, in a study that explored college students' self-injuring patterns, Glenn and Klonsky (2009) found that 46% reported they engaged in 2 to 10 incidents of NSSI across their lifetime, while 16% reported 11 to 50 incidents in their lifetime.

Understanding the frequency of events across one's lifetime is nebulous, given that individuals could have engaged in NSSI for one month while others could have engaged in these behaviors for 30 years. In addition, people are often poor informants on their own behavior when they are not specifically keeping track of every time that they self-injured across their lifespan. Therefore, asking for more precise time frames can provide beneficial information. Specifically, in a sample of college undergraduates and graduates, an average of 35.87 incidents of NSSI engagement in 12 months was found. This equates to an average of three times per month (Wester & McKibben, 2016). However, in a sample of just college freshman, it was found that within a three-month time period students engaged in NSSI an average of 24.46 times, or approximately eight times per month or two incidents per week (Trepal et al., 2015). Finally, in another study of the general public with individuals ranging between 18 and 62 years old, individuals reported engaging in NSSI approximately 65 times across three months (Wester & McKibben, 2016). This averages out to five times per week. While frequency of engagement is important as it can inform you in the degree to which the individual is attempting to cope, frequency of engagement has not been found to relate to an increased risk of suicidal behaviors.

Onset and Prevalence

Ultimately, no age group is immune from NSSI. The age of onset for NSSI is believed to be 13, but the behavior has been reported in younger age groups, as young as 5 years old. Others have begun self-injuring later in life, with the onset in their 30s (Wester & McKibben, 2016). While NSSI typically begins in early adolescence, a trajectory has been proposed with NSSI decreasing or extinguishing by the mid-20s, or soon after individuals leave college. However, there have been reports of NSSI among individuals in their 30s, 40s, 50s, and 60s. These individuals have been labeled "long-term chronic users" of self-injury (Adler & Adler, 2007), tend to use NSSI throughout their life to cope, feel an urge or a need to engage in self-injury, and tend to do so in isolation. That is, they do not often share their behavior with others and may only reach out to discuss their self-injuring behavior in online forums and chat rooms.

NSSI behaviors are highest among inpatient clinical populations, followed by outpatient mental health populations, with estimates ranging from 22% to 40% of individuals seeking outpatient mental health services. However, adolescent and college populations have similar rates of NSSI compared to outpatient clinical populations, even though the majority of individuals who self-injure report *not* being in therapy. Consider any given middle and high school, where 18% to 37% of these youth have self-reported engaging in NSSI behaviors. This breaks down to 2 to 4 students out of every 10 engaging in NSSI. Similarly, college students have reported prevalence rates from 12% to 35%. Finally, the lowest

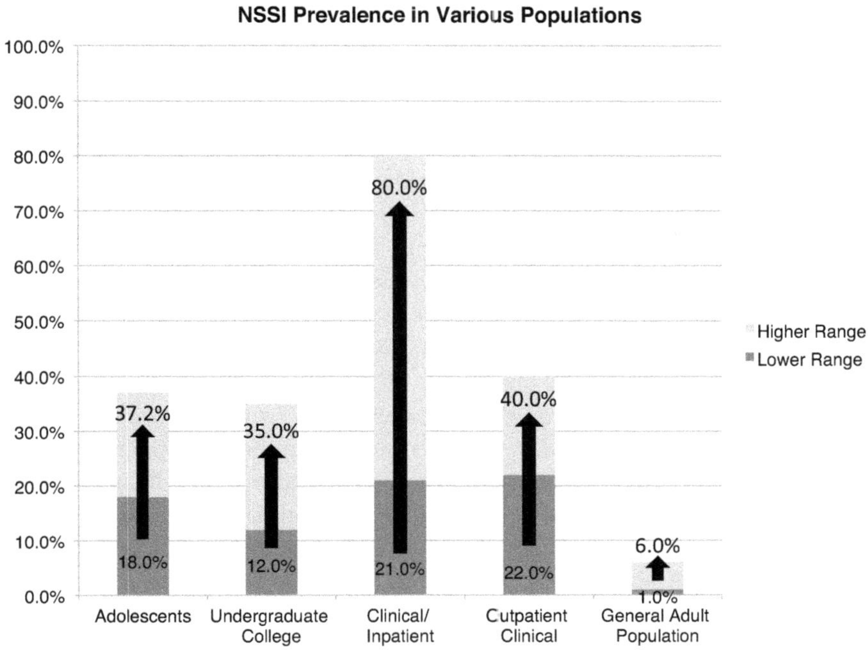

FIGURE 1.2. NSSI prevalence in various populations

rates of self-injury are among individuals within the general population, which is considered to be adults who may or may not be in need of any mental health services.

Similar to differences in definitions of NSSI and self-harming behaviors, rates of NSSI differ based on how they are assessed. Specifically, the most typical way NSSI has been assessed by researchers tends to be lifetime prevalence. This means individuals are asked if they have *ever*, in their lifetime, engaged in NSSI behaviors. Understanding lifetime rates is important as it can provide an overall estimate of the population who have engaged in NSSI behaviors. However, lifetime prevalence assessment can also be problematic due to relying on memory. For example, if someone self-injured in adolescence but is currently in adulthood, they may not remember the behavior clearly in terms of frequency of engagement or the specific methods used, particularly if their engagement in NSSI was not viewed as a significant event. Therefore, while lifetime prevalence is important, it can result in a conservative or unreliable estimate.

Currently, researchers have been asking about more recent NSSI rates, typically based in 12-month time frames, as this matches up with the NSSI diagnostic description (proposed as a condition for further study) in the Diagnostic and Statistical Manual 5. Others have explored NSSI within a 3-month time frame. All time frames have their pros and cons in terms of assessment and research. Some result in a greater reliance on memory and the inaccuracy of recall, while others may rule out individuals who are currently engaging in NSSI behaviors, due to a shorter time frame. Additionally, understanding that a client has engaged in NSSI 20 times over the past 3 months can provide more important information for treatment than 20 times within the past 12 months, unless a more clear understanding of the current behavior is evaluated.

Rates of NSSI have also been found to differ based on how they are assessed. Specifically, most assessments involved one item to determine if an individual engages in NSSI. For example, asking the question: "Have you ever in your life purposefully harmed yourself without the intention to die?" Other assessments have longer self-report or interview protocols (various assessments will be covered in Chapter 4), such as asking specific NSSI method questions. These would ask questions such as "Have you ever purposefully ___ yourself?" with the blank to be filled in with specific NSSI methods such as cut, burn, or pinprick. One-item assessments have actually resulted in lower prevalence rates than multiple-item assessments (Muehlenkamp et al., 2012). It is unknown why lower rates of NSSI are reported when one-item assessments are provided. It may be that some individuals do not identify as a self-injurer, or do not believe the activity they are engaging in is actually self-injury, so they report "no" to a "self-injury" question. But when asked about specific behaviors, such as scratching or cutting, they are more likely to say, "yes, I have engaged in that." It also may be that multiple questions assessing for specific behaviors bring about "yes" responses when in fact the behavior is not NSSI. For example, individuals may report "yes" to preventing wounds from healing, while in some cases it may be more obsessive or compulsive scab picking than it is consciously choosing NSSI behavior. Careful attention is needed when assessing for NSSI. What is known is that prevalence rates are high, and are continuing to get higher.

As an example of the continued increase in NSSI behavior, the authors conducted three studies of incoming freshman at one university. In all three studies, incoming freshman at a university were asked about the NSSI behaviors. The first study was conducted in Fall 2008, the second in Fall 2011, and the third in Fall 2015 (the data provided from 2015 is preliminary data). The goal was to assess trends in NSSI behaviors using a multiple-item assessment, the Deliberate Self-Harm Inventory (discussed in detail in Chapter 4 on intake and assessment). Freshmen were asked both lifetime and current 90-day NSSI engagement. As can be seen in Figure 1.3, lifetime engagement doubled (increased by 2.5 times) across 7 years (from 2008 to 2015). The graph for lifetime NSSI engagement reveals that NSSI engagement overall is increasing, although while doing so more rapidly from 2008 to 2011, it seems to have tapered down in terms of the number of individuals who are reporting having engaged in NSSI at all. However, during the same time frame, the number of college freshman indicating they are *currently* engaging in NSSI has continued to rise at alarming rates. In Fall 2008 only 2.6% of college freshman indicated they had intentionally self-injured within the past three months; however, this quadrupled by 2011, and again doubled to 23% by

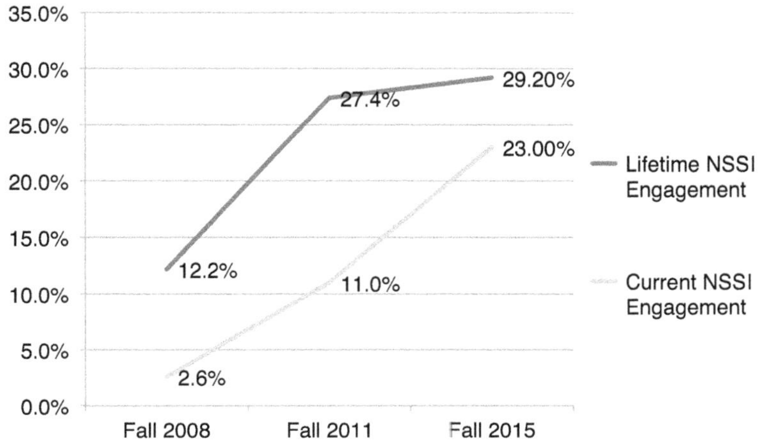

FIGURE 1.3. Prevalence of NSSI across 3 cohorts of university freshman

Fall 2015. So in Fall 2015, nine times the number of college freshman as in 2008 indicated they currently engaged in NSSI.

Demographic Effect on NSSI

The onset of NSSI has remained stable for many decades, with some deviant cases revealing that NSSI can have varying onset for some individuals. What has been less known or researched clinically has been how demographics such as sex and race play a role in NSSI behaviors. Historically, when literature and research was first published on NSSI, it was believed to be a behavior engaged in only by White females. More specifically it was assumed that White female adolescents and young adults who had been sexually abused and were abusing drugs and alcohol were the individuals who were most likely to be engaging in NSSI. In early research studies, it was typically found that more females did in fact engage in self-injurious behaviors than males. More recently, however, limited differences between rates of NSSI engagement have been found between males and females. Males seem to be engaging in NSSI just as frequently as females. Additionally, race does not appear to differentiate NSSI engagement, either.

To provide further examples, consider a study conducted by the authors, which examined NSSI behaviors in 1,325 college freshman. They were asked to self-report their engagement in NSSI behaviors. When exploring sex differences in the entire sample of 1,325 it was found that 9% of females reported self-injuring currently (past 90 days), while 3% of males reported self-injuring currently. It appears based on these percentages that females self-injure more than males. However, sex needs to be taken into context of who responded. More specifically, when comparing the males who self-injure to the total males who participated in the study, and females who self-injure to total females, the rates of NSSI were similar, with 13% of the female respondents indicated engaging in NSSI compared to the female sample, while 11% of the male respondents reported engaging in NSSI compared to the entire male sample. You can see that there is very little difference between the percentage of males and females who engage in self-injury.

The more recent shift of males self-injuring at rates similar to females may be due to males increasing in their level of NSSI engagement, but may also be due to expanding our understanding and definitions of these behaviors. Earlier explanations and definitions of NSSI behaviors frequently focused on behaviors such as cutting. While some males do engage in cutting behaviors, they are less likely to do so than females (Barrocas, Hankin, Young, & Abela, 2012). Males are actually more likely to engage in more purposeful risk taking behavior or more stereotypically masculine behaviors that are acceptable in society. Now considering that some NSSI definitions contain "not socially sanctioned" as part of their definition, this begins to exclude some males who actually engage in NSSI.

As an example of more socially acceptable behaviors being used by males to self-injure, the first author worked with a male adolescent client who, when he was in trouble, would frequently punch a cement wall. Sometimes he punched the wall for less than one minute, while others he punched the wall for over 10 minutes. While this behavior may not be the most appropriate coping method, generally it would be considered socially acceptable for a man. In the larger scheme of things, physical aggression is acceptable for males in most cultures, particularly in the United States. So most individuals never questioned this male adolescent, but instead let him "have his rant." When working with him, I inquired about the time difference. He reported "I punch the wall until my hand hurts." Well, of course, that would seem like a logical solution, but instead as a clinician I delved in further. More specifically I inquired as to what happened when his hand hurt. He reported, "I look for my hand to hurt, because when my hand hurts I focus on that and no longer focus on being angry." In this instance, he used the pain in his hand to regulate the overwhelming feeling of being angry; thus, NSSI behavior. He intentionally engaged in tissue damage (bruising, breaking the skin over his knuckles, and some broken bones over the years) to alleviate his current emotional state. Yet, this was never classified by anyone as self-injury as it did not look like the typical way that most individuals engage in NSSI.

Males more often engage in behaviors that are socially acceptable, but are more risk-oriented. They are more likely to punch or hit themselves. They may even have others punch or hit them, thus not only gaining from NSSI, but also increasing others' perspectives of the "guy code" or male socialization. The second author once worked with a male who burned himself with cigarettes in a group with other members of his military unit. The group engaged in these behaviors separately, but also used the burning as a form of competition or contest to see who could last the longest with the hot cigarette on their arm. Females are more likely to engage in cutting and burning their skin, but do engage in other behaviors as well. However, females are less likely to engage in NSSI as a form of competition.

Little has been explored about race and NSSI behaviors, but more recently, some differences have been found. Most researchers have found that White individuals report greater engagement in NSSI than individuals of other racial backgrounds. One of the first researchers to contradict this finding explored a sample of White and African American adolescents from lower socioeconomic backgrounds (Latzman et al., 2010). In that community, they found that African American adolescents were more likely to engage in NSSI than White adolescents. This finding highlights the importance of taking into consideration an individual's context and larger social system. It is important to consider how one's family, school, or larger community may factor into a person's engagement in self-injury.

In a more recent study exploring NSSI among 1,096 college students, the authors explored race in regards to NSSI (Wester & Trepal, 2015). Specifically, it was found that White, Multiracial, and Hispanic students were more likely to engage in NSSI behaviors than Black/African American, and Asian/Asian American students. However, the number of methods used to self-harm did not differ across race. To explore contextual reasons as to why rates of NSSI differed, it was found that individuals—regardless of race—who felt they belonged to their self-identified ethnic group were less likely to engage in self-injury. Therefore, a sense of belonging was helpful in protecting an individual from engaging in self-injury. What was also determined in this study was that context is important. More specifically, Hispanic and White students were more likely to engage in NSSI than any other group. Although Hispanic students reported a high sense of belonging to their ethnic group, this did not seem to protect them as it did students from other racial backgrounds. Students in this specific study were taken from two separate universities: one was a minority-serving institution that served predominantly White students, while the other was a Hispanic-serving institution which had at least half of the students on campus identifying as Hispanic/Latino. Therefore, when individuals are in a context or setting in which they are the majority, then a sense of connection and belonging to one's ethnic identity no longer serves as a buffer to negative behaviors such as NSSI.

Regardless of this information, our knowledge on how race and sex influence NSSI behaviors is extremely limited and we need to better understand how race, sex, and other demographic factors play into NSSI engagement. We are only beginning to skim the surface of having a grasp on how demographics and identity factor into engagement in NSSI behaviors. Most recently, those having a minority sexual orientation have been found to be a high risk for NSSI engagement, with individuals who are sexual minorities (i.e., lesbian, gay, bisexual, and queer) having been found to self-injure at higher rates than individuals who identify as heterosexual. Having knowledge about how all of these factors intersect and play a role in engaging in NSSI will help clinicians better understand who is at risk and how best to treat and work with them in therapy.

Conclusion

NSSI has been, and will continue to be, discussed among mental health professionals. This is due to a continued increase in NSSI behaviors, which on one hand includes intentional self-infliction of tissue damage that is not socially sanctioned, yet, on the other hand, has become or is becoming a socially normed behavior. The methods of NSSI vary, with individuals typically engaging in more than one method. Additionally, more information is needed on the impact of demographics on NSSI, including how NSSI behaviors may vary across or within demographics. However, we do know how males and females may self-injure differently, and we are also getting glimpses of the impact of race and ethnicity on NSSI engagement.

References

Adler, P. A., & Adler, P. (2007). The demedicalization of self-injury: From psychopathology to sociological deviance. *Journal of Contemporary Ethnography, 36*, 537–570.

Andover, M. S., & Gibb, B. E. (2010). Non-suicidal self-injury, attempted suicide, and suicidal intent among psychiatric inpatients. *Psychiatry Research, 178*, 101–105.

Barrocas, A. L., Hankin, B. L., Young, J. F., & Abela, J. R. Z. (2012). Rates of nonsuicidal self-injury in youth: Age, sex, and behavioral methods in a community sample. *Pediatrics, 130*, 39–45.

Brunner, R., Parzer, P., Haffner, J. Steen, R., Roos, J., Klett, M., & Resch, F. (2007). Prevalence and psychological correlates of occasional and repetitive deliberate self-harm in adolescents. *Archives of Pediatric Adolescent Medicine, 7*, 641–649.

Darke, S., Torok, M., Kaye, S., & Ross, J. (2010). Attempted suicide, self-harm, and violent victimization among regular illicit drug users. *Suicide & Life-Threatening Behavior, 40*, 587–596.

Favazza, A. (1998). The coming of age of self-mutilation. *The Journal of Nervous and Mental Disease, 186*, 259–268.

Glenn, C. R., & Klonsky, D. E. (2009). Social context during non-suicidal self-injury indicates suicide risk. *Personality and Individual Differences, 46*, 25–29.

Graff, H., & Mallin, R. (1967). The syndrome of the wrist cutter. *American Journal of Psychiatry, 124*, 36–42.

Latzman, R., Gratz, K. L., Young, J., Heiden, L. J., Damon, J. D., & High, T. L. (2010). Self-injurious thoughts and behaviors among youth in an underserved area of the southern United States: Exploring the moderating roles of gender, racial/ethnic background, and school-level. *Journal of Youth and Adolescence, 39*, 270–280.

Muehlenkamp, J. J., Claes, L., Havertape, L., & Plener, P. (2012). International prevalence of adolescent non-suicidal self-injury and deliberate self-harm. *Child & Adolescent Psychiatry & Mental Health, 6*. Retrieved from www.capmh.com/content/6/1/10

Trepal, H., Wester, K., & Merchant, E. (2015). A cross-sectional matched sample study of non-suicidal self-injury among young adults: Support for interpersonal and intrapersonal factors, with implications for coping strategies. *Child and Adolescent Psychiatry and Mental Health, 9*, 36. doi: 10.1186/s13034-015-0070-7

Wester, K. L., Ivers, N., Villalba, J. A., & Trepal, H. C. (2016). The relationship between non-suicidal self-injury and suicidal ideation. *Journal of Counseling & Development, 94*, 3–12.

Wester, K. L., & McKibben, B. (2016). Participants' experiences of nonsuicidal self-injury: Supporting existing theory and emerging conceptual pathways. *Journal of Mental Health Counseling, 38*, 12–27.

Wester, K. L., & Trepal, H. C. (2010). Coping behaviors, abuse history, and counseling: Differentiating college students who self-injure. *Journal of College Counseling, 13*, 141–154.

Wester, K. L., & Trepal, H. C. (2015). Non-suicidal self-injury: Exploring the correlations among race, ethnic identity, and ethnic belonging. *Journal of College Student Development, 56*, 127–139.

two
Why NSSI? Models and Theories of Explanation

Mary, a 16-year-old female, reports cutting and burning her skin. She indicates she began harming herself a few years ago. Mary is unable to state the specific purpose of her self-injury, but simply verbalizes that it makes her feel better. She reports self-injury began shortly after she and her uncle starting sexting. She began cutting herself by accident. The first time she accidentally cut herself was when she was outside playing soccer in her bare feet. Feeling both nervous and good (in anticipation) about the sexting, she stepped on a sharp rock and cut her foot. Afterwards, she focused on her foot, and in doing so, realized she was no longer anxious or waiting in anticipation, but instead mesmerized by the pain, the cut, and the blood on her foot. She reported feeling a sense of calmness overtaking her, and liked this experience.

This is a common scenario in counseling, in which clients self-injure but are unclear of the reasons. With non-suicidal self-injury (NSSI) increasing in prevalence, resulting in a rise in clients who are self-injuring entering mental health treatment, the question becomes: Why? What leads an individual to engage in NSSI? Many different explanations have been developed in an attempt to understand NSSI behaviors. There are many different reasons why individuals self-injure. Ultimately, clients are human beings; therefore, they do not all fit within the same box explaining the behavior. However, the models that have been proposed can be used to help better understand possible reasons why our clients engage in self-injury. These models can help mental health professionals know what questions to ask, understand potential factors that may lead or be related to NSSI, or help conceptualize a client who self-injures more holistically.

The majority of individuals, 85–90%, use NSSI to regulate emotions and cognitions (Nock et al., 2010; Wester & McKibben, 2016). This has led the majority of theories proposed to be centered around emotion regulation. Yet NSSI does serve other purposes, including biological, sociological, and relational reasons. Multiple theories and conceptual models explaining and attempting to understand NSSI are described below.

Emotion Regulation Theories

The idea of using self-injury to regulate emotions is one of the more common ideas around the purpose of NSSI. This is supported both by researchers as well as self-reports by individuals who self-injure. As a 32-year-old female reported, "I started burning myself with incense or candle wax as a way to deal with anger. . . . I learned that pain can quickly dull emotions! I switched to cutting myself . . . as a way to deal with negative emotions quickly [which] quickly spiraled into a way to feel in control."

Most theoretical models that posit NSSI as a form of emotion regulation suggest that an individual is presented with a stimulus that results in an emotional or cognitive response (i.e., a stress response). This stress response is most often described as a negative or aversive emotion and includes, but is not limited to, feelings such as anger, shame, jealousy, or sadness. Acts of NSSI have followed feelings of rejection, anger at self or at others, and a sense of numbness (Nock, Prinstein, & Sterba, 2009). This sense of numbness results in a sense of emptiness or being void of emotions. While the stress response can include actual affect, it can also include cognitions, such as rumination or worry. Once this stress response, or emotion, is experienced, it builds in intensity. This intensity could be experienced as over-arousal (i.e., high level of an emotion) or under-arousal (i.e., little to no emotion, feeling void or empty).

In order to cope, or regulate emotions, an individual typically needs to understand the emotion he or she is experiencing. The difficulty here is that NSSI is related to alexithymia (Cerutti, Calabrese, & Valastro, 2013), defined as the inability to identify or describe one's own emotions. An example is when you ask a client what they are feeling before they self-injure, or even what they are feeling while sitting with you. They tend to be unable to label or identify any emotion, and have difficulty describing what the emotion feels like. Being unable to identify or label an emotion can lead to the inability to cope or resolve the emotion. Even if coping strategies are employed, they may be the incorrect ones. For example, there are times when crying may alleviate an emotion and be a helpful coping response (e.g., a small child experiencing fear, therefore crying to get a parent's attention) but in other circumstances it may not be helpful and may instead escalate the situation or the emotion (e.g., a teenager crying in front of a bully).

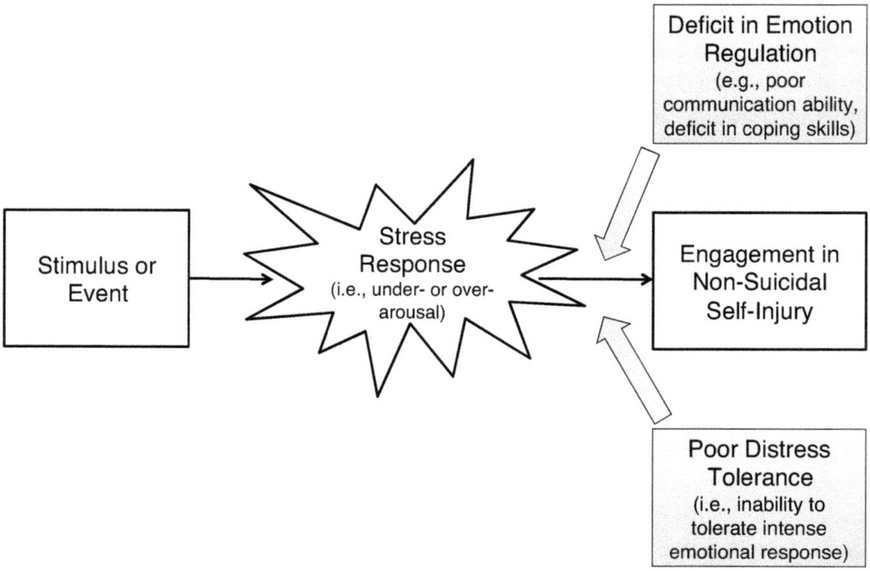

FIGURE 2.1. Basic Summary of Emotion Regulation Models such as Chapman, Gratz, and Brown's (2006) Experiential Avoidance Model of Deliberate Self-Harm and Nock's (2009) Integrated Theoretical Model of the Development and Maintenance of NSSI

Typically, once emotions are identified, coping strategies are employed to resolve the situation or alleviate the emotion. Even if we are unable to identify the emotion, the goal is to feel better, to gain control, or alleviate the over- or under-arousal. However, while using coping strategies may be the means by which most individuals alleviate intense aversive emotions, individuals who resort to NSSI typically lack adaptive or effective coping strategies (Chapman et al., 2006; Nock, 2009; Trepal, Wester, & Merchant, 2015; Wester & Trepal, 2010) and have low distress tolerance (Chapman et al., 2006; Nock, 2009). Low distress tolerance means that the threshold for the amount of stress they can tolerate may be lower than others. Additionally, individuals who self-injure may report not having any other coping methods, may attempt to implement a variety of coping methods but do so ineffectively, or may only use more maladaptive or avoidant coping methods.

Maladaptive coping strategies (e.g., substance abuse, denial, and avoidant behaviors) are employed more by individuals who self-injure to solve their problems or regulate their emotions than by individuals who do not engage in NSSI (Wester & Trepal, 2010). These maladaptive strategies include denial, engaging in eating disorders, holding ice on skin, throwing self into work, taking a shower to alleviate emotions prior to engaging in NSSI, or other avoidant behaviors. Additionally, individuals who self-injure tend to use substances, illicit drugs, prescription drugs, or alcohol in their attempts to cope (Stewart, Baiden, & Theall-Honey, 2014). The use of such maladaptive or avoidant methods to problem solve typically do not resolve the originating concern, subsequently maintaining the intensity of the emotion. When experiencing high levels of aversive emotions or cognitions, the individual's goal at this point is to alleviate this intense aversive emotion. Without the ability to effectively cope, this lends itself to the engagement in maladaptive coping behaviors, such as NSSI.

Application of Emotion Regulation Theories to Client Case: Mary

Using the idea of NSSI as emotion regulation to better understand the case of Mary provided above, she could be regulating either the nervous feeling or the anticipation (or both) of receiving or sending a sext message to her uncle. Regardless of the reason, these emotions would be deemed negative to Mary. For example, she may realize sexting with her uncle is not positive, the behavior may be incongruent with her values, family beliefs, or the law, or she may fear getting caught by her mom, dad, or someone else. Or a sense of nervousness or anxiety may simply be an uncomfortable emotion to Mary.

To understand NSSI through the emotion regulation model would be to believe that the stimulus of sexting with her uncle is creating or resulting in a stress response, one that includes a continual increase in aversive emotions (i.e., anxiety or nervousness), resulting in over-arousal. Due to her inability to cope or regulate these emotions in more effective ways, Mary accidentally falls upon self-injury by inadvertently cutting her bare foot with a sharp rock while experiencing these emotions of anxiety and hope. As can be seen in this scenario, this cut, and resultant pain and blood, is what diverts Mary's attention, allowing her to avoid her emotions. Distraction is one of the two major attentional strategies that help to regulate emotions (Gross, 2007).

While the idea of emotion regulation is one of the more supported reasons for NSSI, there are a few different perspectives. The Experiential Avoidance Model (Chapman et al., 2006) theorizes NSSI in a similar classification as substance abuse and eating disorders. Simply, the reason for engaging in NSSI is avoidance. NSSI then is used to merely avoid the negative affect being experienced, regardless if that is over- or under-arousal of emotion. According to Chapman, self-injury is used to suppress, even if only temporarily, the emotions being experienced in order to increase the current level of functioning.

Experiential Avoidance Model (Chapman and Colleagues)

While Mary may have only engaged in NSSI by accident this one time, the Experiential Avoidance Model (EAM; Chapman et al., 2006) suggests self-injury results in a temporary relief or reduction in the intensity of the emotion. This reduction or removal of the emotion negatively reinforces continued use of self-injury. Therefore, in their EAM, Chapman and colleagues would suggest that Mary would continue to use NSSI in future situations when she experiences intense, aversive emotions, but instead of doing so accidentally, she would purposefully engage in self-harm by cutting herself or using other forms of self-injury. Additionally, engaging in NSSI would become easier, as well as a more automatic coping strategy for her.

Four Functions Model (Nock & Prinstein)

The idea of suppressing, or eliminating, an emotion an individual does not want is supported by other models conceptualizing NSSI. Specifically the Four Function Model (FFM; Nock & Prinstein, 2004) has found that one of the most frequent reasons an individual engages in NSSI is to remove an emotion, thus categorized as automatic negative reinforcement, which has been most frequently cited by individuals as the main reason they self-injure (Klonsky, 2011). Specifically, the FFM suggests that NSSI is used to experience an emotion (positive automatic [affect] reinforcement) or to remove the experience of an emotion (negative automatic reinforcement).

There has been much support for the idea of positive and negative reinforcement of emotions. Specifically, NSSI is predicted by a greater intensity and shorter duration of emotions and thoughts (Nock et al., 2009). Individuals who self-injure experience positive and negative affect differently in regards to intensity and variability (Bresin, 2014). Bresin conducted a study over 14 days where individuals who did and did not self-injure kept diaries of their emotions. He found that overall, individuals who self-injured experienced low levels of positive affect that had low levels of variability. What does this mean? That individuals who self-injure are more frequently experiencing low positive affect that rarely changes. When these individuals did report feeling positive affect, the feelings were short-lived

TABLE 2.1. Functions of NSSI (adapted from Nock & Prinstein [2004])

	Positive Reinforcement	Negative Reinforcement
Automatic (Affective)	To create a desirable state ▪ To feel calm or in control ▪ To increase feeling or feel something when nothing is felt	To remove or reduce negative emotion or thought ▪ To eliminate feeling ▪ To stop intruding memories or thoughts
Social	To gain something socially ▪ Gain attention from peers, parents, or others ▪ A cry for help	To avoid or escape from interpersonal demands ▪ To avoid a task or event ▪ To stop a conflict

and quickly dropped back to the more representative lower level commonly experienced. As an example, if a teenager received a test back with an unexpected A, she may feel a brief moment of excitement or be proud of her achievement; however, that feeling leaves within moments of it being experienced. If she later walked into a lunchroom and had a friend ask her to sit with him at lunch, or if she received a positive text from a friend, her positive affect may increase slightly, but may do so only momentarily (e.g., 1 minute, 20 minutes), quickly turning to low affect. This elation does not continually stay with the person, as it quickly dissipates, if it is even felt at all.

Bresin also found that individuals who self-injured did not experience a persistent negative affect, but instead had frequent fluctuations around a high mean level. Negative affect was also highly variable, suggesting that individuals reacted to situations very differently, therefore not reacting the same in each situation. This suggests their negative affect may, in a sense, be on a roller coaster when they are faced with various stimuli or situations that cause an emotional or stress reaction. For example, take a male teenager. When his alarm goes off in the morning, negative affect may be neutral or low, but may spike suddenly when he arrives in the kitchen to have his mom tell him to make sure he takes his homework to school today. He may slightly decrease in the degree he feels angry or annoyed, but his negative affect may not return to the low level he woke up with. Then at school he walks toward a close friend, only to have that friend turn the other way and walk away. Regardless of the reason (e.g., friend did not want to talk to him; friend did not see him), the appraisal of that action may be negative, such as feeling rejected, which results in a volcanic spike in negative affect. This negative affect may stay elevated, or may decrease by the time he walks to his next class, but the level of negative affect would stay elevated, therefore never fully decreasing. This would continue, like a roller coaster ride, throughout the day with various events and appraisals. In this case, with a lack of effective coping strategies in his toolbox, NSSI may be what is used to regulate this high level of negative affect to bring it down to a lower level. This may result in one NSSI event at one point in the day (e.g., the end of the day; moment his friend walked away from him) or multiple NSSI events throughout the day to control or regulate each event.

While automatic negative reinforcement has been most frequently cited, attempting to remove or decrease current levels of emotions cannot be fully separated from the desire to experience positive emotions (i.e., automatic positive reinforcement, or increasing a sense of calm). Specifically, individuals who self-injure tend to feel better immediately following cutting or harming themselves (Paul, Schroeter, Dahme, & Nutzinger, 2002), including feeling happiness in addition to a sense of peace and calmness (Kemperman, Russ, & Shearin, 1997). While some researchers have found that a combination of positive emotions increase (positive reinforcement) and negative emotions decrease (negative reinforcement) following a NSSI episode, other researchers have found conflicting information, including that negative emotions may in fact stay the same after self-injury even if positive affect increases (Muehlenkamp et al., 2009). This may be due to the increases in guilt and shame feelings experienced by some individuals following a self-injury incident (Paul et al., 2002; Wester & McKibben, 2016).

As mentioned by Chapman and colleagues in their EAM, NSSI is only a temporary relief. Some of the negative affect will arise again as the originating problem was only avoided, not resolved. Also, negative affect can actually increase shortly after cutting or burning oneself due to being frustrated at oneself for actually harming oneself, or saddened that this is how one regulates their emotions and "solves" their problems. These increases in negative emotions have been found to arise as early as one hour after engaging in self-injury (Paul et al., 2002).

Integrated Model of the Development and Maintenance of Non-Suicidal Self-Injury (Nock)

Other theorists offer a slightly different opinion from Chapman and colleagues. Instead of avoidance of emotions, Nock (2004) developed the Integrated Model of the Development and Maintenance of Non-Suicidal Self-Injury (ITM). He suggested NSSI might regulate affect not only by avoiding the emotion but also due to the possibility of using self-injury to self-punish or socially signal. So Nock took the EAM slightly further. He indicated that the difficulties with coping and communication may be a result of family conflict, abuse or neglect, or other distal risk factors in one's history. But more so, he suggested NSSI vulnerability factors. These specifically include the possibilities that NSSI was learned via social learning; therefore, an individual may have learned self-injury from peers, media, or even other family members. He also mentioned that others could consider NSSI pragmatic, which means that the person believes that self-injury "just works" or is the easiest solution compared to other possibilities. Nock suggested pain analgesia, which identifies the idea that individuals who self-injure have a higher pain threshold. Thus, what we may consider to appear painful, in fact doesn't cause them any pain at all.

Similar to positive reinforcement of social functions in the Four Function Model discussed above, Nock also suggests that self-injury can be used for social signaling. Due to poor communication abilities, a final result to get others' attention or cry for help may be to engage in NSSI behaviors. The final two NSSI vulnerability factors Nock mentions includes that NSSI can serve as a form of self-punishment, but that it can also be something that an individual implicitly identifies with. The latter would be true for an individual who labels himself as "a self-injurer," where self-injury becomes part of the person's identity. Other than the addition of the impact of history on interpersonal and intrapersonal behaviors, and the NSSI vulnerability factors, Nock's ITM is similar to Chapman's EAM, as it implies that NSSI is a way to regulate emotional or cognitive distress.

Application of Theory to Client Case: Mary

In the case of Mary, it may be that focusing on the cut and blood is not a way of avoiding the emotion, but Mary may feel placated due to feeling she needed to be punished for her feelings of excitement. The consequential cut on her foot may have fulfilled this belief or need that Mary may have had. Or it may be that Mary may not know how to communicate to her family that she and her uncle are sexting; therefore, she may perceive that this form of self-harm could result in the ability to socially signal others that something is wrong. NSSI has been suggested to be a way to signal or express to others the pain that one is internally feeling in a concrete, physical manner. More specifically, NSSI speaks to a cultural discourse that physical pain may be more privileged than emotional pain (Chandler, 2013). There is an old saying that "if you can't see it, then it must not be real."

Regardless of the reason—avoidance of emotion, social signaling, or self-punishment—both the EAM and the ITM imply that the self-injury would more than likely continue for Mary given the relief she felt from her emotions. This is an example of positive social reinforcement, meaning Mary would be receiving attention from someone based on her NSSI behavior, using NSSI to increase caregiving or gain help from a parent or other individual. However, the FFM and ITM also suggest that using NSSI to communicate can also result in negative social reinforcement, or may stop a particular behavior or interaction with others. It may cause another person to withdraw. As an example, the first author was working with a college student who used self-injury every time she and her boyfriend were fighting. The client found it to be a very effective method of defusing the conflict and resulted in her boyfriend retreating from the argument, leaving the client to "win" the argument every time. She reported that her boyfriend did not want her to self-harm and saw the conflict as the cause of the NSSI; therefore, he felt that if he stopped arguing, her NSSI would stop . . . and usually it did.

The need to use NSSI for social signaling or communication is due to poor communication skills (Nock, 2009). Social signaling has also been related to individuals who have a history of abuse or trauma (Wester & McKibben, 2016). In the words of a 38-year-old female, she reported, "I cut myself when I was 13 or so years old and then stopped a few times. . . . I didn't cut myself again until I was around 26 and just beginning to remember that I was sexually abused by my father beginning at age 3. I cut myself off and on for a few years while dealing with this. . . . [My goal in self-injuring was to] express rage and hurt. I didn't have a voice and wasn't taught or encouraged to express emotions—I was taught to hide them. I had no idea how to begin communicating how much I was hurting. I also cut myself to punish myself for even having emotions and for the wrongs I committed." So as can be seen in this report, the various affective and social reasons for engaging in NSSI can be blended.

Biological/Biopsychosocial Theories

There has been an increased focus on the possibility that NSSI has a biological or biopsychosocial basis. While there is no evidence of genetic predisposition to self-injury, as results of multiple research studies resulted in inconsistent findings (Groschwitz & Plener, 2012), some biological differences have been found between individuals who self-injure versus those who do not. The most consistent biological difference found has been that individuals engaging in self-injury have lower cortisol levels and endogenous opioids prior to engaging in self-harm (Groschwitz & Plener, 2012). This supports some of the emotion regulation models, suggesting that individuals who self-injure, such as Mary, have insufficient bodily stress responses. This also can explain why individuals who self-injure may have higher pain tolerance levels when they engage in self-injury specifically, as endogenous opioids are involved in pain perception and addictive behaviors.

In regards to pain, individuals who self-injure have mentioned not feeling pain when engaging in NSSI. This lack of pain seems to be related to a sense of purpose, intentionality, and control when engaging in NSSI, as the same individuals have mentioned feeling pain when they accidentally injure themselves (Chandler, 2013). Given that endogenous opioids are also related to other addictive behaviors, this can also explain why, for some individuals, NSSI may feel more like a need or a constant urge (Wester & McKibben, 2016), resulting in more process or behavioral addiction for some individuals compared to others. Still, other clients may dissociate when engaging in NSSI. Thus, their tolerance for pain is mitigated by their psychological response.

Typically lower levels of endogenous opioids are a result of childhood neglect or genetic vulnerabilities. Stress during childhood and adolescence can result in changes to the brain, including the inability to adapt and be flexible to the constant changes in life, and an inability or reduced ability to regulate stress (Lupien et al., 2009; Rothschild, 2000). This inability to regulate or cope may be due to a decreased amount of activity in the hippocampus, which has been known to be smaller among individuals who exhibit post-traumatic stress symptoms. Specifically, stress during birth to 2 years old has been found to impact the hippocampus, while stress during adolescence can impact the frontal lobe (Lupien et al., 2009). One of the main purposes of the hippocampus is to regulate emotions, while the main function of the frontal lobe is to carry out higher mental processes such as thinking, decision making, and planning. If these are smaller or impacted during trauma in children and youth, it makes sense that individuals may select NSSI as a coping method due to their inability to effectively use adaptive coping methods to regulate emotions and thoughts.

One proposed biological theory of NSSI posits a neural overlap in the processing of pain and social distress (Eisenberger, 2012). Eisenberger suggested that the unpleasantness of physical pain is processed in the same area of the brain as social pain or distress from loss, rejection, or isolation. This overlap may lead an individual who experiences social pain—for example a rejection from a peer, a loss of a loved one—to result in an activation of the need to process this social pain as a form of physical pain and, thus, NSSI engagement. Leder (1990) spoke of experiencing pain or an uncomfortable sensation as "dysappearance" or where the physical pain experienced can bring attention back to one's body to create a more lived experience. While Leder spoke of this physical pain in a negative, more medical way, Chandler altered the discussion of "dysappearance" in relation to self-injury specifically. She proposed that in regard to NSSI, this physical pain actually is a positive experience of a person as it can regulate the body or allow the person to feel grounded. Ultimately NSSI can increase cortisol levels and increase endogenous opioids, all of which help an individual feel better.

Other researchers have found increased levels of serotonin in individuals who self-harm (Crowell et al., 2008). Serotonin has been related to aggression and violent behavior in general, and self-injury specifically. Thus self-injury would be considered aggression or violence to oneself. While there has been some support for biological reasons for NSSI, it needs to be noted that most researchers examining possible biological reasons for self-injury have done so solely in populations diagnosed with Borderline Personality Disorder (BPD; e.g., Brunner et al., 2010; Jovev et al., 2008; Whittle et al., 2009). While this information is important, it is imperative that we highlight that while self-injury is one of the identifying criteria of BPD, NSSI has been found frequently in non-BPD populations. Therefore, it is difficult to attach these biological findings solely to NSSI without exploring populations with an absence of BPD.

Sociological Theories

While emotion regulation and biological theories explaining NSSI tend to be more pathological or medical model based, more recently theories have been emerging that highlight the sociological aspects of NSSI. Discussions of NSSI can be traced back to ancient Greek and biblical times, with references to self-injury in the Bible (Favazza, 1998). Only recently in the past few decades has NSSI received much more public scrutiny, attention, and research. This inquiry has led to more media attention, including NSSI being portrayed in fiction and nonfiction books, represented in films and television shows, stories and reports of NSSI in various fashion, developmental, and clinical magazines, along with newspaper articles, and a surge of NSSI on social media, including websites, Twitter handles, foundations, Facebook and MySpace groups, and many chat rooms with an emphasis on NSSI.

Due to the swell in attention to NSSI in society and the media, it has been suggested that this is the start of NSSI being less about pathology and psychological mental illness and more about NSSI being a form of sociological deviance (Adler & Adler, 2007; Hodgson, 2004). Sociological explanations for NSSI take into consideration the influence of society and culture, along with the interaction with other people. Thus these theories consider the overall social context when attempting to explain how or why individuals engage in NSSI.

Four reasons have been highlighted as explanations of why NSSI is becoming more of a sociological rather than a medical or psychopathological phenomenon. These include: (1) An increasingly diverse population engages in self-injury; (2) individuals are learning about self-injury in new ways, including social learning; (3) NSSI is not just an impulsive act, but is being used in instrumental and planful ways; and (4) there is a subculture around the acceptance of NSSI (Adler & Adler, 2007).

Earlier depictions of NSSI suggested that individuals who self-injured were intelligent, middle or upper class females ranging from adolescence to middle age (Favazza, 1998; Zila & Kiselica, 2001) who were abusing substances, were engaging in sexually risky behavior, or had previously been abused (Klausner, Rosenthal, Renzler, & Walesh, 1972), and exhibited self-loathing through criticism, guilt, or low self-esteem (Simpson, 1980). However, the population of those who self-injure has become more diverse, including both younger and older individuals—starting as early as 5 years old, even though the typical onset is around 13 years old, but also including long-term chronic self-injurers and those who self-injure later in life. Additionally, a smaller percentage than originally expected report histories of trauma and abuse, with some individuals reporting no childhood trauma, and instead reporting "perfect" childhood and family experiences (Adler & Adler, 2007; Wester & McKibben, 2016). While some individuals have been found to abuse substances or have low self-esteem and high self-criticism, others have been found to have high self-efficacy and be high achievers (Walsh, 2006). Additionally, NSSI is not just a female behavior, but instead males and females have been found to self-injure at similar rates. This speaks to the increasingly diverse population engaging in self-injury, signifying a larger societal issue rather than just a pathological concern.

Due to NSSI being represented through various venues, such as films, magazines, books, and social media, individuals are provided new ways to learn about NSSI. NSSI has historically been considered a symptom of larger mental health concerns, which is why originally it was only found in the Diagnostic and Statistical Manual IV-TR (APA, 2000) as a symptom of Borderline Personality Disorder. Historically, researchers and clinicians believed that NSSI was learned in isolation, where individuals felt they either accidentally learned NSSI or they "invented" it (Hodgson, 2004). More recently, however, a greater number of individuals are learning NSSI more socially, from others. More specifically, individuals are learning about NSSI from reading books and stories in magazines such as *Psychology Today* and *Seventeen*; teens are hearing about NSSI through discussions in health education classes, through speeches and media depictions of artists and Hollywood stars reporting their use of NSSI, along with films, television shows, and music lyrics depicting NSSI. NSSI is becoming more mainstream culture. It has been discussed on news channels such as CNN and ABC, and represented in newspapers. A search on YouTube.com in 2016 for "self-injury" led to "about 139,000" videos found (up 19,000 videos from the same search in 2015, which found "approximately 120,000"), and the number continues to increase. Multiple anti- and pro-NSSI websites, chat rooms, and message boards exist on the Internet. Therefore, the chances to hear and learn about NSSI are becoming easier as it exists as a phenomenon on a societal level.

Researchers are increasingly finding that individuals are engaging in NSSI in more instrumental, purposeful, and planful ways than originally proposed. While impulsivity still remains a concern for individuals who engage in NSSI behaviors, there are some who are very mediated and planful about their engagement in NSSI. Specifically, matching up to the emotion regulation theories indicated earlier, a meaning of "an effective way to deal with the world" (Hodgson, 2004, p. 170) has been suggested by individuals who self-injure. NSSI has been suggested to be a normed behavior, and an acceptable way of dealing with emotions such as sadness, confusion, guilt, and anger (Adler & Adler, 2007). As Chandler (2013) mentioned, NSSI speaks to a cultural discourse that physical pain is more privileged than emotional pain.

Finally, the fourth rationale for why NSSI is more a sociological deviance than a medical or psychological concern is the increasing subculture of acceptance around the behavior. It is believed to be a voluntary choice and lifestyle by some, not just a symptom of distress or problems. Some individuals have an explicit identity as a self-injurer (Adler & Adler, 2007; Nock ITM; Wester & McKibben, 2016). Taking from the Four Functions Model (FFM), individuals use NSSI to communicate to others either to socially signal or to belong to a group. This latter purpose may be to belong to a social group or connect with peers, while NSSI has also been found to spread in an environment such as a school. This is referred to as social contagion—thus when a popular individual in the school or peer group engages in self-injury others may try out the behavior in order to fit in, to belong, or simply because they are curious. Curiosity has been found to be a reason why some individuals engage in and continue utilizing NSSI (Hodgson, 2004). Additionally, pro-NSSI websites have emerged that are encouraging the behavior and providing tips on how to engage in various forms of NSSI as well as manage or hide it from others. While most individuals have hidden the behavior from others (Hodgson, 2004), more recently some wear and engage in NSSI as a badge of honor and support others in engaging in NSSI; this represents an increase in an affirming subculture around NSSI. This is similar to what occurred in the 1980s around eating-disordered behavior, another form of deliberate self-harm.

Application of Sociological Theories to Client Case: Mary

While the example of Mary provided above lends itself more to an emotion regulation explanation, what is unknown at this point is whether Mary actually heard about self-injury through readings, movies, peers, or artists who sing her favorite songs. While cutting her foot on the rocks while playing soccer barefoot may have been accidental, it may be that Mary could relate that experience to other settings where she heard or read about self-injury from others. Hearing about it from others, whether that be an artist held in high esteem, a peer in her school setting, or a stranger in a film or magazine article, this previous knowledge may lead to an increased possibility of maintaining the self-injuring behavior of cutting due to a previous social learning of self-injury. Therefore, understanding Mary's interactions with others, previous knowledge, and surrounding environment in relation to NSSI is important to better understand the acceptance and support her continued engagement.

Other Theories

Relational–Cultural Theory (RCT)

The first author has suggested seeing NSSI through the lens of relational–cultural theory (RCT; Trepal, 2010). RCT is a feminist and developmentally informed approach that considers both the individual's relational and societal contexts (Jordan, 2010). While most traditional developmental theories suggest that individuals grow up, become independent, and function best separately, RCT proposes that the ultimate goal in development is increased and relationally complex connections with others. According to RCT, people suffer in isolation and shame. At the heart of the theory, life is about connections. Connections with others do great things—they give people increased energy, empowerment, and the sense of wanting to continue to connect. Therefore, it makes sense that people long for these connections; however, based on past life experiences (called relational templates) people act in ways to keep themselves safe in relationships. Thus, although people intensely desire connections, they act in ways that keep them out of the very relationships they so desire. These methods are called strategies of disconnection (Jordan, 2010), and NSSI can be considered one of them. In this model, a strategy of disconnection can distance one from oneself and others, despite an intense underlying desire to connect.

Another aspect of RCT is the concept of societal stratification. Society has oppressed and marginalized groups of people so that connection is not always possible. Trepal (2010) suggests that these societal disconnections are especially powerful for women due to historical objectification and silencing. However, men are not immune. For example, men can be socialized to safely express feelings such as anger. Other emotions, such as fear, guilt, shame, and sadness are culturally feminized. Thus, men may be culturally disconnected from feeling and expressing a wide range of emotions, leading them to turn inward and self-injure (Trepal, 2010). In addition, we know that clients also exist at the intersections of various life demographics and identity statuses (race, ethnicity, sex, gender, affectional status, socioeconomic status, ability status, among others). When society privileges or marginalizes aspects of one's identity, people can be further isolated and disconnected from others, as well as from what they perceive to be mainstream society.

For example, consider an adolescent who identifies as bisexual and was bullied at school. They may initially feel a range of things from fear to shame to anger. The youth comes home and tells their parent about the bullying and tries to express their feelings. The parent responds with silence or anger—telling the child that the bullying is "their own fault." If the child hadn't been so different, so "gay," then they would not have been bullied. Over time and with repeated results, the child learns that emotional safety does not exist in close relationships or, from their perspective, within society. They cannot be their authentic self in relationships or in society. The adolescent then discovers NSSI and disconnects from their feelings and their bodies, and others, through self-harm. This case represents various aspects of NSSI—the development of relational templates (the parent's reaction to the youth's sharing of feelings), cultural disconnections (the bullying and the parent's emphasis on the child as *different* from others), and the development of a strategy for disconnection (the NSSI develops in an attempt to stay safely disconnected both in relationships and the world).

Using RCT as a theoretical frame, mental health professionals can work with clients who self-injure to enhance their self-empathy, explore relational templates that relate to their strategies for disconnection, and encourage them to represent themselves authentically in relationships with the ultimate goal of increasing connections and decreasing isolation and the use of NSSI. In addition, prevention efforts can focus on identifying and ameliorating aspects of culture and society that serve to isolate and disconnect clients from themselves and others (Trepal, 2010).

Application of Relational–Cultural Theory to Client Case: Mary

In Mary's case, if we were to apply relational–cultural theory, we need to consider how the self-injurious behavior that she accidentally used (and let's say continues to use) impacts or associates with her relations to herself and to others. For example, while she is hopeful as well as anxious regarding sexting with her uncle, does the cut on her foot that calmed her down help her to disconnect from those internal, unbearable feelings? Thus ultimately disconnected from her body, will she not be as attuned with herself? Additionally, how does NSSI help her relate, or disconnect, with others? Take the relationship with her uncle, for example. While she is excited and hopeful on one hand about this possible relationship developing through texting, her NSSI behaviors may be a way to purposefully disconnect from this relationship, maybe put her uncle off or make her body unattractive. Additionally, if the sexting is exciting for Mary because this engagement provides her with attention she has not received in other places, sexting along with NSSI can be a result of a desire to connect but not understanding how to do so in a more appropriate manner. Her uncle, of course, is only one relationship to consider, but in therapy, clinicians need to consider many other relationships, including familial and peer.

Systemic Perspective

While researchers have suggested the possibility of an environmental perspective, this has rarely been explored or discussed outside of the Four Functions Model (FFM) of positive and negative reinforcement of affect and social functions. In the FFM, Nock mentions how individuals use NSSI to influence individuals and the environments around them. What is not discussed extensively, however, is how the larger environment influences why and how an individual selects and continues to engage in NSSI. A larger systemic model would lead to helping researchers and clinicians better understand a holistic, contextual picture of the client and his or her engagement in NSSI.

A larger systemic model can be supported through findings from individual studies. Researchers have explored components of larger systems in smaller individual fragments. These include history of abuse, family criticism and conflict, family interpersonal connectedness, sense of belonging to one's ethnic group, and more recently the suggestions that NSSI continues to increase due to societal norming of NSSI behaviors (Adler & Adler, 2007; Wester, Ivers, Villalba, & Trepal, 2016; Wester & Trepal, 2010). More specifically, when each variable or context is explored individually, they have been found to explain NSSI, albeit only smaller percentages of NSSI behavior. However, if combined, or explored altogether, they may explain greater amounts of NSSI engagement. In particular, the combination of contextual and individual factors may begin to help clinicians better understand the behavior and how to best address it for each client.

It may be helpful to begin thinking of NSSI on a larger systemic perspective, considering blending some of the existing models and explanations of NSSI with a larger ecological theory, such as Bronfenbrenner's Ecological Systems Theory (Figure 2.2). Doing so would take into consideration the individual along with the interactions and relationships they have with individuals surrounding them, the larger environment and culture, as well as the timing of various events.

Application of the Systems Perspective to a Client Case: Mary

Taking this systemic model into consideration, it would suggest that it is not just Mary and her internal processes and reasons of why she accidentally found NSSI while playing soccer, why it may have worked to regulate her emotions of anticipation and anxiety, or why she continued to engage in NSSI. Instead it would explore the larger context around her. This would include better understanding Mary's microsystem, but also understanding her larger surroundings. More specifically, what is going on in the family, including but not limited to her relationships with her immediate family members (e.g., mom, dad, siblings), along with extrafamilial family members (e.g., uncle, aunt). It would explore her school environment, relationships with peers, significant others such as boyfriends or girlfriends, as well as prevalence of NSSI in her school (i.e., is she aware of others engaging in

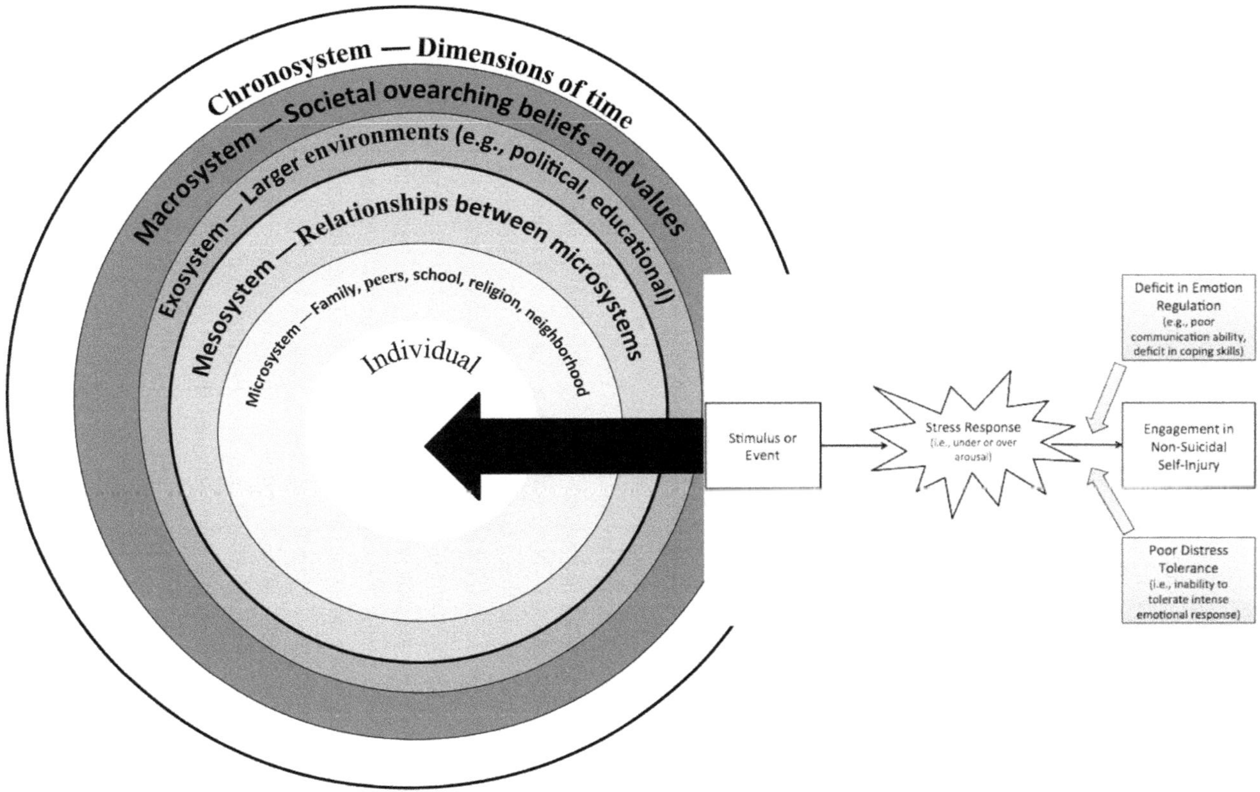

FIGURE 2.2. Systems perspective of NSSI

the behavior). Exploring and understanding the microsystem would even consider her religious affiliations and beliefs, along with current neighborhood environment (e.g., violence, community atmosphere). The clinician would then connect the information from the microsystem with the macrosystem. This means exploring the relationships between the systems. In Mary's case, this might be exploring how the family interacts or engages with Mary's peers, or the school Mary attends, or how her immediate nuclear family interacts or values the extrafamilial family, messages that have been provided in interacting with other family members (e.g., always listen to your family, do what they say).

Along with the immediate environments that Mary interacts with, this larger systemic perspective would take into consideration the exosystem, or the messages and beliefs that are in the larger systems. While Mary may not directly interact with these messages or environments, they would impact her. For example, has state government recently cut funding to the educational system, which may result in less administrative or teacher oversight in the schools? This may result in less one-on-one interaction between teacher and student, or a decrease in the availability of a school counselor, therefore allowing Mary to slip under the radar in the school setting. The exosystem may also entail a parent losing a job, which may result in decreased financial support to gain mental health or medical treatment; it may have resulted in a parent changing jobs, which may have resulted in less parental supervision of Mary, all of which could have resulted in either her NSSI or sexting behaviors.

Larger cultural and societal beliefs, values, and events are also considered in the systemic perspective (i.e., macrosystem). This would explore what is currently occurring culturally and on a larger societal level for Mary. In this case, media has increased portrayal and discussion of NSSI versus what was present a few decades ago, which may make it more likely that Mary has heard about, or is accepting of, NSSI behavior. Finally, Bronfenbrenner discussed the chronosystem, which includes timing of events. This includes timing of what is occurring in Mary's life, as well as chronologically, and how time interacts with all of the other systems. This would encourage a clinician to consider events that may have occurred at specific moments in development for Mary, asking such questions as: Was Mary abused in her life, and if so, at what age and developmental stage? Given that sexting with her uncle is occurring at 16 years old, what developmental considerations need to be given regarding the impact of this engagement, along with why NSSI may have been selected as a coping method. The chronosystem would suggest that clinicians should also consider how events in the microsystem interact with the individual, the events, and the macrosystem.

Conclusion

This chapter presented various theoretical explanations for why individuals engage in NSSI. Each model proposes a slightly different understanding of why and how an individual selects, and continues to engage in, NSSI. These theories can help clinicians to better conceptualize what the specific individual may need, thus helping to drive treatment. Consider the various emotion regulation models. If a clinician understands NSSI from the Experiential Avoidance Model (Chapman et al., 2006), then they would believe that an individual has low distress tolerance while experiencing high aversive emotions, while lacking effective coping strategies. Thus, an increase in problem-focused coping and relaxation techniques, along with the ability to tolerate distress, would decrease the overall use of NSSI. However, if a clinician understands NSSI from more of the Four Functions Model (FFM; Nock & Prinstein, 2004), then questions inquiring if NSSI is serving more social or automatic/emotive functions would help drive interventions. This would help a clinician know if they needed to help increase communication ability (social functions of NSSI) versus emotion regulation strategies (automatic functions of NSSI). Therefore, clinicians may implement treatment such as dialectical behavior therapy or problem solving therapy (discussed in Chapter 7) to alleviate the causes of NSSI, or may select various interventions (discussed in Chapter 8) that match up with how they conceptualize the onset of NSSI for the client.

If clinicians did not view NSSI through the lens of emotion regulation models, but instead believed NSSI is a result of biological reasons, then more pharmacological treatment to adjust the levels of serotonin or cortisol levels might be necessary. If a clinician approached understanding NSSI from a systems perspective, then treatment may result (after assessment) in a focus on communication or coping strategies, but also family communication or interventions that are larger organization- or school-based. Thus, it can be seen how understanding the reasons and theories behind NSSI can drive treatment implications.

References

Adler, P. A., & Adler, P. (2007). The demedicalization of self-injury: From psychopathology to sociological deviance. *Journal of Contemporary Ethnography, 36*, 537–570.

American Psychiatric Association. (2000). *Diagnostic and statistical manual of mental disorders* (4th edition, text revised). Washington, DC: Author.

Bresin, K. (2014). Five indices of emotion regulation in participants with a history of nonsuicidal self-injury: A daily diary study. *Behavior Therapy, 45*, 56–66.

Brunner, R., Henze, R., Parzer, P., Kramer, J., Feigl, N., Lutz, K., & Stieltjes, B. (2010). Reduced prefrontal and orbitofrontal gray matter in female adolescents with borderline personality disorder: Is it disorder specific? *NeuroImage, 49*(1), 114–120.

Cerutti, R., Calabrese, M., & Valastro, C. (2013). Alexithymia and personality disorders in the adolescent non-suicidal self-injury: Preliminary results. *Procedia—Social and Behavioral Sciences, 21*, 372–376.

Chandler, A. (2013). Inviting pain? Pain, dualism and embodiment in narratives of self-injury. *Sociology of Health & Illness, 35*(5), 716–730.

Chapman, A. L., Gratz, K. L., & Brown, M. Z. (2006). Solving the puzzle of deliberate self-harm: The experiential avoidance model. *Behaviour Research and Therapy, 44*, 371–394.

Crowell, S. E., Beauchaine, T. P., & Linehan, M. M. (2008). A biosocial developmental model of Borderline Personality: Elaborating and extending Linehan's Theory. *Psychological Bulletin, 135*, 495–510.

Eisenberger, N. I. (2012). The neural bases of social pain: Evidence for shared representations with physical pain. *Psychosomatic Medicine, 74*, 126–135.

Favazza, A. R. (1998). The coming of age of self-mutilation. *The Journal of Nervous and Mental Disease, 186*, 259–268.

Groschwitz, R. C., & Plener, P. L. (2012). The neurobiology of non-suicidal self-injury (NSSI): A review. *Suicidology Online, 3*, 24–31.

Gross, J. J. (Ed.). *Handbook of emotion regulation.* New York: Guilford Press.

Hodgson, S. (2004). Cutting through silence: A sociological construction of self-injury. *Sociological Inquiry, 74*, 162–179.

Jordan, J. V. (2010). *Relational–cultural therapy*. Washington, DC: American Psychological Association.

Jovev, M., Garner, B., Phillips, L., Velakoulis, D., Wood, S. J., Jackson, H. J., & Chanen, A. M. (2008). An MRI study of pituitary volume and parasuicidal behavior in teenagers with first-presentation borderline personality disorder. *Psychiatry Research, 162*(3), 273–277.

Kemperman, I., Russ, M. J., & Shearin, E. (1997). Self-injurious behavior and mood regulation in borderline patients. *Journal of Personality Disorders, 11*(2), 146–157.

Klausner, E., Rosenthal, R., Renzler, C., & Walesh, R. (1972). Wrist cutting syndrome: The meaning of a gesture. *American Journal of Psychiatry, 128*, 1363–1368.

Klonsky, E. D. (2011). Non-suicidal self-injury in United States adults: prevalence, sociodemographics, topography, and functions. *Psychological Medicine, 41*, 1981–1986.

Leder, D. (1990). *The Absent Body*. Chicago, IL: The University of Chicago Press.

Lupien, S. J., McEwen, B. S., Gunnar, M. R., & Heim, C. (2009). Effects of stress throughout the lifespan on the brain, behavior and cognition. *Nature Reviews Neuroscience, 10*, 434–445.

Muehlenkamp, J. J., Engle, S. G., Crosby, R. D., Wonderlich, S. A., Simonich, H., & Mitchell, J. E. (2009). Emotional states preceding and following acts of non-suicidal self-injury in bulimia nervosa patients. *Behavior Research and Therapy, 47*(1), 83–87.

Nock, M. K. (2009). Why do people hurt themselves? New insights into the nature and functions of self-injury. *Current Directions in Psychological Science, 18*, 78–83.

Nock, M. K., & Prinstein, M. J. (2004). A functional approach to the assessment of self-mutilative behavior. *Journal of Consulting and Clinical Psychology, 72*(5), 885–890.

Nock, M. K., Prinstein, M., & Sterba, S. (2009). Revealing the form and function of self-injurious thoughts and behaviors: A real-time ecological assessment study among adolescents and young adults. *Journal of Abnormal Psychology, 118*, 816–827.

Nock, M. K., Prinstein, M., & Sterba, S. (2010). Revealing the form and function of self-injurious thoughts and behaviors: A real-time ecological assessment study among adolescents and young adults. *Psychology of Violence, 1*, 36–52.

Paul, T., Schroeter, K., Dahme, B., & Nutzinger, D. O. (2002). Self-injurious behavior in women with eating disorders. *American Journal of Psychiatry, 159*, 408–411.

Rothschild, B. (2000). *The body remembers: The psychophysiology of trauma and trauma treatment.* New York, NY: W. W. Norton & Company, Inc.

Simpson, M. (1980). Self-mutilation is indirect self-destructive behavior. In N. L. Farberow (Ed.), *The many faces of suicide* (pp. 257–283). New York: McGraw-Hill.

Stewart, S. L., Baiden, P., & Theall-Honey, L. (2014). Examining non-suicidal self-injury among adolescents with mental health needs, in Ontario, Canada. *Archives of Suicide Research, 18*, 392–409.

Trepal, H. C. (2010). Exploring self-injury through a relational–cultural lens. *Journal of Counseling & Development, 88*(4), 494–499.

Trepal, H. C., Wester, K. L., & Merchant, E. (2015). A cross sectional matched sample study of non-suicidal self-injury among young adults: Support for interpersonal and intrapersonal factors, with implications for coping strategies. *Child and Adolescent Psychiatry and Mental Health, 9*, 36.

Walsh, B. (2006). *Treating self-injury: A practical guide*. New York: Guilford Press.

Wester, K. L., & McKibben, B. (2016). Participants' experiences of nonsuicidal self-injury: Supporting existing theory and emerging conceptual pathways. *Journal of Mental Health Counseling, 38*, 12–27.

Wester, K. L., & Trepal, H. C. (2010). Coping behaviors, abuse history, and counseling: Differentiating college students who self-injure. *Journal of College Counseling, 13*, 141–154.

Wester, K. L., Ivers, N., Villalba, J. A., & Trepal, H. C. (2016). The relationship between nonsuicidal self-injury and suicidal ideation. *Journal of Counseling & Development, 94*, 3–12.

Whittle S., Chanen, A. M., Fornito, A., McGorry, P. D., Pantelis, C., & Yücel, M. (2009). Anterior cingulate volume in adolescents with first-presentation borderline personality disorder. *Psychiatry Research, 172*(2), 155–160.

three
Non-Suicidal Self-Injury and Suicide

Non-suicidal self-injury (NSSI) is often mistaken for or confused with a suicide attempt, which makes the treatment of NSSI difficult. To mistake NSSI as suicide could result in implementing inappropriate, and potentially expensive, treatment, such as sending an individual to an inpatient behavioral treatment center. It could also create potential ethical quandaries related to breaking the confidentiality of minor clients. While at times this type of treatment is helpful for NSSI, it is not necessary in most cases. Yet to completely ignore the overlap or connections between NSSI and suicide would be problematic as well, as NSSI is one of the predictors of suicidal behavior.

NSSI and suicide differ by definition. While they appear similar in behavioral actions, they are distinctly different in purpose. Both behaviors fall under the larger umbrella of *self-directed violence*. Self-directed violence is defined by the Centers for Disease Control and Prevention (CDC) as the intentional use of physical force or power against oneself, which either results in or has a high likelihood of resulting in injury, death, psychological harm, maldevelopment, or deprivation. Self-directed violence encompasses a wide range of behaviors including NSSI and suicidal behaviors. Suicidal behaviors encompass acts of fatal and nonfatal suicide and suicidal ideation.

The CDC has labeled self-directed violence as a major public health problem in the world, as suicide (only one form of self-directed violence) is the 11th leading cause of death in the United States, but the third leading cause of death among persons aged 15 to 24 (Crosby, Ortega, & Melanson, 2011). More individuals are hospitalized due to nonfatal suicidal behavior and NSSI behaviors. Some NSSI behaviors are mislabeled as suicide attempts by clinicians and health providers. Although many individuals have received medical care in hospital emergency departments, greater than 50% of persons engaging in suicidal behaviors never seek health services (Crosby et al., 1999), and 80% of individuals who currently engage in NSSI are not reaching out for mental health services (Wester & Trepal, 2010). Therefore, while it is helpful to understand the nuanced differences between suicidal and non-suicidal self-injurious behaviors, it is also important for mental health professionals to engage in advocacy around self-directed violence (see Chapter 12 for more information about advocacy for NSSI).

What makes it difficult to parcel out suicidal and non-suicidal self-injurious behaviors is that they can look similar (e.g., a cut from a razor on one's arm) and both have similar predicting factors. Predicting factors for NSSI and suicidal behaviors include depression, anxiety, post-traumatic stress, sexual or physical abuse, externalizing behaviors, and family problems. Both suicide and NSSI have been found to co-exist, and are highly related. More specifically, 10% of pre-adolescents, 35% of adolescents, and 16% to 25% of adults engaged in NSSI also reported suicidal behaviors (Hamza, Stewart, & Willoughby, 2012). Rates of NSSI and suicide co-existing have been as high as 92% among adults, with 57% of individuals reporting both NSSI and suicide attempts and 35% reporting NSSI and suicidal ideations (Wester & McKibben, 2016). With so much co-occurrence, it is important to be able to discern the differences between the behaviors.

By definition NSSI and suicide differ. Specifically, NSSI is defined as intentional, self-inflicted harm that causes immediate damage to body tissue with no suicidal intent. However, suicidal behavior is defined as behavior that is self-directed and deliberately results in injury or the potential injury to oneself with implicit or explicit evidence of wanting to die. NSSI and suicidal behaviors have been found

Box 3.1 Suicide and NSSI Definitions

Non-Suicidal Self-Injury (NSSI)

Intentional, self-inflicted harm that causes immediate damage to body tissue with no suicidal intent.

Suicidal Behavior

Behavior that is self-directed and deliberately results in injury or the potential injury to oneself with implicit or explicit evidence of wanting to die

TABLE 3.1. Differences Between Suicidal and Non-Suicidal Self-Injury

	Non-Suicidal Self-Injury	Suicide
Prevalence	Widespread, more prevalent	Prevalent in a smaller subset of the population
Frequency	Performed dozens, hundreds, or thousands of times by one individual	Performed once or a few times
Methods	Range of methods, such as cutting or burning, but all methods cause immediate tissue damage; type of method may change based on purpose or tolerance	Includes methods that can cause immediate tissue damage but also non-tissue damage methods such as overdose or self-poisoning; type of method rarely differs per attempt
Severity	Rarely leads to lethal injury or needs medical attention	Usually needs medical attention and can result in lethal injury
Intent/ Purpose	To maintain or temporarily increase functioning, without death	To die; to end all experiences

to differ on five dimensions. These include prevalence, frequency, methods, severity, and function/purpose (see Table 3.1).

Frequency and Prevalence

While suicide is a leading cause of death, NSSI is engaged in more frequently by a greater number of individuals. Consider an individual who may be engaging in both suicidal behaviors and NSSI concurrently. This individual may self-injure with no suicidal intent ten, twenty, or even ninety times before engaging in one act of self-injury with the intent to die as a result of the behavior. An individual has been found to engage in NSSI an average of 80 times in one year (Nock & Prinstein, 2004), while the mean number of lifetime suicide attempts is 2.8 (Nock, Joiner, & Gordon, 2006). Therefore, NSSI is more frequently engaged in compared to suicidal behaviors. Additionally, even when rates of co-occurring suicide and NSSI are high, there are individuals who report engaging in NSSI without ever having suicidal ideation or attempts (Wester & McKibben, 2016). While suicidal behaviors and NSSI do co-occur, thoughts of NSSI and suicide rarely co-occur at the same moment. Thus, when Barbara is having thoughts of cutting herself to regulate her emotions and gain control of her thoughts (i.e., NSSI) she typically is not also having thoughts of killing herself (i.e., suicide). Thoughts of NSSI and suicide occur together less than 5% of the time (Nock, Prinstein, & Sterba, 2010). When they do, it appears that NSSI is being used to thwart or delay attempts of suicide.

Methods

While suicidal behavioral methods and NSSI often mimic each other, they also differ. Most individuals utilize more than one method to engage in NSSI behaviors. The average number of methods used by adolescents and young adults is two to three, with some reporting as many as eleven methods throughout their lifetime. One individual may be cutting and burning to self-harm, with no suicidal intent, while another may report a wider range of methods, ranging from wound picking and hair pulling to cutting and burning. This process of switching may be using each method for a particular reason, such as cutting oneself to regulate emotions but burning oneself to self-punish; or it may be due to an increase in tolerance. That is, the individual may need to engage in a more severe form of NSSI in order to achieve the same result (e.g., regulate emotions). Regardless of how many methods are used to engage in NSSI, each of the methods causes immediate tissue damage (e.g., hair pulling causes tissue damage to a hair follicle, cutting to the skin and underlying tissue).

Individuals who attempt suicide more than one time tend to use the same method; thus they are not switching methods each time they attempt to self-inflict death (Berman et al., 2006). Furthermore, the methods used to engage in suicidal behavior are sometimes different than those selected for NSSI, although at times they look the same. For example, methods used to attempt suicide include both those that cause immediate tissue damage (e.g., cutting self with a razor blade), but also those that do not (e.g., self-poisoning, overdosing). When a person uses the same type of method to self-harm both for NSSI and suicidal purposes, the method may differ slightly. It may be a subtle difference though, such as a horizontal cut versus a vertical cut on a forearm, or cutting on one's leg versus cutting on a vein, or even cutting using scissors versus a razor blade in the same location on the body.

Severity and Intent

The severity of the injury is related to the purpose. That is, the purpose of NSSI is to continue to live, to function, to engage in life and with others; while the purpose of suicide is to end all life, to stop living. Therefore, the severity of harm done when attempting suicide is much more severe than with NSSI. It is important to note that NSSI can accidentally result in severe or mortal wounds, without intention. When this occurs it is typically due to impulsive behavior, having such a high level of aversive emotions or thoughts that one feels out of control and engages in reckless or thoughtless behavior, or being under the influence of other substances such as drugs or alcohol. Therefore, it is helpful to assess clients for impulsive behaviors, along with assessing for severity of NSSI methods (e.g., using a scalpel versus dull scissors), checking for severe wounds or wounds the individual is not allowing to heal, determining if NSSI is chronic in nature (i.e., length of time engaging in NSSI), assessing for the development of tolerance to previous or current methods, and whether the individual engages in NSSI under the influence of other substances, in order to assure that accidental death, infections, or serious injuries are not being inflicted unintentionally. More about assessment related to NSSI can be found in Chapter 4.

Although NSSI and suicidal behaviors are different, NSSI has been found to be a robust predictor of suicidal behaviors. It is a stronger predictor of suicidal behavior than other predictors, including depression, hopelessness, post-traumatic stress, and history of child abuse (Hamza et al., 2012). Both lifetime and current NSSI engagement have been found to predict suicidal ideations and attempts (Andover & Gibb, 2010; Glenn & Klonsky, 2009; Nock et al., 2006; Wester, Ivers, Villalba, & Trepal, 2016; Whitlock & Knox, 2007). More recently it has been found that current engagement in NSSI behaviors is a stronger predictor of suicidal ideations than lifetime NSSI (Wester et al., 2016). It is not just current NSSI engagement but also the number of methods used to self-injure that predicts suicidal ideation. The more methods one uses to NSSI, the more likely they are to be having suicidal ideations as well. Let's consider this practically. It means that if a person was to scratch themselves, cut themselves with a razor blade, and burn their skin to self-injure, they would be more likely to have suicidal ideations than someone who is only self-cutting. The use of multiple methods can be because each method has a different purposes, or it can be related to the development of tolerance for existing methods used.

Considering the emotion regulation models discussed in Chapter 2, NSSI provides temporary relief from the original presenting concern. Yet, eventually tolerance to methods can be built up (Wester & McKibben, 2016), resulting in the need to increase the severity of the current method or switch to an entirely different method. One 32-year-old female shared her story of self-injury, revealing her development of tolerance to her various methods across time.

> "I started burning myself with incense or candle wax in seventh grade as a way to deal with anger. . . . I learned that pain can quickly dull emotions! I switched to cutting myself, first with an X-Acto knife and then with dismantling disposable razor blades in eighth grade. By sophomore year in high school, I was carrying razor blades with me everywhere I went and cutting multiple times a day. What started as a way to deal with negative emotions quickly spiraled into a way to feel in control. Cafeteria doesn't have what they said they would? Cut. Homework not right? Cut. Your sister left you in a parking garage downtown for three hours? Cut cut cut. By the end of high school, I was cutting so much that I would lose small periods of time. I was very secretive and smart about my cutting. Thighs. Breasts. Torso. Places no one had to see. I was having to cut more and deeper though, to get the same effect."

Her experience shows how methods can change and shift across time, but that she needed to self-harm more frequently, as well as more severely, in order to get the same effect of sense of control from NSSI as she did initially with burning her skin. Another example of tolerance is provided by a 45-year-old female who discusses her trajectory into NSSI: "I started self injuring at the age of 4 with safety pins. Throughout early childhood I did impassive things like bang my head against doors and jab my palm with pencils. At 10 . . . I used a nail to cut out a loose baby tooth. At 12, I switched to razor blades and honed that trance state by engaging in ritual (using same blades and rags, playing certain music, looking into the mirror, cutting for a similar amount of time)." You can see from this case that she started with minor self-injury (i.e., safety pins) that caused minimal tissue damage but across time escalated to more severe NSSI, using razor blades to cut.

To increase tolerance is to change methods or engage in more severe NSSI (e.g., cutting deeper) due to the method of choice no longer working, no longer regulating emotions, or no longer serving the original purpose or goal of the behavior. If NSSI is being used to cope or to regulate emotions, and this method is no longer working, then a sense of hopelessness can set in, a sense that nothing is going to get better and nothing the person is doing is working. This can result in suicidal ideation—a desire to end life—as the individual cannot see a way out of the current emotion/s or situation. While the number of methods has been found to positively relate to suicidal behaviors, specific methods have been found to relate, as well. More severe NSSI methods such as cutting, burning, or carving in one's skin are greater predictors of suicidal behavior compared to less severe or moderate forms of NSSI, such as pulling one's hair or biting oneself (Favaro et al., 2008; Lloyd-Richardson, Perrine, Dierker, & Kelley, 2007; Tang et al., 2011).

Interestingly, while engagement in NSSI, and number and type of methods used, have been found to be strong predictors of suicidal behavior, the frequency of NSSI engagement is not related at all (Nock et al., 2006; Wester et al., 2016). That is, suicidal ideations or attempts do not seem to be impacted regardless of whether a person has engaged in NSSI one time or one thousand times. It may be less about the number of times one engages in NSSI and more about whether the engagement is actually working. For example, if Sam has cut himself because he has received a lower than expected grade on his paper, and cutting himself resulted in a sense of relief or control, then he may continue to do this every time he receives a lower than desired grade on any exam or homework assignment. He may even transfer the use of NSSI to other situations, such as football or soccer, where he feels he has performed less than perfect. Therefore, his frequency of cutting may increase. However, if cutting works for Sam, and therefore continues to calm him down, to help him gain a sense of control, then this continual use of cutting may never result in a sense of hopelessness or suicidal ideations, as his selected method of coping (i.e., NSSI) is currently working for him. If cutting stops working for Sam, or he needs to cut more, cut deeper, or even switch to another method, such as burning himself, to gain the same sense of calm, this then reveals that his original method of cutting or NSSI is no longer working for him. Sam may be gaining a tolerance to the original cutting behavior he selected. Thus, it is less about the frequency of NSSI engagement that seems to predict suicidal behaviors and more about the actual engagement or the number of methods.

Theories Linking NSSI and Suicide

In order to explain *why* NSSI and suicide are linked, various theories have been proposed. While the full exploration of these theories is not in the scope of this book, some highlights as to how these are connected are provided through a brief discussion of three theories: the Gateway Theory, the Interpersonal-Psychological Theory of Suicide, and the Third Variable Theory.

Gateway Theory

The Gateway Theory, originally proposed by Stanley, Winchell, Molcho, and Simeon (1992), suggests that NSSI and suicidal behavior exist on a continuum, both sharing similar behavioral and experiential qualities, although the intent is different. This theory posits that NSSI precedes the development of suicidal behaviors and that suicidal behaviors actually stem from escalating or increasing NSSI behaviors, including frequency or severity. This model is grounded in other models of self-harm, including substance abuse. For example, researchers have suggested that marijuana is a gateway drug for more extreme, severe drug use. The Gateway Theory has been supported in that lifetime and current NSSI engagement, number of methods, and type of methods predict suicidal behaviors.

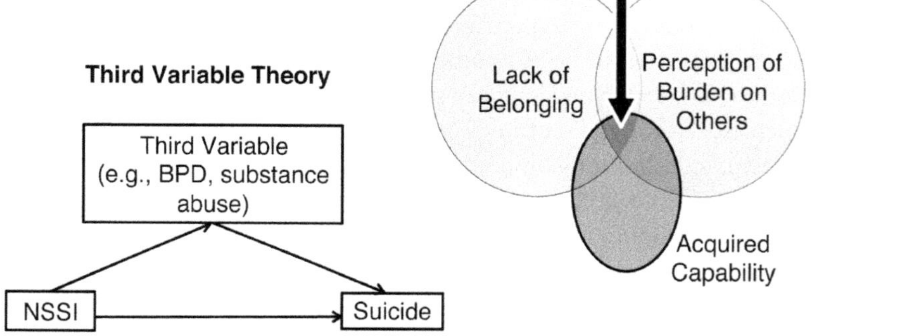

FIGURE 3.1. Altered figures of theories of suicide

Interpersonal-Psychological Theory of Suicide

Joiner agreed to some extent with Stanley et al. (1992) in his Interpersonal-Psychological Theory of Suicide, as he suggested that in order for an individual to engage in a behavior such as suicide, which requires the ability to intentionally harm oneself, the individual needs to overcome the fear of causing oneself harm or physical pain. He calls the process of overcoming the fear and being able to engage in suicidal behaviors *acquired capability*. NSSI is one of the many ways in which an individual can acquire the capability to harm oneself. Other ways he suggested include, but are not limited to, multiple surgeries, domestic violence, and other forms of bodily harm. NSSI is one way in which a person can become desensitized to the fear of causing harm or pain to one's body—which is needed typically for engaging in suicidal behaviors. Acquired capability is not the only component of Joiner's Interpersonal-Psychological Theory of Suicide, but is only one factor he deemed to be necessary to move from suicidal ideations to suicide attempts. This theory has also been supported by research.

Third Variable Theory

Another theory that links NSSI and suicide is the Third Variable Theory (Hamza et al., 2012). It is suggested that ultimately suicide and NSSI are not related at all, but that in fact they are linked through some spurious external variable, such as psychological disorder (e.g., Borderline Personality Disorder) or behavior (e.g., substance abuse) which increases the risk for both NSSI and suicidal behaviors, resulting in a correlation simply because they are co-occurring but not directly related. Another example of how to consider this is that researchers have found consumption of ice cream to be positively related to theft and robbery; that is, as the sales and consumption of ice cream increases, so does the number of thefts and robberies. While this relationship doesn't make any sense, as most individuals do not consume ice cream, then pull up to a vacant home to break and enter with the desire to steal, the relationship between these two behaviors is really temperature or weather. Specifically, more ice cream is consumed during summer months when the weather is nicer and the temperature is hotter. This is also the time when families leave their homes for vacations and time away, which increases the ability for thefts and robberies to occur. Therefore, both eating ice cream and robberies are related to weather and higher temperatures, but are not necessarily related to each other. The relationship is spurious. This is the idea behind the Third Variable Theory. This theory has also been supported through exploration in psychological disorders such as Borderline Personality Disorder (BPD), where individuals seem to have an increase of both NSSI and suicidal behaviors (Jacobson, Muehlenkamp, Miller, & Turner, 2008; Nock et al., 2006), with these behaviors being linked more to BPD than to each other.

Hamza and colleagues (2012) suggest that ultimately all three of these NSSI-Suicide models need to be blended into a larger integrated model, that "third variables" such as BPD need to be considered and controlled for in research, as well as in clinical assessment of NSSI and suicidal behavior, understanding that these third external variables actually increase the risk of NSSI and suicide co-occurring. They also suggested, however, that with so much research backing NSSI predicting suicidal behavior, this link simply cannot be ignored and considered to be completely spurious. Rather, the fact may be that NSSI is a gateway behavior that helps one acquire capability to engage in suicidal behaviors. So, it may be the combination of all of these models to create the perfect storm for NSSI to transfer or result in suicidal behaviors.

It needs to be noted, however, that even if NSSI desensitizes an individual to engage in suicidal behaviors, that suicidal behavior or attempt is not the end of the continuum. While most theorists have suggested NSSI and suicide to lie on a continuum, it should be considered more of a cycle. Individuals may begin with mild or moderate forms of NSSI (e.g., scratching self, pulling hair, punching self), but as tolerance increases they seek out more severe methods (e.g., cutting, burning methods), which links to and increases suicidal ideations. If an individual attempts suicide, they may continue engaging in NSSI to alleviate aversive, intense emotions or to control social situations; however, they may not attempt suicide for an extended period of time or ever, although past suicide attempts do predict future suicide attempts. Therefore, it is important to understand that NSSI and suicide may lie on a continuum and *are* related; yet this relationship has many other factors to consider in the context of the relationship.

Finally, while they are related and NSSI predicts suicidal behaviors, it is important to note that NSSI has also been found to protect against the actual attempt of suicide. More specifically, 37% of individuals reported that they engaged in NSSI to halt or delay their attempt to kill themselves, knowing that if they could delay the desire to attempt suicide, the yearning to die and end life would dissipate. As one 18-year-old female indicated, "At times, self-injury was the only thing standing between me and suicide. It was kind of like a compromise or a half-way point. Like if I couldn't actually kill myself, hurting myself was enough for a while." A 21-year-old male directly stated "injuring myself stopped me attempting suicide on numerous occasions." Therefore, it is important *not* to remove the NSSI behavior prior to allowing an individual to gain other coping skills first.

Differentiating Suicide and NSSI

So the question becomes how to tell suicide and NSSI apart when working with a client. Given that NSSI and suicide have some of the same predictors, including past trauma such as physical or sexual abuse, depression, relational or family conflict, impulsivity, isolation or sense of being alone, or various psychological disorders or symptoms, along with the similarity of self-inflicted behaviors, it can be difficult during assessment to differentiate. This also leads to the need to assess each episode of self-harm individually, as while one episode may be NSSI, another may be suicide. Then to muddy the waters even further, another episode may be a mix of the two forms of self-directed violence, with an individual intentionally setting out to kill himself, then to decide he only wants to inflict harm in order to continue living, or vice versa.

The first course of assessment is to inquire from the client or patient him- or herself about the behavior and intention behind the behavior. How do they describe the form of self-harm? Was it purposefully to kill oneself or to continue living life? Therefore, it is important to separate the questions "Do you want to or have you ever harmed yourself?" and "Do you want to kill yourself? Have you ever attempted to kill yourself?" Separating these questions can serve two purposes. One is to clarify if the individual has attempted, or is currently considering, killing him- or herself, providing you as the clinician with crucial information. Secondly, it also indicates to your client that you are well aware that there is a difference between suicide and NSSI behaviors, making them more likely to report NSSI to you. Being able to open this line of communication between the clinician and client is imperative so that the client is willing to share more about his or her self-injuring behavior, including purpose, reasons, functions, methods, and more. One client shared with the first author that she used NSSI to help her feel better, to feel more calm. She used both cutting and burning to help her alleviate extreme feelings of anger and anxiety, as well as when she felt abandoned by her mother. She also reported increases in NSSI behaviors when she started dating a peer who also engaged in NSSI, but when she ended the relationship her frequency of self-harm decreased as well, although was still present. However, through these discussions of methods, frequency, purpose, functions, and situational connections it was also revealed where she hid her tools for self-injury. For example, when she started self-harming with more frequency she reported hiding her razor blades in the battery of her cell phone so that she could take them to school and her parents would not find them easily. Throughout these conversations, after multiple sessions, this client also revealed when her thoughts of NSSI would shift into suicidal ideations. This open line of communication with clients is helpful, not only to understand the function NSSI is serving, but also to parcel out what is NSSI versus what is suicide.

In addition to inquiring about actual suicidal and NSSI behaviors, suicidal ideations need to be asked about separately, thus separating out the actual engagement in NSSI, attempts of suicide, as well as thoughts about suicide or self-harm. Suicidal ideations relate both to NSSI and to suicide attempts (Muehlenkamp & Gutierrez, 2004), with the only factor really clearly distinguishing between these two groups being outlook or perception of life. Specifically, individuals who felt more repulsion toward life were more likely to have attempted suicide. Repulsion toward life is a negative attitude toward life and also accounts for the amount of negative experiences an individual has in life, per their perception. Therefore, the more negative experiences an individual reports, the more likely she will be to have loathing toward life, and potentially attempt suicide. On the other hand, individuals who had a more positive perception on life were more likely to engage in NSSI behaviors only.

While both suicide and NSSI have similar predictors, individuals who engage in both NSSI and attempt suicide consistently have higher levels of depression, hopelessness, impulsivity, and suicidal ideations than individuals who only engage in NSSI with no suicide attempts in their past (Dougherty et al., 2009; Muehlenkamp & Gutierrez, 2004). Therefore, assessments that gather information about levels of depression, impulsivity, and hopelessness, along with suicidal ideations and client self-report would be important to consider in identifying whether the behavior is more likely suicide versus NSSI. As mentioned above, it is also important to assess methods of self-harm, as methods used to attempt suicide rarely change across attempts, but may slightly differ from the methods used to inflict non-suicidal self-harm. Chapter 4 contains more detailed information on the assessment of NSSI.

Conclusion

While NSSI and suicide are, by definition, different, they are similar in respect to predictors and some behaviors used to engage in self-harm. NSSI has been theorized to lead to suicidal behaviors, and ultimately has been empirically revealed as one of the stronger predictors of suicidal behaviors. Yet, they are not the same thing, and at times NSSI has been used to guard against actual engagement in suicidal behaviors. Therefore, it is imperative that clinicians gain a true understanding of an individual's behavior through a thorough assessment, and understand for each individual client how suicide and NSSI may be linked.

References

Andover, M. S., & Gibb, B. E. (2010). Non-suicidal self-injury, attempted suicide, and suicidal intent among psychiatric inpatients. *Psychiatry Research, 178*, 101–105.

Berman, A. L., Jobes, D. A., & Silverman, M. M. (2006). *Adolescent suicide: Assessment and intervention* (2nd edition). Washington, DC: American Psychological Association.

Crosby, A. E., Cheltenham, M. P., & Sacks, J. J. (1999). Incidence of suicidal ideation and behavior in the United States. *Suicide and Life-Threatening Behavior, 29*, 131–140.

Crosby, A. E., Ortega, L., & Melanson, C. (2011). *Self-directed violence surveillance: Uniform definitions and recommended data elements*. Atlanta, GA: Center for Disease Control and Prevention, National Center for Injury Prevention and Control.

Dougherty, D. M., Mathias, C. W., Marsh-Richard, D. M., Prevette, K. N., Dawes, M. A., Hatzis, E. S., Palmes, G., & Nouvion, S. O. (2009). Impulsivity and clinical symptoms among adolescents with non-suicidal self-injury with or without attempted suicide. *Psychiatry Residency, 30*, 22–27.

Favaro, A., Santonastaso, P., Monteleone, P., Bellodi, L., Mauri, M., Rotondo, A., Erzegovesi, S., & Maj, M. (2008). Self-injurious behavior and attempted suicide in purging and bulimia nervosa: Associations with psychiatric comorbidity. *Journal of Affective Disorders, 105*, 285–289.

Glenn, C. R., & Klonsky, E. D. (2009). Social context during nonsuicidal self-injury indicates suicide risk. *Personality and Individual Differences, 46*, 25–29.

Hamza, C. A., Stewart, S. L., & Willoughby, T. (2012). Examining the link between non-suicidal self-injury and suicidal behavior: A review of the literature and an integrated model. *Clinical Psychology Review, 32*, 482–495.

Jacobson, C. M., Muehlenkamp, J. J., Miller, A. L., & Turner, J. B. (2008). Psychiatric impairment among adolescents engaging in different types of deliberate self-harm. *Journal of Child and Adolescent Psychology, 37*, 363–375.

Lloyd-Richardson, E. E., Perrine, N., Dierker, L., & Kelley, M. L. (2007). Characteristics and functions of non-suicidal self-injury in a community sample of adolescents. *Psychological Medicine, 37*, 1183–1192.

Muehlenkamp, J. J., & Gutierrez, P. M. (2004). An investigation of differences between self-injurious behavior and suicide attempts in a sample of adolescents. *Suicide and Life-Threatening Behavior, 34*, 12–23.

Nock, M. K., Joiner, E. E., Gordon, K. H., Lloyd-Richardson, E., & Prinstein, M. J. (2006). Nonsuicidal self-injury among adolescents: Diagnostic correlates and relation to suicide attempts. *Psychiatry Research, 144*, 65–72.

Nock, M. K., & Prinstein, M. J. (2004). A functional approach to the assessment of self-mutilative behavior. *Journal of Consulting and Clinical Psychology, 72*, 885–890.

Nock, M. K., Prinstein, M. J., & Sterba, S. K. (2010). Revealing the form and function of self-injurious thoughts and behaviors: A real-time ecological assessment study among adolescents and young adults. *Psychology of Violence, 1*, 36–52.

Stanley, B., Winchell, R., Molcho, A., Simeon, D., & Stanley, M. (1992). Suicide and the self-harm continuum: Phenomenological and biochemical evidence. *International Review of Psychiatry, 4*, 149–155.

Tang, J., Yu, Y., Wu, Y., Du, Y., Ma, Y., Zhu, H., et al. (2011). Associations between non-suicidal self-injuries and suicide attempts in Chinese adolescents and college students: A cross sectional study. *PLoS One, 6*(4), e17977. Retrieved from http://dx.doi.org/10.1371/journal.pone.0017977.

Wester, K. L., Ivers, N., Villalba, J. A., & Trepal, H. C. (2016). The relationship between non-suicidal self-injury and suicidal ideation. *Journal of Counseling & Development, 94*, 3–12.

Wester, K. L., & McKibben, B. (2016). Participants' experiences of nonsuicidal self-injury: Supporting existing theory and emerging conceptual pathways. *Journal of Mental Health Counseling, 38*, 12–27.

Wester, K. L., & Trepal, H. C. (2010). Coping behaviors, abuse history, and counseling: Differentiating college students who self-injure. *Journal of College Counseling, 13*, 141–154.

Whitlock, J., & Knox, K. L. (2007). The relationship between self-injurious behavior and suicide in a young adult population. *Archives of Pediatric Adolescent Medicine, 161*, 634–640.

Section II
Assessment and Diagnostic Considerations

four
Intake, Initial Assessment, and Therapeutic Relationship

While a higher prevalence of people report engaging in non-suicidal self-injury (NSSI), it is important to note that only about 20% of these individuals may seek mental health services, and of those, only half may report to their clinician that they self-injure (Wester, Downs, & Trepal, 2016; Wester & Trepal, 2015). So the questions that need asking are "Why are individuals who self-injure not seeking treatment?" and "When they do seek treatment, why are they not sharing with their clinician that they self-harm?"

Unfortunately the answer is simple. Most clients do not share NSSI with their clinician, or any other health care provider, for a variety of reasons: the behavior is conducted in isolation or secrecy, the person may fear judgment of the behavior or may already feel guilty about the behavior himself, previous negative reactions and judgments have been received when others found out about NSSI, fear that the NSSI will be confused as suicidal behavior, or fear of losing autonomy over the choice to engage in NSSI. Regardless of the reason, mental health professionals need to be aware of the lack of reporting and engage in behaviors with clients that may increase their desire to report NSSI, as well as work on it within therapy.

Reaching out for help is not necessarily limited to mental health and medical professionals. Help can be sought out from many different places, including teachers and professors, clergy, family, and friends. Yet, not everyone seeks out help from another person regarding his or her NSSI behavior. Specifically, 23% of individuals reported they have *never* reached out for help concerning self-injury, while others have reached out minimally (to an average of only two people; Wester & McKibben, 2016), with the most frequent person being reached out to being . . . a friend. Friends can be helpful. They tend to be an individual in whom we confide and trust with knowing things about us that we may not trust other people to know (including clinicians). However, friends can also be individuals who engage in NSSI, potentially increasing the behavior and social contagion of self-injury. All of these relations and aspects surrounding NSSI need to be better understood and assessed within the therapeutic context. Nevertheless, a client will not begin to share detailed or intimate information about their NSSI with a clinician unless a strong therapeutic alliance is felt.

Even outside of the idea of NSSI, the therapeutic relationship and alliance with clients is key to better outcomes in counseling. The development of a strong therapeutic alliance allows clients the trust to share things with clinicians they may have never shared with others in their life. This alliance also provides the clinician with the ability to have tough conversations and confront the client when therapeutically necessary.

There are many reactions that mental health professionals may have to NSSI behaviors. These include, but are not limited to, disgust, fear, horror, confusion, reluctance, anger, and even curiosity. Some of these reactions can be due to lack of knowledge of NSSI, including the forms, functions, and ultimate goals of the behavior. Others may be due to mistaking NSSI as a form of suicidal behavior, which of course it is not (although it is a strong predictor of suicidal behavior). And innately, the idea and engagement of NSSI goes against our internal idea of self-preservation. The idea that someone would engage in purposeful and intentional physical self-harm with immediate consequences does not always seem to make sense. However, reminding oneself that NSSI is in fact, for most individuals who engage, a self-preserving and coping behavior is important and may calm some of the negative judgments and reactions felt.

These negative reactions from mental health professionals are not helpful to the client or to the therapeutic alliance. Typically a client who engages in NSSI experiences emotional distress. Therefore, to experience another's negative judgment on top of that initial distress can feel overwhelming. It may result in retreating into oneself to further hide the NSSI behavior, avoiding sharing information for fear that it will overwhelm the clinician, or may conversely stimulate a positive reaction where the client is pleased she has caused such a reaction in the clinician and may continue to engage in NSSI or report extreme forms of NSSI to cause additional negative reactions solely for shock value. This latter tends to be less common but can occur.

Early in her career, the first author had a male teenage client who reported self-harm. While she did not reveal a great deal of shock or negative reaction to his reports of NSSI, he continued to escalate what he reported. First he reported, and showed, scars and recent marks, caused by scratching his arms with fingernails and rocks. When she did not react with a lot of emotion (negative or positive) but became inquisitive, the client upped the ante with his reporting of self-harm. His reports (not his current behavior) continued to escalate to all the NSSI he had done, including deeper cuts, cutting with razor blades, as well as self-harm during sexual encounters. To this day, the counselor is uncertain what was true versus embellished by the client, but what became obvious in this moment (and through further work and questioning with this client) was that this client received many reactions of shock and horror. Some of the adults in his life, including his immediate family, rejected him and called him mentally ill, indicating they no longer wanted him around or as part of the family. Therefore, part of his grandiose expression of NSSI (both actual behaviors, as well as verbal reports of NSSI behaviors) was mostly due to assisting the rejection of others. His goal was to isolate himself on his own terms, rather than wait for the individual (including this clinician) to reject him first. His belief was that the more elaborate and grand his stories and actual NSSI behaviors were, the more likely that an individual would not want to associate with him. Historically, for this client, this in fact worked. However, once he realized that this clinician was not going to reject him, nor react in horror, his examples and stories of extreme NSSI stopped, and his actual engagement in NSSI behaviors decreased (although it did not extinguish).

While this story is an important one to understand, it is also not the most typical example of a client you will have in counseling. However, this case is similar to others in the fact that this client feared rejection, negative reactions, and judgments about his NSSI behaviors. His fear was that in reporting this behavior, he would be rejected and alone. While this fear led this particular client to provide more lavish stories, for most clients fear causes them to refuse to disclose NSSI behavior at all, or to minimize their reports of engagement. Therefore, most commonly clients underreport NSSI behaviors, if they report them at all.

Clients either come to therapy of their own voluntary accord, or because they are mandated by others (e.g., parent, other professional, court). The reason an individual is coming to counseling does not necessarily mean they will be more or less willing to talk about NSSI. However, being mandated into counseling may mean they are being forced to talk about NSSI when they may not have been ready to disclose the behavior to another (e.g., a worried parent has referred them to talk to you about their NSSI; a teacher has brought a student to you because she found out about the NSSI while the student was in her class). Seeking therapy voluntarily does not mean a client is ready to disclose NSSI behaviors to the clinician, either. Again, the importance of the development of the therapeutic relationship, the establishment of trust, as well as the initial intake and assessment is what is important here. The combination of these aspects within a counseling room will create an environment where it may be more encouraging for a client to disclose NSSI engagement rather than withhold the information.

Therapeutic Relationship

Entering into a therapeutic relationship with a client who self-injures is no different than entering into a relationship with any other client. Typically the difference is in the clinician's reaction to self-injury. Thus, clinicians need to internally reflect on their reactions and beliefs about self-injury, engage in education around self-injury to truly understand the purpose and function of self-injury generally, but also engage with each client to understand the unique purpose of self-injury to her.

One way to establish a therapeutic relationship with a client who engages in self-injury, particularly if he is hesitant to talk about NSSI, is to validate the use of NSSI. Validation does not mean that you approve of the behavior, but simply that you understand and empathize with the need for NSSI in this particular client's life; that you understand, or want to understand, the circumstances that have led to the need to use self-injury; and that you recognize that NSSI may currently be one of the few, if not the only, method/s that may be working for her to help her cope or navigate this/these difficult situations.

In addition to empathy and validating the client's current circumstances, allowing for client autonomy is important. Autonomy will be discussed further in Chapter 6 when discussing ethics in working with clients who self-injure, but for the purpose of the therapeutic relationship, one thing a clinician can do to immediately drive a wedge between themselves and the client is to insist that they stop engaging in NSSI or assert that reducing or extinguishing NSSI *needs* to be a therapeutic goal.

Typically, as mental health providers, we are taught that long-term counseling goals are usually determined by the client, or in collaboration between clinician and client. When asked, most clients actually would like to reduce or extinguish their use of NSSI (Nafisi & Stanley, 2007). Thus, in these circumstances, reducing and working on NSSI in therapy is the client's goal. However, there are times when reducing or stopping the use of NSSI is not the client's goal, or the client may adamantly refuse to stop engaging in these behaviors. If, at this point in time, the clinician steps in and requires the client to work on NSSI, therapy will at least be ineffective, and potentially could be harmful to the client; that is, harmful in regards to the clinician pushing her own agenda and values on the client, the client terminating therapy early, and the possibility that the client will not seek future mental health treatment.

During assessment, which is discussed in this chapter, the goal is to understand the NSSI behavior of each client. There are times when it is imperative that a clinician does require reducing NSSI as a therapeutic goal because the behavior is life-threatening. Although NSSI by definition is not intended to kill oneself, through the use of severe methods, deep wounds, or wounds that may be infected, the client can accidentally kill her- or himself. If it is the case where NSSI is actually life-threatening based on the types of behaviors the client engages in, once the clinician validates the use and need for NSSI, ethically they need to engage in a conversation providing education and exhibiting concern for the client. This conversation may not stress the need to stop NSSI, but instead to reduce it to behavior that at minimum is no longer life-threatening. Nafisi and Stanley (2007) talk about how to have this conversation compassionately and nonjudgmentally. They indicate that typically the fear of reducing or stopping NSSI is because nothing else has worked for the client in terms of regulating emotions or numbness, and her ability to communicate her internal thoughts and emotions has been difficult to ineffective. This collaboration can be done through providing education on the implications of the severe wounds, compassionately discussing concern over the severity of the current behavior, and collaborating and compromising on what the client is willing to do within the boundaries of the clinician's determination of what is no longer considered life-threatening NSSI engagement.

Intake and Assessment

NSSI assessment can occur on two levels. The first level is more informal or natural in the sense of general questions or a typical intake. This is typically done through behavioral screening questions, allowing clients to provide yes/no responses. The second level is a more formal and detailed assessment once it is determined that an individual self-injures.

Informal or Initial Intake

In most outpatient, and sometimes inpatient, mental health settings, the intake consists of multiple questions. These questions characteristically include some related to self-harm and/or suicidal behavior. However, frequently, the NSSI and suicidal questions are not adequately separated. Therefore, the first step in building trust with a client who self-injures is to separate intake questions that ask about suicide and NSSI behaviors so that they are aware that you understand these behaviors are different. In most outpatient settings the authors have worked in, the intake form typically asks a question such as, "Have you ever wanted to kill or harm yourself?" Given the fear that some individuals may have that their NSSI behaviors will be perceived as suicidal in nature, resulting in negative judgments or even more intense treatment (i.e., referral to an inpatient crisis setting), clients may be less likely to indicate they engage in NSSI behaviors when "self-harm" and "suicide" are asked in the same question. Separating out these behaviors is important to encourage clients to be honest about self-injury. Even if a client says "no" to the self-harm or NSSI question during intake, the clinician has opened a door for the client by revealing that he understands the innate difference between suicidal and NSSI behaviors. Box 4.1 provides an example way in which these questions can be naturally sequenced or separated during an intake.

Keep in mind that a client can actually engage in *both* suicidal and NSSI behaviors concurrently. So in this line of questioning, and in the subsequent formal, detailed NSSI assessment, it is important to differentiate behaviors that are suicidal versus behaviors that are specific to NSSI. Finally, it should be noted that some clients need more of an explanation when given a question about NSSI. If the clinician asks the client if they have ever attempted to harm themselves without the intent to kill themselves and the client asks, "What do you mean?" the clinician should be ready with a follow up (e.g., cutting yourself, burning yourself, picking at your skin, etc.).

Box 4.1 Examples of Separate Suicidal Behavior and Non-Suicidal Self-Injurious Behavior Questions During Initial Intake, and Subsequent Assessments

- *Have you ever attempted to kill yourself?*
- *Have you ever attempted to harm yourself, with no intention to die as a result of the self-harm?*

When clients reveal that they in fact do engage in NSSI during the initial intake or questioning, clinicians (as stated above) need to be aware of and possibly temper their reactions. Clients may pick up microsecond nonverbal reactions of shock or disgust and can determine these to be a negative judgment by the clinician. In Caroline Kettlewell's autobiography, *Skin Game*, she suggests that clinicians should approach an affirmative response with "respectful curiosity."

While it is ideal that a client (or student) may self-report their engagement in NSSI, at times these behaviors come to a clinician's attention through other means. This may be through our own suspicion, but also through reports by parents, friends or peers, teachers, or physicians. Similar to affirmative self-report, respectful curiosity works well in inquiring about NSSI among individuals when clinicians are asking for more details or the possibility of NSSI. Indicators of NSSI are multiple, although no one indicator points to NSSI alone, as the signs of NSSI listed in Table 4.1 are also signs of other behaviors, such as suicidal behavior, depression, eating disorders, substance abuse, oppositional defiant disorder, and more. However, when these signs exist, it can be helpful to approach the individual with curiosity, specifically asking (and separating) the NSSI and suicidal questions.

Once a client, or individual, indicates he engages in NSSI, the goal is to respond with a calm, low-key, dispassionate demeanor (Walsh, 2007). We have discussed the consequences of reacting negatively or judgmentally to clients who report NSSI behaviors. However, Barent Walsh also suggested that to respond in an excited, overly interested manner could inadvertently reinforce the NSSI behavior due to the interest in the behavior. Therefore, if a client is looking for connection and approval, he may interpret a clinician's interest in NSSI as a behavior that will gain him attention in treatment. Accordingly, it is important to validate NSSI, empathize with a client's situation or emotion, and conduct a formal, detailed assessment of NSSI behavior to better understand the uniqueness for this client, while also not overly expressing attention to the behavior.

TABLE 4.1. Signs and Indicators of Non-Suicidal Self-Injury

Physical	Behavioral
▪ Scars	▪ Difficulty in interpersonal relationships
▪ Fresh wounds (cuts, scratches, bruises)	▪ Keeping sharp objects on hand
▪ Burn marks or erasure scabs	▪ Hidden or secretive behaviors
▪ Reports of "cat scratches"	▪ Isolating oneself socially
▪ Hair loss or bald spots (e.g., scalp, arm, leg, eyebrows, eyelashes)	▪ Overdependence on one person or friend
Clothing and Accessories	▪ Claiming frequent accidents
▪ Wearing clothes too warm for the season (e.g., long sleeves in hot weather, long pants)	**Affective**
▪ Bracelets, scarves, or other accessories constantly worn in the same location	▪ Inability to identify or label emotions
▪ Avoiding activities where arms or legs may be exposed (e.g., swimming)	▪ Over-focus on one emotion (e.g., only emotion can identify is anger, or anxiety)
▪ Refusal to get undressed in front of others	▪ Continual mood swings or constant low affect
	▪ Irritability

Formal, Detailed NSSI Assessment

Once it is determined that the client engages in NSSI (and possibly suicidal behavior as well), a more detailed assessment is necessary. This detailed assessment helps to determine the next steps in a treatment plan, as well as how severe or ingrained the NSSI behavior is and if the client is at risk of accidental severe injury or death.

A few formal NSSI assessments exist, some of which will be discussed below. The difficulty in some of the formal assessments is that they include other non-NSSI behaviors such as suicide attempts, suicidal ideations, eating-disordered behaviors, substance abuse, or other high-risk behaviors. For some clinicians, depending upon the client or the setting, these other assessments or measures may be a helpful way to pull apart NSSI from other self-harming behaviors. However, if the assessment is specifically focused on NSSI behaviors, then the questions regarding other behaviors may not be as important. A few of these measures are discussed below, but the assessment provided in this chapter is solely for NSSI behaviors (and can be used to differentiate NSSI behaviors from suicidal behaviors if needed). This assessment is based on a conglomeration of other assessments, reports, and suggestions from other researchers and clinicians, as well as clinical experience. First we will take a moment and discuss a few measures that already exist, which may or may not be publically or freely accessible.

NSSI Measures and Assessments

Various deliberate self-harm, self-violence, and NSSI measures have been developed across the past three decades. These include the Inventory of Statements about Self-Injury, the Non-Suicidal Self-Injury Assessment Tool, Self-Harm Inventory, Functional Assessment of Self-Mutilation, Deliberate Self-Harm Inventory, Self-Harm Behavior Questionnaire, Self-Injury Questionnaire, Self-Injurious Thoughts and Behaviors Interview, and Suicide Attempt Self-Injury Interview. Each of these will be briefly discussed below, followed by specific questions that clinicians can ask to gain a more detailed perspective of a client's NSSI behaviors.

Functional Assessment of Self-Mutilation (FASM)

The FASM is a self-report instrument designed to assess methods, frequency, and functions of NSSI developed by Lloyd and colleagues (1997). The FASM has two sections, the first of which asks individuals to indicate whether and how often they engaged in 12 different NSSI behaviors across the past year. If the individual indicates they have engaged in at least one form of self-injury, they are instructed to answer 22 additional questions that assess the function of the NSSI behavior(s). These items are rated on a Likert scale (0=never to 3=often) to assess whether participants engage in NSSI for positive or negative reinforcement and affective/automatic or social reasons (i.e., the Four Functions Model discussed by Nock and Prinstein, which can be found in Chapter 2). Therefore, the FASM provides information on recent engagement in NSSI, frequency of recent NSSI episodes, as well as the function of the NSSI in general. The FASM was validated further by Nock and Prinstein (2004) on a group of adolescents admitted to a psychiatric inpatient facility.

Self-Harm Inventory (SHI)

The SHI is designed to measure general self-harming behaviors, of which one is NSSI. It is a self-report inventory that assesses behaviors such as substance use (e.g., abused prescription medication, abused alcohol), suicidal behaviors (e.g., overdosing), high-risk behaviors (e.g., intentional reckless driving), eating disorders, excessive exercising, and other self-harm behaviors. Individuals indicate yes or no to each item, and summing all of the items derives a final score. Randy Sansone and colleagues (1998) validated the SHI primarily on individuals with borderline personality disorder (BPD) from other studies (e.g., a study on obesity, BPD clients with other self-inflicted violence behaviors, and a study of moms diagnosed with BPD).

Deliberate Self-Harm Inventory (DSHI)

The DSHI was developed to specifically measure lifetime engagement and frequency of NSSI behaviors. Kim Gratz (2001) validated the DSHI on a sample of college students. The self-report inventory contains 17 items, 16 of which are specific NSSI behaviors in which individuals indicate yes or no to using the method to engage in intentional self-harm with no intention to die. The 17th question asks if they have done anything else to harm themselves and provides a space for the individual to write what behavior they engaged in. For the last question, it is important for clinicians to determine whether the behavior is actually considered NSSI, as sometimes individuals will indicate they attempted suicide, overdosed, engaged in asphyxiation, purged, or purposefully wrecked their car. While the behaviors reported by individuals are important to assess, as it provides information regarding their current risk of self-inflicted violence, suicidal behavior, and other high-risk behaviors, it is important to determine if the behaviors noted are actually NSSI-specific. If a person indicates they have used a behavior, they are asked to indicate how frequently across their life they have engaged with that specific behavior, providing a lifetime frequency count of NSSI behaviors. The outcome of the DSHI is a combination of dichotomous indication of whether a person has engaged in NSSI (yes/no based on individual indicating yes to engaging in *any* of the NSSI behaviors noted), a count of the number of methods an individual has used to engage in NSSI across their lifetime, and a frequency count of the number of lifetime NSSI episodes.

The DSHI has been adapted and used with other populations by the current authors in multiple studies. Specifically, some of the original 17 items were combined, as they reflected the same behavior with different instruments (e.g., burned with cigarette and burned with lighter or match were combined into burned self with an object [e.g., lighter, match, cigarette]). This resulted in a total of 11 items, 10 of which are specific NSSI behaviors, while the final item is an open-ended response item asking if they have done anything else to engage in NSSI. Additionally, this adapted version asks about lifetime engagement, but shifted the frequency of episodes to a self-report of recent NSSI behaviors (i.e., within the past 3 months) given the problem with memory recall over a longer period of time. We have validated this briefer and adapted measure of the DSHI (i.e., DSHI-Adapted) with college students, clients in outpatient mental health settings, adolescents in inpatient settings, and the general public.

Self-Harm Behavior Questionnaire (SHBQ)

Peter Gutierrez, Osman, Barrios, and Kopper (2001) developed the SHBQ as a self-report questionnaire. Individuals are asked to report their NSSI, suicidal behaviors, suicide threats, and suicidal ideation. The number of items on this questionnaire is unclear, but the SHBQ is divided into four sections, one section for each type of ideation, thought, and behavior as noted. For each affirmative answer (e.g., if the individual indicates "yes" to have you ever experienced suicidal ideation), then follow up questions are asked in that section that inquire about methods used, intent of the behavior, frequency of engagement, if medical treatment was required, age of onset and age of most recent episode, and whether anyone else was aware of the behavior. The authors created each section so that it could be rated and ranked with an overall score to indicate severity or risk of behavior. The SHBQ was validated on undergraduate college students.

Suicide Attempt Self-Injury Interview (SASII)

The SASII, developed in 2006 (Linehan and colleagues) contains 42 questions that ask in-depth information about self-harm behavior. This assessment is done through a formal structured interview. It assesses NSSI and suicide by asking the function and intention behind the self-harm behaviors that individuals indicate they have engaged in. It contains 4 screening questions about whether the person has intentionally harmed him- or herself and the time frame of this self-harm. The screening questions also inquire about how many episodes or isolated times the individual has self-harmed, as each of the remaining questions will go through each episode in detail. Therefore, if the client has two episodes of NSSI or suicidal behavior, then the interview form will be gone through two times, one time for each event of self-harm. The questions on the SASII inquire about descriptions of the method used to self-harm, intent and outcome expectations (to determine if NSSI or suicide), lethality of methods, physical conditions post-injury, medical treatment received or needed, preparations prior to self-harm, and functional outcomes of the behavior. Questions are asked in myriad formats, including open-ended questions that need scoring by the rater, checklist questions, Likert-scale format, forced choice answers, and yes/no responses. The responses can be compiled into four scaled scores: suicidal intent, rescue likelihood (the likelihood that the individual would have been found or rescued when they self-harmed), suicide communication (the degree to which they talked about suicidal behaviors prior to engaging), and lethality. The SASII was validated with patients of a psychiatric inpatient unit who had attempted suicide, individuals who presented in an emergency department for suicide attempt, and clinical trials for females who met criteria for borderline personality disorder. The SASII, along with scoring, can be found on the University of Washington's website: http://blogs.uw.edu/brtc/publications-assessment-instruments/

Self-Injury Questionnaire (SIQ)

The SIQ, developed by Santa Mina and colleagues (2006), contains 30 questions that focus on self-harm in general. Thus the SIQ is not NSSI-specific, but assesses behaviors across a self-inflicted violence spectrum, including substance abuse, purposeful high-risk behaviors, NSSI, and suicidal behaviors. Participants are asked whether they have engaged in specific self-harm behaviors, the frequency of their engagement, and the intentions behind the self-harm. The intentions behind self-harm behaviors span across six factors, including emotion regulation, coping, self-protection, stimulation, and dissociation. They validated this measure using a sample of clients admitted to an inpatient and crisis facility for self-harm behaviors.

Self-Injury Thoughts and Behavior Interview (SITBI)

The SITBI contains 169 questions conducted through a formal structured interview format. It contains five sections: suicide plans, suicide gestures, suicide attempts, suicidal ideation, and non-suicidal self-injury. Therefore, the majority of the assessment inquires about suicidal behaviors, with a portion of it focused on NSSI. Each section contains a screening question, which if the individual responds "yes," follows with questions that inquire about the frequency, characteristics of the suicidal or NSSI behaviors, functions of each self-harm behavior, factors that contributed to the behavior (e.g., work, school, family, friends), and context of the self-harm (e.g., experience of physical pain, use of substances prior to or during self-harm episode). The interview can be used with adolescents or adults, and when working with youth the interview does have a parent version where the parent can be asked similar questions about their child in a separate room. Nock, Holmberg, Photos, and Michel (2007) validated this interview with individuals in a psychiatric inpatient facility as well as with the general public through recruitments in newspapers, community bulletin boards, and social media message boards.

Inventory of Statements about Self-Injury (ISAS)

The ISAS, developed by Klonsky and Glenn (2009), consists of two sections that assess lifetime engagement in NSSI behaviors, along with the functions of these behaviors. The functions of the behaviors appear to be modeled on the Integrated Theoretical Model by Nock, and the Four Functions Model by Nock and Prinstein, discussed in Chapter 2. The ISAS is a self-report measure that provides individuals with 12 NSSI behaviors, asking if they have ever intentionally engaged in any of these behaviors without suicidal intent. Therefore, this measure does not assess for suicidal behaviors specifically. If an individual says yes, they have used any of the 12 NSSI behaviors, they are asked to indicate the frequency in which they have used them across their lifetime. Additional questions in this section inquire about age of onset, pain felt during NSSI episodes, whether NSSI is performed alone or with others, time between urge to self-injure and actual engagement, and whether the individual would like to stop engaging in NSSI behaviors. These questions are asked in a multiple-choice format. The second section of the ISAS asks individuals to indicate the reasons they engage in NSSI behaviors (if they indicated in section one that they engaged in at least one NSSI behavior). This section contains 39 items that assess 13 functions of NSSI on a Likert scale from 0 (not relevant) to 3 (very relevant). These functions are then condensed into two overarching functions (although they can be examined as individual functions as well): interpersonal and intrapersonal. The interpersonal functions scale consists of the individual functions of autonomy, interpersonal boundaries, interpersonal influence, peer bonding, revenge, self-care, sensation seeking, and toughness. The intrapersonal functions scale involves the affect regulation, anti-dissociation, anti-suicide, marking distress, and self-punishment functions. The ISAS has been validated on an undergraduate psychology college student population.

Non-Suicidal Self-Injury Assessment Tool (NSSI-AT)

The most recent NSSI assessment tool developed is the NSSI-AT by Whitlock and colleagues (2014). The tool can be found online for free access at the Cornell Research Program on Self-Injury and Recovery website: http://www.selfinjury.bctr.cornell.edu/perch/resources/fnssi.pdf. The NSSI-AT was validated on students from public and private universities. The NSSI-AT is designed to be a structured interview consisting of 39 questions provided across 12 modules. These modules include a screening question inquiring about 15 types or methods used to self-injure, followed by the functions, age of onset and recent NSSI behaviors, whether the individual was able to cease NSSI behaviors at any point, wound locations, motivations and functions of NSSI, frequency of engagement, practice patterns (e.g., NSSI alone, location preferences, accidental severity), treatment experiences, and whether other individuals are aware of their NSSI behaviors.

Summary of Formal NSSI Assessments

As can be seen in the review of measures above, many measures have been developed to assess self-harming behavior. Not all of the measures focus specifically on NSSI behaviors, but most tend to inquire about a myriad of forms for inflicting self-violence. All are important, but not all truly separate out NSSI behaviors. Additionally, most measures inquire about lifetime NSSI. This can be important information, as it can provide a clinician with the development of the behavior, length of time which a client has engaged, as well as the potential progression of behavior (e.g., has tolerance increased, causing NSSI to become more severe or methods to change). Moreover, NSSI that occurred well over a year ago may be less relevant in treatment than NSSI that has occurred within the past few weeks or months. Therefore, it is important to distinguish between NSSI and other forms of self-inflicted violence, as well as determine other clinically relevant features of NSSI, such as age of onset, total number of methods currently used, progression of methods across time (i.e., tolerance), severity, frequency of episodes, functions of NSSI, and precipitating events, to mention a few. It is also important to understand if suicide and NSSI are co-occurring, and how they may or may not be connected for the person (e.g., is NSSI a protective factor against suicidal behavior, or one that is leading up to suicidal behaviors).

A few of the assessments noted above do in fact focus on all of these important clinical aspects of NSSI, and some of them are free and available to use (these are noted above with web addresses). Here we will discuss specific questions that you can use to inquire about NSSI behaviors, and questions that can be used to gain important clinical information that can assist in either referrals or treatment planning, depending upon your setting. Additionally, each of the questions or topics that we indicate are important to ask are addressed in detail below about how or why it may be important to ask this question of a client or student, and what you may do with that information.

The questions provided in Box 4.2 provide an outline and examples of questions that can be asked. It needs to be noted that these questions may be more in-depth and detailed than some settings necessitate (e.g., assessing a student in a school) but less detailed than other settings may require (e.g., client admitted for inpatient treatment). Regardless, example and context-specific questions are provided that could be asked regardless of setting, as well as questions that may help with treatment formulation.

NSSI and Suicidal Screening Questions

First it is important to begin the assessment with screening questions that distinguish between NSSI and suicidal behaviors. Some of the self-harm assessments include screening questions that follow up with more detailed questions once a client affirms that she has engaged in some form of self-harm behavior. These screening questions should be separate, which means keeping the suicidal behavior and the NSSI questions apart so that a client can indicate yes or no to each behavior individually. As mentioned earlier this helps you, and the client, understand that these behaviors are in fact distinct and different.

If a client or student affirms he is in fact suicidal, has attempted suicide, or currently is having suicidal ideations, the clinician should continue in a suicide assessment (not provided here). If a client affirms he has engaged in NSSI, then continue with the existing follow up questions noted in Box 4.2 and discussed below. If a client asserts he has attempted suicide or had suicidal ideations *and* engages in NSSI, part of the next task is to differentiate which behaviors are in fact suicidal in nature, the degree to which the client's suicidal and NSSI behaviors overlap and are divergent, and how the behaviors connect (if they do at all; see Figure 4.1). For example, is the client currently experiencing both suicidal ideations and engaging in NSSI? Has NSSI and a desire to kill oneself occurred at the same time? How does the client see NSSI and suicide as similar or different in her own life? Has the client ever used NSSI to delay or avoid attempting suicide? Has a client begun with NSSI and it escalated to a suicide attempt?

NSSI Follow Up Assessment

NSSI Methods, Frequency, Severity, and Tolerance

Once a client indicates she has engaged in self-harm, the first task is to determine what she has actually done. More specifically, to determine which methods she has used, and whether these methods are specific to NSSI or whether they are

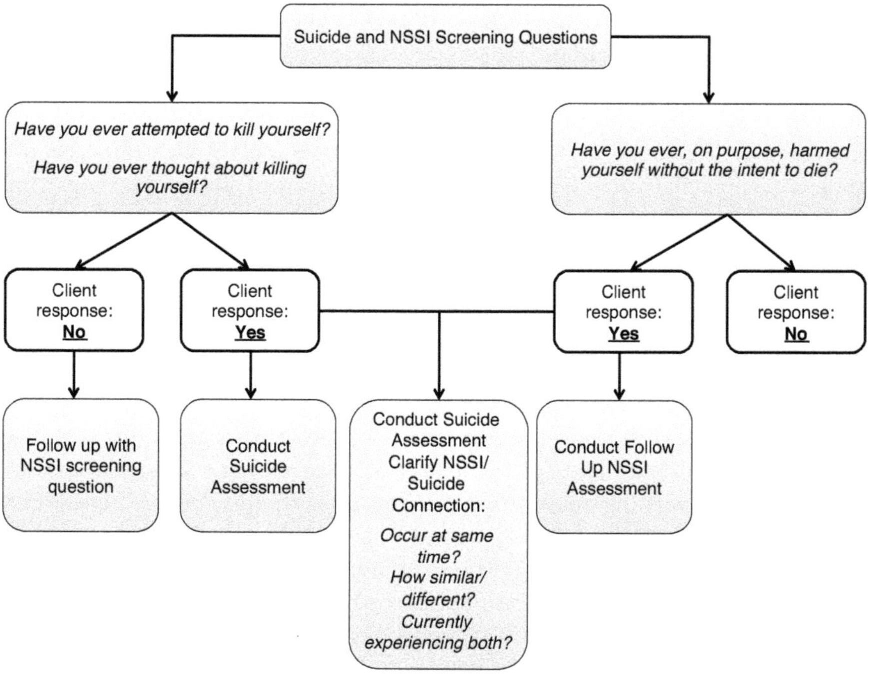

FIGURE 4.1. Flow of NSSI/suicidal behavior screening questions

indicative of other forms of self-inflicted violence, such as substance abuse or eating disorders. Form 4.A can be copied and provided to a client to have her check off which NSSI methods she has used in her lifetime, in the past year, and more recently. There is an open-ended question indicating "other" so that the client can write in any other behavior she may engage in to purposefully hurt herself; however, please determine if this behavior is actually a form of NSSI and not another self-harm behavior (e.g., eating disorders, substance abuse, high-risk activities). Other forms of self-harm should be followed up on, but the follow up questions on the NSSI assessment are not as relevant to those forms of deliberate self-harm.

It is important for many reasons to obtain detailed information regarding the specific methods used to engage in NSSI. This helps to ascertain the severity of NSSI behaviors, to distinguish NSSI versus other self-harm behaviors, and the number of methods has been found to predict suicidal ideations (with more methods used indicating greater likelihood of suicidal ideations). Some NSSI methods cause more severe damage, such as cutting with razor blades, scalpels, or knives; while other forms of NSSI cause more minor tissue damage, such as pins and needles. Assessing for specific methods, therefore, can help you understand the **severity** of the behavior, as well as the need for an immediate focus on the NSSI if necessary.

Form 4.A

Methods Used to Self-Injure

What specific methods have you used to self-injure, without the intention to die or kill yourself? Please indicate each method you have used across your lifetime, in the past year, as well as more recently. ✓ if yes (leave blank if no). Please indicate the frequency in which you have used each method during the past year and more recently.

Have you intentionally, on purpose, without an intent to kill yourself …	**... in your life?**	**… in the past year?**		**… in the past 3 months?**	
	✓ if yes	**✓ if yes**	**If yes, how many times**	**✓ if yes**	**If yes, how many times**
Used an object to cut yourself?					
Used something to burn your skin?					
Pulled out your hair?					
Rubbed something into your skin to make it raw?					
Carved or erased your skin?					
Pricked yourself with a pin or other sharp object?					
Severely scratched yourself with your fingernails or another object?					
Bitten yourself to where it leaves a mark or an open wound?					
Banged or hit yourself to the point of bruising or other injury?					
Hit yourself with another object to the point of bruising or other injury?					
Broken your own bones?					
Prevented wounds from healing?					
Engaged in a fight or other high-risk activity with the sole purpose of getting hurt?					
Done anything else that is not mentioned on this list? If so, please indicate: ______________					

An average of using two methods to self-injure is common; however, some individuals have reported up to 11 (Wester et al., 2016). What is important in the assessment of methods is both the number of methods (due to the relationship between number of methods and suicidal ideation) but also to determine **how methods have changed** across time. For example, when the client started self-injuring, what method did she use? Has she selected more methods to self-injure than what she started with? Have these methods increased in severity? As an example, one participant in a study discussed starting with pin pricking and scratching and increasing to cutting with a razor blade, followed by throwing herself down the stairs in an attempt to hurt herself or break her bones. She talked about this increased severity and progression of NSSI over a period of years. This example provides an indication of how NSSI has progressed throughout since onset, specifically how her use of NSSI has increased in severity. This can be assessed in part from the responses on Form A, but additional questions need to be asked to determine how things have shifted across time. Specifically, some of these questions assess for **tolerance** of the NSSI behavior. Is more severe behavior needed (in methods or severity/depth of wounds) to achieve the same effect desired?

Assessing lifetime NSSI helps a clinician gain a holistic picture of the progression of the behaviors for each client. Inquiring about 12-month NSSI behavior helps to connect it to the proposed condition for further study in the DSM-5 (see more about NSSI diagnosis in Chapter 5). And probing about more recent NSSI behaviors (e.g., within 3 months) can get at what is currently going on for the client, and potentially how immediate NSSI may be in helping them to cope or regulate emotions.

Sometimes it may be helpful to hand Form 4.A to a client regardless of their response on the NSSI screening question. While the screening question is helpful, we have found that a general screening question typically results in a more conservative report, or less likelihood that someone will affirm NSSI than if asked about specific behaviors. This may be due to the myth that NSSI really only consists of "cutting," as this is typically what it is referred to in the general public and social media. Thus, asking about specific behaviors can help clinicians gain a more accurate picture. However, if Form 4.A is used in lieu of the NSSI screening question, make sure to follow up on intentions behind the behavior to rule out any behavior that is solely engaged in mindlessly or as a result of compulsive behavior rather than intention to purposefully self-harm.

Asking about **where on the body** a person self-injures is helpful, as a clinician can gain information about the possibility of the behavior resulting in accidental death versus no risk of mortality, how secretive the behavior may be, or the connection NSSI may have to others or to previous trauma. For example, if a client uses a razor blade to cut herself and does so on her wrist, this has the possibility of resulting in accidental death, particularly if the client is impulsive, has low self-awareness or dissociates when self-injuring, or tends to have deep wounds after cutting. However, if she pulls hair out on her eyebrows, this results in minor tissue damage and tends not to be a threat of immediate or accidental loss of life. If she scratches or cuts on her breasts or genitalia, where others are less likely to look, then she may be hiding her NSSI from others or may be associating the behavior with another event. A client may engage in NSSI in a location that she has been abused, physically or sexually, as a form of punishment to herself, in an attempt to own or take back her body, or in an effort to disfigure that portion of her body so no one else will abuse her or find that part of her body desirable. In addition, diagnostically, it is important to further assess behaviors such as hair pulling, skin picking, and head banging specifically, as they may be the result of certain diagnoses (e.g., trichotillomania, excoriation, stereotypic movement disorder). Specific parts of the body indicated may include the head, face, eyebrows, and eyelashes.

Context of NSSI

Once a clinician has a better grasp on the severity and intention behind self-harm behavior, a better understanding of the context is necessary. This specifically entails asking questions about substance abuse, immediate surroundings such as location (e.g., room, building) and other individuals, and patterns of injury. Questions about substance use are important, as they can help determine how much control an individual may have over when he self-injures. Does he only self-injure when under the influence of substances, and if so, then it may be that when he is using substances his inhibition and control decrease, resulting in NSSI engagement. This also may indicate that he may have less control in the moment over self-injury, resulting in more severe harm than he originally intended. Engagement in NSSI while under the influence of a substance can increase the risk of accidental death.

Using substances may be linked to a client finding wounds on her body without recollection of engaging in these behaviors, as NSSI may have occurred during high intoxication or a blackout. However, not remembering engaging in NSSI could be due to a client engaging while dissociating. Blacking out, dissociating, or engaging in NSSI while intoxicated tend to increase the risk of mortality due to the inability to recall what was occurring at the moment of NSSI engagement.

Understanding an individual's urges to self-harm and his ability to delay engagement can help understand self-control, the ability for the client to cease self-injury, as well as whether other coping mechanisms may have been attempted. If a client has been able to delay engaging in self-injury, this shows promise for the ability to continue delaying and implementing alternative problem solving strategies. This may also show the desire to cease NSSI behaviors. Having an awareness of what other problem solving strategies a client has attempted to implement, successfully or unsuccessfully, is important, as it can provide a window into what they have tried and how hopeless they may feel if nothing else has worked. As will be talked about in the treatment chapters (7 and 8), individuals who self-injure report using more adaptive and maladaptive coping strategies. What this reveals is the potentially ineffective way in which these coping strategies are being implemented or the possibility that a client is employing the wrong coping strategy for the emotion being felt (e.g., attempting to burn off anger through exercising when in fact they are sad).

Recognizing impulsivity versus control over the behavior is also important. This can be achieved by asking the above-stated questions regarding delay in engagement, but clinicians can also gain this information by asking about rituals or locations in which the client engages in NSSI. For example, consider the following scenario: A fight occurs at school with an adolescent's best friend. She experiences an immediate escalation of both anxiety and anger, which she feels is intolerable. While sitting in her math class, she continues to ruminate on the fight, as well as feeling overwhelmed by her emotions. The question is whether she can hold out long enough for the school day to end and for her to go home and self-harm in her bedroom; or does the emotion feel so overwhelming that she cannot stand it and requests to go to the bathroom and self-injures at school? This scenario presents information related to whether the client has enough control over NSSI as well as the level of distress tolerance she may have. Now consider the same scenario where this adolescent doesn't even leave math class to self-harm but does so while sitting in her desk. She may still be able to hide the self-harming behavior (e.g., digging fingernails into the palm of her hand, scratching underneath her shirt sleeve, cutting her arm underneath her desk) or she may self-harm in plain sight of others. This may depend on her purpose of NSSI (e.g., social or affective reasons).

NSSI tends to be more secretive behavior, where individuals are less likely to engage in these behaviors when others are around. However, Glenn and Klonsky (2009) determined that individuals who self-injure when by themselves are at a higher risk of suicidal behaviors. Additionally, self-injuring around peers may reveal a social function of NSSI (i.e., social contagion, peer approval, need for attention, or forcing others to withdraw).

Ability to Cease NSSI

While it is important to understand a client's ability to delay NSSI engagement, it is also important to understand if a client has been able to stop or cease NSSI behavior. This can also help you understand if they desire to stop self-injuring, and the strengths the client has in their ability to stop. Even if they have begun engaging in NSSI again, at one point they were able to stop the behavior. Stopping can be for days, months, or even years. Similarly, it is important to ask a client if she/he has any desire to stop NSSI, as this helps you determine if NSSI cessation is a goal for the client.

Along with the ability or desire to cease NSSI altogether, it is important to understand a client's ability to stop self-injuring during each episode. Does a client stop in the moment because she feels pain? Because she has exactly five cuts on her arm? Or because she saw blood? Understanding the stopping point for each episode can help a clinician understand how to intervene or help a client delay NSSI engagement. More specifically, Chapter 8 discusses how to use various distraction methods to delay NSSI engagement. However, it is recommended that these distraction methods align with the purpose or stopping points of NSSI for each individual client.

Functions of NSSI

Many other assessments indicate, as is the sole purpose of the FASM discussed above, that understanding the functions or purpose of NSSI for each client is important. Knowing a client's purpose for engaging in NSSI can help in determining a treatment plan that may be effective. For example, if a client self-injures to communicate to others his internal pain, then working on effective communication skills and enhancing relationships may be helpful. If a client engages in NSSI to regulate emotions or stop ruminating thoughts, then various coping skills and emotion regulation strategies may be most helpful in helping them decrease or extinguish NSSI. A client who indicates she needs or craves NSSI to fully function may be exhibiting a possible behavioral addiction to NSSI. A client who displays a possible behavioral addiction may require a different treatment plan in counseling than a client who struggles with communicating to others. Form 4.B can be provided to a client to indicate the reasons why he generally engages in NSSI behavior. Keep in mind that rarely does a client use NSSI for only one reason; however, it is important to note primary reasons for NSSI.

All clients need to be considered individually. Therefore, this NSSI follow up assessment provides a template, as do other self-harm and self-injury assessments discussed above. This template can help clinicians understand the context of a situation or of the NSSI behavior for each client, gain information on the severity of the behavior, as well as understand NSSI's connection (or not) to suicide for each client. The answers to these questions can help determine follow up questions where you need more information, but also can assist in the development of a treatment plan that will be effective for the client.

There are other things to consider in the assessment. If you are working with youth and you have a parent, legal guardian, or other family members in the room, a youth may not provide you with honest answers. It may be that the family is unaware of the self-injury, so the youth does not want them to become apprised; or the family may be aware of the youth's engagement in NSSI but may not be aware of the frequency or severity of the behavior; or the family may be one of the main causes of the youth engaging in NSSI and to discuss it in front of the family

Box 4.2 NSSI Follow Up Assessment

Screening Questions

Have you ever attempted to kill yourself?
Have you ever had thoughts of wanting to kill yourself?
Have you ever intentionally, on purpose, harmed yourself, but did not have the intention to die?

NSSI Follow Up Assessment

NSSI Methods, Frequency, Severity, and Tolerance

At what age did you begin self-injuring?
How did you begin (e.g., how did you learn about self-injury)?
What methods or behaviors have you engaged in, lifetime, 12 month/year, more recently? [use Form 4.A or ask individual questions]

- For each method noted, make sure you ask the *specific intent of the method*. Was/Is the method used without the intention to die as a result of the behavior, in order to clarify that this is in fact NSSI and not suicidal behaviors (e.g., *And when you cut, have you ever had any intention of killing yourself?)*
- For each method noted, inquire as to the extent of the self-injury, including:
  - What instruments has the client used to engage in this form of self-harm? (e.g., *When you cut, what do you typically cut with?*)
  - Where on the body the does the client use that form of NSSI? (e.g., *Where do you or have you burned yourself?*)
  - How has that form of NSSI changed across time? (e.g., *You indicated you sometimes prick yourself with a pin. Has this behavior remained the same since you have started using it? If it has changed, how has it changed [in frequency of episodes, in severity of wounds]?*)
  - Is there a need for medical care? (e.g., *Has cutting yourself ever led to the need for medical care? Have you ever needed medical care, but not sought it out? If you have needed medical care before, how many times have you needed it [that you have sought it out or needed but not sought it out]?*)
- Additional prompts and questions to ask about in regards to the specific methods of NSSI are to inquire about the number of methods used across time (e.g., *I notice that the number of methods has increased/decreased throughout your life. Can you tell me about that? What has led to this increase/decrease? Has the frequency or the need*

to engage in NSSI increased or decreased? Has the severity of wounds or methods increased/decreased along with the change in methods?)

Context of NSSI

Have you ever used substances such as drugs, prescription medication, or alcohol prior to self-harming?

Have you ever used substances such as drugs, prescription medication, or alcohol when you were self-harming?

- If yes, approximately what percentage of episodes of self-harm do you believe you were using any drugs, alcohol, medication, or other substances during?
- Please describe some of these times.

Have you ever found a recent wound on your body that you had no recollection of inflicting? Please describe at least one time. Any others?

When you feel an urge or a need to self-injure, how long are you able to wait or delay until you actually engage (e.g., cut, burn yourself)?

- If not, have you ever wanted to delay engaging in NSSI but were unable to do so?
- If yes, what have you done during the time you were able to delay engaging in NSSI even though you wanted to?
- Have you ever attempted to use any other coping strategy or solve the problem in any other way? If so, what have you tried?

When you engage in self-injury, is there a process to engage in any of the methods you indicated using or specific locations you prefer to self-injure (e.g., bedroom, home, current location)?

When you self-injure is anyone else around or are you typically by yourself?

- *If someone else is around, who is typically with you?*

Ability to Cease NSSI

Have you ever been able to stop engaging in NSSI? If so, what led you to stop? What helped? What led to you engaging in NSSI again?

Do you want to stop self-harming?

When you are self-harming, how do you know when enough is enough? How do you know when to stop in the moment? What do you look for (e.g., sensation, sight of blood or wound)?

Functions of NSSI

In general, what are some of the reasons you self-injure? [Provide client with Form 4.B.]

Form 4.B

Reasons You May Self-Injure

Please take a moment and indicate the reasons that you engage in self-injury. There are many reasons why an individual may engage in self-harm so you may have more than one reason.

Please indicate the relevance of each reason listed below to why you self-injure. If the reason you engage in self-injury is not on this list, please feel free to include it at the bottom.

I self-injure at times . . .	**No relevance to me**	**Some relevance to me**	**Very relevant to me**
..to feel better			
..to decrease the feeling I am experiencing (e.g., anger, sadness, anxiety)			
..to stop the constant flow of thoughts in my mind			
..to feel connected to my body or to feel real			
..because I deserve it			
..because I need to be punished			
..so others will notice me			
..to stop a fight or other interaction with another person			
..to withdraw or be alone			
..to communicate			
..because I crave or need it			

would result in a more severe or frequent engagement in NSSI which the youth may be attempting to avoid. Therefore, it is important to assess NSSI with and without the family present.

This does *not* mean that you *only* assess NSSI without the family present. NSSI should be assessed with the family present as well, as the family may have information that the youth may not provide to you. So for the clearest picture of NSSI, it is important to assess NSSI *both* with the family present as well as without the family.

When working in inpatient facilities or other residential facilities (e.g., residential treatment, correctional facilities), individuals can become savvy to what they need to say. Therefore, an individual can indicate they engaged in a specific self-harm behavior without the intent to die even if they in fact were suicidal, as he knows the consequences or treatment required for NSSI may be less intense than for suicidal behavior. Additionally, clients can make NSSI more secretive in nature to keep clinicians and family members from knowing they still self-harm. While working in a juvenile correctional facility, the first author was informed by one male youth that he was no longer self-harming, when in fact he was continuing to cut but was doing so in more private places (e.g., in his groin area and armpits) where most correctional personnel would not be able to see it. His secretive nature of cutting was determined when he went to the emergency room due to an actual suicide attempt. During admission to the inpatient crisis unit, it was discovered that he had continued to cut but in more secretive ways.

Finally, when asking the reasons why an individual engages in NSSI, or the precursor events or situations to engaging in NSSI, most clients may not be aware. This is due to a combination of being less conscious or mindful, as well as due to alexithymia (the inability to identify or label emotions). Therefore, using an NSSI behavior log can be helpful for clients to write down and list times when they engaged in NSSI or had the urge to engage in NSSI over a certain period of time. This can help clinicians understand the contextual circumstances of NSSI, as well as help bring awareness to the client regarding his/her NSSI behavior. See Form 4.C for an example NSSI behavioral log.

Conclusion

There are a variety of ways in which one can assess and inquire about NSSI behaviors. Specifically, mental health professionals need to be cognizant of separating out and ensuring their clients understand they are aware of the similarities and differences in suicide and NSSI behaviors. Additionally, a very thorough follow up on NSSI behaviors specifically can assist in determining the client's risk of severe injury or accidental death, and help in treatment planning and determining which interventions are more appropriate. Finally, attention to the development of the therapeutic relationship is key in working with clients who self-injure.

Form 4.C

NSSI Behavioral Log

	Episode 1	Episode 2	Episode 3	Episode 4	Episode 5
NSSI Description					
What method was used?					
What physical wound occurred on body?					
How did you know or when did you stop?					
Was anyone with you?					
Context of NSSI					
What caused urge or need to self-injure?					
What feeling did you have?					
Who was part of this situation?					
Where did the situation occur? (e.g., home, school)					
Were you able to delay self-injuring?					

References

Glenn, C. R., & Klonsky, E. D. (2009). Social context during nonsuicidal self-injury indicates suicide risk. *Personality and Individual Differences, 46*, 25–29.

Gratz, K. L. (2001). Measurement of deliberate self-harm: Preliminary data on the deliberate self-harm inventory. *Journal of Psychopathology and Behavioral Assessment, 23*(4), 253–263.

Gutierrez, P. M., Osman, A., Barrios, F. X., & Kopper, B. A. (2001). Development and initial validation of the self-harm behavior questionnaire. *Journal of Personality Assessment, 77*(3), 475–490.

Klonsky, E. D., & Glenn, C. R. (2009). Assessing the functions of nonsuicidal self-injury: Psychometric properties of the inventory of statements about self-injury (ISAS). *Journal of Psychopathological and Behavioral Assessment, 31*, 215–219.

Linehan, M. M., Comtois, K. A., Brown, M. Z., Heard, H. L., & Wagner, A. (2006). Suicide attempt self-injury interview (SASII): Development, reliability, and validity of a scale to assess suicide attempts and intentional self-injury. *Psychological Assessment, 18*(3), 303–312.

Lloyd, E. E., Kelley, M. L., & Hope, T. (1997, April). *Self-mutilation in a community sample of adolescents: Descriptive characteristics and provisional prevalence rates.* Poster session presented at the annual meeting of the Society for Behavioral Medicine, New Orleans, LA.

Nafisi, N., & Stanley, B. (2007). Developing and maintaining the therapeutic alliance with self-injuring patients. *Journal of Clinical Psychology: In Session, 63*(11), 1069–1079.

Nock, M. K., Holmberg, E. B., Photos, V. I., & Michel, B. D. (2007). Self-injurious thoughts and behaviors interview: Development, reliability, and validity in an adolescent sample. *Psychological Assessments, 19*(3), 309–317.

Nock, M. K., & Prinstein, M. J. (2004). A functional approach to the assessment of self-mutilative behavior. *Journal of Consulting and Clinical Psychology, 72*(5), 885–890.

Sansone, R. A., Wiederman, M. W., & Sansone, L. A. (1998). The self-harm inventory (SHI): Development of a scale for identifying self-destructive behaviors and borderline personality disorder. *Journal of Clinical Psychology, 54*(7), 973–983.

Santa Mina, E. E., Gallop, R., Links, P., Heslegrave, R., Pringle, D., Wekerle, C., & Grewal, P. (2006). The self-injury questionnaire: Evaluation of the psychometric properties in a clinical population. *Journal of Psychiatric and Mental Health Nursing, 13*(2), 221–227.

Walsh, B. (2007). Clinical assessment of self-injury: A practical guide. *Journal of Clinical Psychology: In Session, 63*(11), 1057–1068.

Wester, K. L., Downs, H., & Trepal, H. C. (2016). Counseling outcomes of non-suicidal self-injury for eight clients in outpatient treatment: A retrospective case study. *Counseling Outcome Research and Evaluation, 5*, 1–18.

Wester, K. L., Ivers, N., Villalba, J. A., & Trepal, H. C. (2016). The relationship between non-suicidal self-injury and suicidal ideation. *Journal of Counseling & Development, 94*(1), 3–12.

Wester, K. L., & McKibben, B. (2016). Participants' experiences of nonsuicidal self-injury: Supporting existing theory and emerging conceptual pathways. *Journal of Mental Health Counseling, 38*, 12–27.

Wester, K. L., & Trepal, H. C. (2015). Non-suicidal self-injury: Exploring the correlation among race, ethnic identity, and ethnic belonging. *Journal of College Student Development, 56*(2), 127–139.

Whitlock, J., Exner-Cortens, D., & Purington, A. (2014). Assessment of nonsuicidal self-injury: Development and initial validation of the Nonsuicidal Self-Injury—Assessment Tool (NSSI-AT). *Psychological Assessment, 26*(3), 935–946.

five
Diagnostic Considerations

What's in a name? In Chapter 1, we learned that *self-injury*, *self-harm*, *self-mutilation*, *suicidal behavior*, and *parasuicidal behavior* are all terms that have been used fluidly and interchangeably, in some instances, to describe NSSI. This lack of a common nomenclature presents a complicating factor in that researchers and clinicians have had problems identifying and classifying these behaviors. Recently, *non-suicidal self-injury* has become the more accepted term (yet more so in the United States and Canada, but not necessarily in the United Kingdom or Australia). Part of the reason for this change was the inclusion of NSSI in Section III, as a "condition for further study," in the Diagnostic and Statistical Manual of Mental Disorders (DSM-5; American Psychiatric Association, 2013, p.783).

According to Zetterqvist (2015), attempts to define an independent NSSI diagnosis in previous editions of the DSM have been going on since the 1980s. These early advocates for a stand-alone NSSI diagnosis recognized the important role of impulses, preoccupation with wanting to self-harm, the cycle of anticipation–harm–relief, repetitiveness, and the differentiation from suicidal behaviors.

NSSI having its own diagnostic category would accomplish several goals. First and foremost, a distinct diagnosis would separate NSSI from both suicidal behaviors and the sole diagnostic connection with borderline personality disorder (BPD). Clinicians, clients, and researchers could speak the same language, so to speak, since there would be clear descriptors in the NSSI diagnostic category. Secondly, it would certainly improve the chances for gathering relevant research findings if one definition was put forth. More specifically, it would lead to research on evidence-based treatments for NSSI behaviors that did not solely include clients who were diagnosed with BPD, which in turn may lead to improvements in client care and outcomes in treatment. Given that there are over 150 diagnoses in the current issue of the DSM-5, and future revisions of the manual aim to continue to clarify and make diagnostic criteria more clear, researched, and purposeful, developing a stand-alone NSSI diagnosis may be a daunting task.

DSM-5 NSSI Diagnosis, Condition for Further Study

The current proposed DSM-5 (2013) NSSI criteria include (p. 803):

- Engaging in NSSI incidents on five or more days within the past year
- With at least one of the following expectations: to seek relief from a negative feeling or cognitive state, to resolve an interpersonal difficulty, or to induce a positive state
- The behavior must also be associated with one of the following: interpersonal difficulty or negative feelings and thoughts (e.g., depression, anxiety), premeditation, and/or ruminating on NSSI
- Scab picking, nail biting, and socially sanctioned behaviors like body piercing and tattooing do not qualify for the diagnosis
- The behavior or resulting consequences cause clinically significant distress or disruption in functioning
- The behavior does not occur during psychosis or while the person is intoxicated or withdrawing from substances and is not better explained by another disorder or condition (see differential diagnosis below).

Figure 5.1 is an overview of the topics of NSSI functions, motivations, and emotions inherent in the proposed criteria. The proposed criteria include the concepts of *frequency* (over a certain period; over the lifetime), *function* (the purpose served by these behaviors) and *motivation* (related to the feelings, thoughts, or cycle of these behaviors). Let's examine each of these three core concepts.

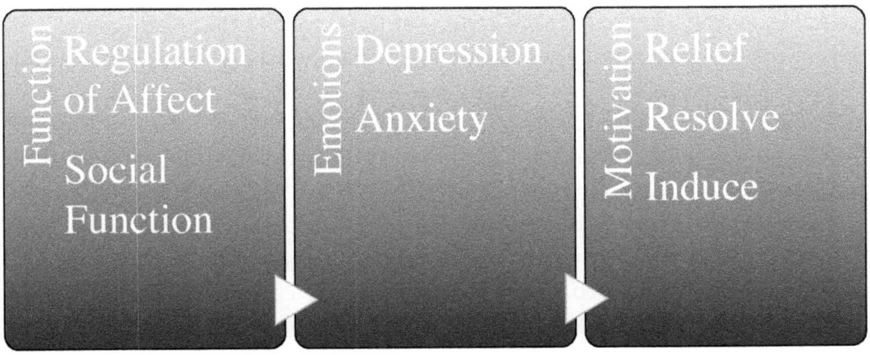

FIGURE 5.1. NSSI Function, Motivation, Emotion

Frequency

The proposed criteria for NSSI disorder include NSSI incidents on five or more days within the past year. Frequency is an important concept, as clinicians would not want to diagnose someone who overate at a Thanksgiving meal with binge eating disorder. They would also not want to diagnose a client who engaged in NSSI once in the past year with a mental disorder. Frequency shows a clinically significant pattern of engaging in a behavior and is one hallmark of the diagnostic process, along with impairment in functioning.

Function

It is commonly known that NSSI behaviors serve functions. A chief function is affect regulation. This means that engaging in self-harm relieves negative affect or powerful negative emotions (e.g., anger, rage, fear, sadness, etc.). Another common function of NSSI is social regulation. This means that engaging in self-harm serves a social purpose (e.g., communication, connection). Other functions include to stop dissociation, feel relief or excitement, alleviate boredom, engage in self-punishment, or stop suicidal thoughts (among others). Lloyd-Richardson, Perrine, Dierker, and Kelley (2007) report that most clients who self-injure identify more than one function served by this behavior. This makes sense given that feelings don't exist in isolation. A person may feel rage and want to seek relief at the same time.

Motivation

The concept of motivation involves the cyclical nature of self-injury. Negative thoughts and feelings (such as depression) exist, a client engages in pre-meditation, and may also engage in rumination about these behaviors well in advance of self-harming. The person may have a certain ritual associated with the behaviors, or they may quickly decide to do so without much prior thought in their conscious awareness. Finally, it is important to remember that some clients will combine the engagement in self-harm with using or abusing substances, so both function and motivation may become less clear. Finally, as mentioned in Chapter 1, the proposed diagnostic criteria differentiate those NSSI behaviors that are socially sanctioned (e.g., tattooing and body piercing), as these are more globally accepted forms of tissue damage.

When the DSM was being revised prior to 2013, there was some debate over whether NSSI should receive its own diagnostic category. Muehlenkamp (2005) cited the idea that NSSI behaviors exist on the suicidal behaviors continuum and that there is high comorbidity with other diagnoses (e.g., eating disorders, BPD) as among the most common reasons that people felt there was not enough evidence of uniqueness for a stand-alone diagnosis. Thus, the new listing of NSSI in the

DSM-5 addresses some of these concerns by outlining clear criteria for frequency, function, and motivation and lists borderline personality disorder, suicidal behavior disorder, trichotillomania, stereotypic self-injury, and excoriation (skin picking disorder) as differential diagnoses. Given that this proposed NSSI diagnosis is in need of research to validate the existence of this constellation of functions, emotions, behaviors, and motivations, mental health professionals still need to grapple with diagnostic issues when working with clients who self-injure. Before examining diagnostic issues that clinicians have used to capture self-injury, a discussion of various dimensions of diagnosis is needed.

The Diagnostic Dilemma

Because NSSI is not currently classified as a mental *disorder* in the DSM-5, nor is it listed in the ICD codes, clinicians are left with a bit of a dilemma when trying to figure out the best ways to classify this constellation of behaviors. As mentioned at other times in this book, each individual who self-injures is unique. Therefore, a one-size-fits-all approach to diagnosis will not work.

Why Diagnose?

Mental health professionals use diagnosis to help conceptualize clients' behaviors and presenting symptoms. Diagnoses often help clinicians to guide treatment planning (see Figure 5.2). There are both positive and limiting aspects to diagnosis.

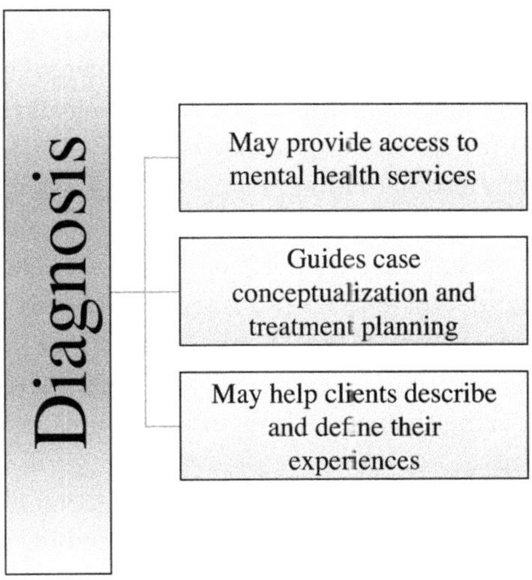

FIGURE 5.2. The Importance of Diagnosis

Labeling

Have you ever had a new physical or mental symptom, not known what was wrong, and immediately turned to Google to start searching for answers? Likely, this only intensified your worries or made you more nervous and concerned. On the positive side, you may have located some information or been more prepared to talk to your doctor or mental health professional.

Consider the concept of labeling. When someone uses the label "cutter" it can have positive (identity, notoriety) and negative aspects (a person is reduced to the label, stigma). In her book *Down Came the Rain: My Journey Through Postpartum Depression*, actress Brooke Shields describes what it was like finding out that what she had been feeling and experiencing (she was diagnosed with postpartum depression) had a name. She was able to release some of the self-blame she had been feeling. She found out that knowing the name of the disorder helped her. In this instance, the label was positive and helped to provide information and free the client from emotional distress.

When the negative aspects of a label are prominent, people can't see other facets of the person who self-injures beyond the label. Narrative therapists call this the dominant story (e.g., she *is* manipulative, he *is* a borderline). The label and the accompanying story do not allow clients or others in their lives to allow for exceptions to their problems (or labels). This lack of ability to experience or see exceptions can reduce both hopefulness and self-agency. Thus, it is easy to understand why some mental health professionals either offer diagnoses cautiously or tend to avoid them when possible, for fear of the labeling game. Sometimes, having a certain diagnosis can limit one's opportunities (e.g., entrance to the military or certain occupations).

Now, it is not always possible, probable, or even helpful to avoid diagnosis. Often, mental health professionals are reimbursed for their work through insurance companies. Those institutions require a code in order to know how many sessions or how much money to allot to justify the expense of mental health services. Other times, clients seek services at grant- or government-funded agencies, or wish to be eligible for certain programs, where only those who are diagnosed with the target concern receive funding.

The medical model has been deemed reductionist in nature (reducing clients to their symptoms) instead of incorporating contextual factors such as developmental, multicultural, and societal influences (Eriksen & Kress, 2006). From a strengths-based and wellness approach, mental health professionals take those contextual factors into account. Clients are seen from a holistic, biopsychosocial profile instead of reducing them to a cluster of symptoms in an attempt to make sense of their concerns.

Ethically, mental health professionals have the obligation to discuss the role of diagnosis in their client's treatment. As will be discussed in Chapter 6, the process of informed consent provides clients with the information needed to make a decision about whether or not to enter into treatment. The same is true with diagnosis.

Mental health providers should discuss the role of diagnosis with clients—what it is, what diagnosis may and may not be covered by insurance or third-party payers, who may have access to their mental health and diagnostic records (including insurance companies, courts, etc.), and how diagnostic labels can be both positive and limiting (Kress, Hoffman, Adamson, & Eriksen, 2013).

Another note about diagnosis and classification: In October 2015, entities and providers covered by HIPAA (Health Insurance Portability and Accountability Act) became mandated to use the International Classification of Diseases (ICD-10) classification system. The World Health Organization (WHO) created and supports the ICD codes in order to help with the classification of mental health disorders around the globe. The ICD codes give providers the opportunity for more specificity in their classifications. This doesn't mean that the DSM-5 is obsolete! The DSM contains much more detailed diagnostic information than the ICD codes and outdated codebook. The transition is easy for most mental health professionals, as the DSM-5 contains both the ICD-9 and ICD-10 codes alongside the DSM diagnosis. The ICD-10 has one code (Z91.5 Personal history of self-harm) that specifically reflects self-injury.

History of NSSI Classification

Although self-injuring behaviors have been documented since biblical times, their classification has clearly been a work in progress. Favazza (1998) developed an early initial classification system (see Table 5.1). He attempted to delineate the behaviors into three categories—major, stereotypic, and superficial/moderate—in order to help clinicians differentiate treatment options.

Almost a decade ago, Trepal and Wester (2007) asked mental health professionals how they diagnosed clients who self-injured. Here is what they reported: Most felt that NSSI could be related to more than one diagnosis. The most commonly reported were borderline personality disorder, depression (including major

TABLE 5.1. Favazza's (1998) NSSI Classification System

Classification	Description	Associated Diagnosis/Condition
Major NSSI	Severe (e.g., auto-enucleation—removal of one's eye)	Psychosis
Stereotypic NSSI	Repetitive; lacks emotions or meaning; associated with neurological concerns or developmental disability	Autism Stereotypic movement disorder
Superficial/Moderate NSSI	Superficial tissue damage; involves emotion or social function; *most common	Impulse control disorder Trichotillomania

depression and dysthymia), post-traumatic stress disorder, anxiety disorders, bipolar disorder, and substance abuse. Eating disorders, conduct disorder, and other childhood disorders such as autism were also reported, although were not as prevalent.

As mentioned earlier, the proposed criteria for NSSI include borderline personality disorder, suicidal behavior disorder, trichotillomania, stereotypic self-injury, and excoriation (skin picking disorder) as differential diagnoses. Various researchers and clinicians have also attempted to diagnostically categorize self-injurious behaviors through existing disorders to include the following: addictions (specifically process addiction), eating disorders, anxiety disorders, and obsessive-compulsive and related disorders. Each of these diagnostic frameworks will be explored in detail.

DSM-5 Listed Differential Diagnoses

Differential diagnoses are used to help clinicians consider whether one diagnosis or another best accounts for a client's presenting symptoms. The following diagnoses are listed in the DSM-5 as differential (to also be weighed) when attempting to classify NSSI.

Borderline Personality Disorder (DSM-5 Listed Differential Diagnosis)

Borderline personality disorder (BPD) is defined as "a pattern of instability in interpersonal relationships, self-image, and affects, and marked impulsivity" (DSM-5, 2013, p. 645). Personality disorders are also thought to be longstanding problematic patterns of relating to oneself and the world. Perhaps the most common diagnostic association for NSSI is this disorder. This is true for a number of reasons. Chiefly, in past editions of the DSM, self-injurious behaviors were termed "self-mutilation" and were listed as one of the diagnostic criteria for borderline personality disorder. This limitation tended to connect NSSI and BPD in ways that were both helpful and limiting. For example, because NSSI could be used as one of the supporting criteria for BPD, clients who self-injured were often recognized as having BPD. Although certainly not all clients diagnosed with BPD self-injured and not all clients who self-injured met the diagnostic criteria for BPD. In fact, up until the most recent (5th) edition of the DSM, this was the only time that self-injury was mentioned in the manual.

Diagnostic parameters for BPD include five or more of nine criteria that indicate a diagnosis for this disorder. The criteria address mood instability, fears of abandonment, identity disturbance, impulsivity, anger, problematic patterns with interpersonal relationships, paranoid ideation/dissociation, and self-harm. In fact, criterion 5, "Recurrent suicidal behavior, gestures, or threats, or self-mutilating behavior" (DSM-5, 2013, p. 663), specifically addresses NSSI; however, these behaviors are termed "self-mutilation" and listed in the same criteria as suicidal behavior/s. The diagnostic criteria also explicitly state that self-mutilating behavior associated with efforts to avoid abandonment or done impulsively should not be indicated—these behaviors have their own criteria. Thus, a BPD diagnosis for a client who self-injures can be very complicated and must be carefully and dimensionally assessed.

The second author once worked with a client who had self-injured and had been diagnosed with BPD. The client frequently self-injured, especially when she was punishing herself about something. For example, when she missed a few questions on an exam, she would cut herself over and over in a pattern related to the specific number of questions she got wrong. Thus, she would cut herself in patterns of 3 if she got 3 items wrong. She would report feeling that she was "bad" or going to be kicked out of college whenever she didn't perform to perfection. She had very reactive moods. Additionally, she reported feeling unable to make friends, lived alone in her dorm room, and reported always feeling empty and not having a "sense of self." She had seen several other counselors at the college counseling center prior to working with the second author. Each time she would make some progress, or come to the summer break when the center was closed, she would "fire" her counselor by sending them an email saying that she preferred to work with someone else. Feelings of abandonment were pervasive for this client and she often self-injured by either cutting or burning herself in attempts to control her feelings about separation or perceived rejection.

In the DSM-5 (2013) glossary of terms, *negative affectivity* is defined as "Frequent and intense experiences of high levels of a wide range of negative emotions (e.g., anxiety, depression, guilt/shame, worry, anger), and their behavioral (e.g., self-harm) and interpersonal (e.g., dependency) manifestations" (p. 825). Given that negative emotionality and emotion dysregulation appear to be common both in those who self-injure and in those diagnosed with BPD, it makes sense that they have sometimes been connected. For clinicians, it may be important to make sure to rule out a personality disorder when trying to categorize a client's self-injury if they present with these symptoms and concerns.

Trichotillomania (DSM-5 Listed Differential Diagnosis)

Trichotillomania is a DSM-5 diagnosis characterized by the repetitive desire to pull out hair. There also exists tension prior to pulling out the hair and relief once the cycle is complete. Thus, it is easy to see how trichotillomania meets some of the proposed diagnostic criteria for NSSI. In addition, skin tissue is being damaged when clients pull out their bodily hair. The diagnosis of trichotillomania is specifically related to bodily hair; however, this diagnosis may also co-occur with anxiety disorders (such as obsessive-compulsive disorder) and others.

The second author once had a client who pulled out all of the hairs on one of her eyebrows while traveling to Florida over spring break. When she came back to counseling, she recounted the trip in vivid detail. She was in a car with three other friends. She remembered feeling bored, irritated, and annoyed at the long drive to get to their hotel. She started to pull out hairs (as she had done before) from her eyebrow. Her method was very intense. She would pull the hair, twirl it around in between her thumb and index finger three to four times, look at the root, and then eat the hair. She described doing this for each of the hairs that she pulled out. As you can imagine, pulling out all of those hairs and engaging in this intense process must have taken quite some time. The client also reported that, as she was engaging in the process, her friends started to notice what she was doing. They began commenting how shocked they were, saying things like "Eww, it is so gross that you are eating your eyebrow hairs!" The client reported that she became increasingly embarrassed, but this only increased her anxiety and drove her to continue to pull out the hairs.

Excoriation (Skin Picking) Disorder (DSM-5 Listed Differential Diagnosis)

Excoriation disorder involves recurrent picking of one's own skin, despite attempts to stop or lessen the behavior. It is common in adolescence and may begin around changes in the skin, such as acne. Excoriation disorder may share some common elements with other forms of self-harm (e.g., ritual, done to alleviate negative feelings or change an emotional state, done in isolation, and is also associated with obsessive-compulsive disorder [DSM-5, 2013, pp. 254–255]). This diagnosis may be made if the client generally focuses on skin picking or interfering with wound (i.e., scab) healing and does not engage in other forms of self-injury (e.g., cutting, burning, etc.). However, underlying medical conditions or substance use should always be investigated (Lester, 2012).

Suicidal Behavior Disorder (DSM-5 Listed Differential Diagnosis)

Suicidal behavior disorder is also listed in the DSM-5 Section III, Conditions for Further Study. As mentioned throughout this book, NSSI and suicidal behaviors have a complex relationship. This complexity in thoughts, intent, behaviors, and consequences complicates symptoms (for clients) and diagnosis (for clinicians). The proposed criteria for suicidal behavior disorder include: a suicide attempt in the last 24 months (the person's intention was to cause their own death, a different intention from NSSI [to change mood state]), differs from suicidal ideation or preparation, and the attempt was not made for political or religious reasons, or during delirium (DSM-5, 2013, p. 801). It appears that this condition for further study may actually help differentiate suicidal behavior and NSSI even further. In essence, the proposed disorder attempts to clarify and distinguish a suicide attempt by intention (to end one's life) rather than focus on specific behaviors (cutting, burning) or suicide methods (gunshot, drowning, overdose). As stated throughout this book, the relationship between NSSI and suicidal behaviors can be complex. Clients can engage in NSSI (without the intent to die) and also have suicidal ideation or have attempted suicide. Chapter 3 provides more information.

Stereotypic Movement Disorder (DSM-5 Listed Differential Diagnosis)

Stereotypic movement disorder is included in the Neurodevelopmental Disorders section of the DSM-5. The hallmark of these disorders is related to developmental discrepancies in the areas of intellectual abilities, communication, social functioning, attention, learning, and motor skills. Thus, clinicians who consider this diagnosis related to NSSI are clearly focused on the client's developmental functioning. These disorders are usually first diagnosed in children. Criteria for stereotypic movement disorder includes "repetitive, seemingly driven, and apparently purposeless motor behavior" (DSM-5, 2013, p. 77) that interferes with functioning, has an early onset, and is not better accounted for by another disorder or condition.

The diagnostic criteria for stereotypic movement disorder include an important specification as to whether the disorder is presenting with or without self-injurious behavior. An example of non-self-injurious stereotypic movement would be a child who rocks their body repetitively and without purpose. An example of self-injurious stereotypic movement would include repetitive head banging or eye poking. In addition, movements can be combined (e.g., rocking and head banging in the same episode). Although some stereotypic movements are common in childhood, those diagnosed with this disorder experience impairment in their functioning. There are two other specifications: 1) if the disorder is associated with a medical, genetic, neurodevelopmental disorder or condition or an environmental factor and 2) the current severity (DSM-5, 2013, pp. 77–78).

Other Associated Diagnoses

Comorbidity

A very important diagnostic consideration is the fact that problems often do not exist in isolation. Therefore, mental health professionals should always look for co-occurring or comorbid symptoms and diagnoses in order to formulate the best diagnosis so that their clients can get the most appropriate treatment. Comorbidity represents the existence of two diagnoses or conditions at the same time. It is

Box 5.1 Comorbid Diagnoses With NSSI

Research indicates that NSSI is comorbid with the following diagnoses

- Eating disorders
- Anxiety disorders
- Depressive disorders
- Borderline personality disorder
- Substance abuse disorders

Box 5.2 Comorbid With NSSI

Research also indicates that NSSI is comorbid with the following

- Physical/Sexual abuse
- Neglect
- Family discord

important for clinicians to be able to accurately assess for the presence of both diagnoses/disorders in order to make appropriate treatment decisions.

Given that negative emotionality and emotion dysregulation are common characteristics underlying a few diagnoses, it makes sense that people who self-injure may also meet the criteria for the disorders listed in Box 5.1.

While the factors listed in Box 5.2 are not diagnostic categories, they do represent important information that can help mental health professionals to develop an accurate diagnosis and treatment plan for NSSI. If any of the following are present, clinicians should assess the client's history of adverse childhood experiences and trauma history.

The following diagnoses have been either found to be comorbid with NSSI or used by clinicians to diagnostically explain self-harming behaviors.

Addictions

The elements of addiction include (a) compulsivity or impaired control, (b) tolerance and withdrawal, (c) impairment in social functioning, and (d) continued use of the substance or behavior in spite of negative consequences (DSM-5, 2013). In the DSM-5, substance use disorders are defined and diagnosed in relation to the specific substance used (e.g., alcohol, cannabis, opioids, etc.). While engaging in self-harm certainly can be done under the influence of a substance, it does not generally involve the compulsive use of substances into a cycle of tolerance and withdrawal. The behavioral cycle present in engaging in NSSI and substance use may share some elements. The DSM-5 does note that "behavioral addictions" (p. 481) are not included in the substance use disorders diagnostic category as they lack the research support to qualify for mental disorders (e.g., stand-alone diagnosis). The notable exception is gambling disorder.

Hagedorn (2009) reveals that process addictions—or what some refer to as behavioral addictions—are a type of addictive behavior (e.g., gambling addiction, food addiction, exercise addiction, Internet addiction, sexual addiction) that do not involve ingesting substances (p. 110). They are addictions to a process, or to *the doing* of something. In fact, some formerly so-called process addictions (eating addiction, gambling) have recently evolved into new diagnoses in the current edition of the DSM. Internet gaming disorder is also now included as a condition for future study (DSM-5). Binge eating disorder earned its own diagnostic category in the DSM-5 (APA, 2013). In the past edition of the DSM, binge eating disorder was listed as a condition for further study. Mental health professionals were able to categorize individuals who met the criteria under "eating disorder not otherwise specified." However, having a new diagnostic category for binge eating disorder will now allow for more specific diagnosis and subsequent treatment planning, overall hopefully leading to improved client outcomes.

Buser and Buser (2013) make the case that NSSI could, indeed, be a form of a process addiction. Research supports that the following addiction characteristics are present in some who self-injure: compulsivity, loss of control, continued use despite negative consequences, and tolerance (Buser & Buser, 2013). However, research supporting the presence of these addictive elements in some people who self-injure does not mean that there is a one-size-fits-all model of NSSI. As you can see, it is understandable that some mental health professionals choose to conceptualize and treat NSSI from an addictions framework. While more research is needed, one way to clinically consider whether NSSI may be a process addiction is to assess whether the client implicitly identifies as a self-injurer (I *am* a self-injurer), feels constant need or urges to engage regardless of activating event or situation, discusses continued increased tolerance for NSSI behaviors, as well as discusses consequences when NSSI is not engaged in (e.g., withdrawal effects). This does not rule in or out NSSI as a process addiction, but may help clinicians determine if working with a client from an addiction-based treatment model versus an affective, problem-focused treatment model may be more effective for a client.

Eating Disorders

Eating disorders are among the most lethal of mental health concerns. They range from anorexia (restricting eating) to bulimia (eating and then disposing of the contents of the stomach) to binge eating disorder (increased episodes of eating) with several sub-types.

Svirko and Hawton (2007) maintain that there is a strong association between self-injury and eating disorders. They conducted a review of the research on both at the time and concluded that they share a number of factors, including a need for control, increased impulsivity, negative emotionality, emotion dysregulation, and obsessive-compulsive characteristics. They also point out that those who struggle with NSSI and/or eating disorders may share common family dynamics and background experiences.

The second author once worked with a client who struggled with this very issue. The client was engaged in bulimia for several years. Over the past 6 months, she had been actively decreasing her episodes of bulimia through increasing mindfulness and other coping skills. However, as the bulimia decreased, the client's self-injury began to increase. It was as if she was replacing one behavior with the other.

Obsessive-Compulsive and Related Disorders

Obsessive-compulsive disorders include those conditions that have both obsessions and compulsions. Obsessive-compulsive and related disorders have been used to diagnose self-injury, as this category includes both trichotillomania and excoriation. Specific diagnostic criteria for both were detailed earlier in this chapter. However, obsessive-compulsive disorder (OCD) and generalized anxiety disorder (GAD) both include symptoms that clients who self-injure may present with, a pattern of intense thoughts, urges, or action that aim to alleviate distress and anxiety or another feeling. Thus, it is easy to see why some mental health professionals may choose to diagnose and work with self-injury from this framework.

Finally, anxiety disorders are very common and are often comorbid with those in the Obsessive-Compulsive and Related Disorders category. The diagnoses in this category are often associated with fear and avoidance as motivation for engagement in behaviors. The second author has used unspecified anxiety disorder to diagnose a client who self-injured when they did not meet the full criteria for another anxiety disorder (e.g., GAD) but anxiety, worry, and irritability were present along with the NSSI behaviors. The client was a performance art student who was very fearful and apprehensive about her talents being judged and frequently worried herself into episodes of NSSI where she would burn her stomach with a hot iron. She reported feeling anxiety and irritability most of the time (although she did not engage in NSSI most of the time to resolve these feelings).

Some clinicians have also used other-specified impulse control disorder to account for self-injury. Caution is to be noted that the Disruptive, Impulse Control, and Conduct Disorders category primarily focuses on problems with controlling emotions and behaviors that violate the rights of others (DSM-5, 2013, p. 461). Those who self-injure are mainly seeking to harm themselves, so clear diagnostic criteria would need to differentiate these disorders and the NSSI.

Finally, depression and anxiety have a lot in common. It is often said that depression and anxiety are the opposite hands of the same glove; whenever you see signs of one, you should assess for the presence of the other. Clients who self-injure may report that they experience co-occurring symptoms of both depression and anxiety. Since NSSI is comorbid with many other diagnostic categories, it is important for mental health professionals to clearly cross-assess for each.

Conclusion

The diagnosis of non-suicidal self-injurious behaviors is often a complex and multi-factored process. The *Diagnostic and Statistical Manual of Mental and Emotional Disorders* (DSM-5) and the ICD-10 codes are some of the main tools that mental health professionals use to form a diagnosis. However, accurate assessment (including both formal and informal aspects) is an important diagnostic foundation.

As we saw in the previous chapter on assessment, there are many ways to approach a particular set of behaviors, problems, and concerns in a client's life. Behaviors cannot be better accounted for by medical and substance abuse origins. A biopsychosocial assessment provides an overview of different intersecting domains of a client's life and gives a well-rounded view of different aspects of their functioning in different areas. Clinicians should also be mindful of a client's cultural background, including their developmental trajectory and gender, among other aspects. A specific assessment of NSSI behaviors (e.g., a functional assessment that addresses thoughts, functions, urges, intentions, and history) provides very detailed information related to the history, course, and specifics of the behavior. So, how do mental health professionals appropriately diagnose those who self-injure? As mentioned before, there is not a one-size-fits-all option, as clients who self-injure are all unique.

In sum, the process of NSSI diagnosis is complicated. However, accurate diagnosis is an important step on the road to finding appropriate treatment and resources. Given the inclusion of **Non-Suicidal Self-Injury** as a condition for further study in the DSM-5, it is more important than ever that researchers and clinicians partner to investigate the possibility of a stand-alone official NSSI diagnosis.

References

American Psychiatric Association. (2013). *Diagnostic and statistical manual of mental disorders* (5th edition). Washington, DC: Author.

Buser, T. J., & Buser, J. K. (2013). Conceptualizing non-suicidal self-injury as a process addiction: Review of research and implications for counselor training and practice. *Journal of Addictions & Offender Counseling, 34*, 16–29.

Eriksen, K., & Kress, V. E. (2006). The DSM and the professional counseling identity: Bridging the gap. *Journal of Mental Health Counseling, 28*(3), 202–217.

Favazza, A. (1998). The coming of age of self-mutilation. *Journal of Nervous and Mental Disease, 186*, 259–268. doi: 10.1097/00005053-199805000-00001

Hagedorn, W. B. (2009). The call for a new diagnostic and statistical manual of mental disorders diagnosis: Addictive disorders. *Journal of Addictions and Offender Counseling, 29*, 110–127.

Kress, V. E., Hoffman, R. M., Adamson, N., & Eriksen, K. (2013). Informed consent, confidentiality, and diagnosing: Ethical guidelines for counselor practice. *Journal of Mental Health Counseling, 35*, 15–28.

Lester, R. J. (2012). Self-mutilation and excoriation. *Encyclopedia of Body Image and Human Appearance, 2*, 724–729. doi: 10.1016/B978-0-12-384925-0.00114-0

Lloyd-Richardson, E., Perrine, N., Dierker, L., & Kelley, M. (2007). Characteristics and functions of non-suicidal self-injury in a community sample of adolescents. *Psychological Medicine, 37*, 1183–1192. doi: 10.1017/S003329170700027X

Muehlenkamp, J. J. (2005). Self-injurious behavior as a separate clinical syndrome. *American Journal of Orthopsychiatry, 75*, 324–333.

Svirko, E., & Hawton, K. (2007). Self-injurious behavior and eating disorders: The extent and nature of the association. *Suicide and Life-Threatening Behavior, 37*(4), 409–421.

Trepal, H., & Wester, K. (2007). Self-injurious behaviors, diagnoses, and treatment methods: What mental health professionals are reporting. *Journal of Mental Health Counseling, 29*, 363–375.

Zetterqvist, M. (2015). The DSM-5 diagnosis of nonsuicidal self-injury disorder: A review of the empirical literature. *Child and Adolescent Psychiatry and Mental Health, 9*, 31. doi: 10.1186/s13034-015-0062-7 six

Ethical Considerations for Treatment

Ethics are a cornerstone of mental health counseling practice. They are developed by professions to guide clinicians in making ethical decisions about clients and their treatment. Various mental health professions (e.g., counseling, social work, marriage and family therapy, psychology) and other organizations (e.g., American School Counselor Association, National Board of Certified Counselors, state licensing boards) have developed official sets of ethical codes to help practitioners navigate these dilemmas.

Foundations of Ethical Codes

According to Kitchener (1984), there are five core moral principles that serve as the foundation for ethical codes and ethical decision-making processes. These include:

Autonomy: The client's independence and their right to chose
Nonmaleficence: The counselor's obligation to do no harm
Beneficence: The counselor's obligation to help the client, to be of benefit to the client (goes beyond doing no harm)
Justice: Treating clients the same under the same conditions
Fidelity: The counselor's loyalty, faithfulness, and trustworthiness in support of their clients

These principles serve as the foundation for professionals making decisions about clients' care and treatment. State laws also influence these decision-making processes. The relationship between state laws and professional codes of ethics is also complex.

Sometimes, professional codes of ethics are infused (codified) into state counseling laws or detailed in counselor rules and regulations. For example, at this time, nineteen states have adopted the American Counseling Association (ACA, 2014) Code of Ethics into the foundation of their state counseling rules and regulations. In the other states, this is not the case. In addition, there may be times where state laws and ethical codes conflict. In those cases, clinicians are reminded to consult with as many stakeholders as possible before reaching their decisions and outlining their course of action. A model for ethical decision making will be presented later in this chapter. First, let's examine some potential ethical issues that may be related to non-suicidal self-injury.

Ethical Issues Associated with NSSI

Although this list is by no means exhaustive, there are several common ethical concerns, including respect for client autonomy, informed consent, confidentiality, working with minors, and clinician reactions/competence, that may arise when working with clients who self-injure. Various authors (Hoffman & Kress, 2010; Lloyd-Richardson, Lewis, Whitlock, Rodham, & Schatten, 2015; White, McCormick, & Kelly, 2003) have underscored these ethical issues associated with NSSI and each will be considered in turn below.

Client Autonomy

Ethical Issue—Client Autonomy

American Association for Marriage and Family Therapy (2015) Code of Ethics 1.8

"Marriage and family therapists respect the rights of clients to make decisions and help them to understand the consequences of these decisions."

American Counseling Association (2014) Code of Ethics A.1.c

"Counselors and their clients work jointly in devising counseling plans that offer reasonable promise of success and are consistent with the abilities, temperament, developmental level, and circumstances of clients. Counselors and clients regularly review and revise counseling plans to assess their continued viability and effectiveness, respecting clients' freedom of choice."

American Psychological Association (2010) Ethical Principles of Psychologists and Code of Conduct Principle E

"Psychologists respect the dignity and worth of all people, and the rights of individuals to privacy, confidentiality, and self-determination."

National Association of Social Workers (2008) Code of Ethics 1.02

> "Social workers respect and promote the right of clients to self-determination and assist clients in their efforts to identify and clarify their goals. Social workers may limit clients' right to self-determination when, in the social workers' professional judgment, clients' actions or potential actions pose a serious, foreseeable, and imminent risk to themselves or others."

The respect for the client's autonomy and their ability to make independent decisions is essential to the clinical relationship and, as mentioned earlier, serves as a foundation for ethical decision making. All clients, including those who self-injure, have the right to make decisions for themselves (independence) and to make choices about their treatment (including the right to refuse treatment). With respect to NSSI, other people in the client's world, including teachers, parents, and physicians, may believe that the client should stop self-injuring. However, this ethical principle comes into play in that the client may not feel that they want to stop self-injuring, or may not feel ready to stop the behavior at this point in time. According to Kress and Hoffman (2008), clients may not be ready to change their behaviors or may not feel that these behaviors are problematic issues for treatment. During these situations, clinicians are faced with a potential ethical dilemma. Consider the case of Enrique, described in Box 6.1. Clinicians may be concerned with risk management—is the client self-harming in a way that puts them in increased risk of medical complications? Are they practicing other self-harming behaviors while self-injuring (e.g., substance abuse)? Is the client also suicidal or expressing suicidal ideation in addition to the NSSI? Clinicians must weigh the client's right to autonomy and to make choices about their treatment in the face of these dynamics. These types of questions and concerns may make it difficult for a counselor to interpret their course of action.

Box 6.1 Client Case Example: Enrique

Enrique is a 19-year-old college student who comes to see you for counseling. He has filled out some routine paperwork prior to his initial session where he indicates that he is experiencing depression, has recently broken up with a girlfriend, and that he self-injures. In the initial session, you talk with Enrique about his goals for counseling. He states that he wants to focus on the breakup with his girlfriend. He explains that the self-injury is a coping skill that he has used since early adolescence and that he engages in the behaviors more often when he is struggling with managing his emotions. However, at this time, he is not interested in trying to stop self-injuring.

Mental health professionals need to balance the principles of autonomy and nonmaleficence when determining client treatment. A clinician needs to consider the purpose of the NSSI (e.g., self-soothing, coping mechanism) versus the consequences and harm that could be done (e.g., could the NSSI result in accidental death or severe harm or disfigurement). As Hoffman and Kress (2010) state: "... the counselor must determine if passive action and respecting a client's treatment decisions (autonomy) could cause significant harm to the client (nonmaleficence). When the significance of the harm outweighs client autonomy, action must be taken to keep clients safe" (p. 348).

Thus, in Enrique's case described above, the counselor must balance the client's autonomy (his decision not to want to stop self-injuring) with the principle of nonmaleficence (the potential for significant harm due to the self-injury). The complex relationship between NSSI behaviors and ethical principles such as autonomy and nonmaleficence leads to a discussion of risk management.

Risk Management—Identifying Risk Factors in Treatment

Risk management is a term that strikes fear into the heart of many clinicians and their supervisors. While ethical codes serve as a guide for clinicians' decision making processes, risk management concerns may be more practically focused. However, there are certain ethical principles that are commonly considered to be associated with risk management concerns. Mental health practitioners who work with clients who are suicidal, or whose self-injury is undertaken in a way that is medically compromising, may have to wrestle with the ethical principle of *nonmaleficence* (do no harm). The decisions that they may have to make regarding assessment and exploring options for involuntary treatment may leave them wondering if they have made the right choice—one that does not harm their client.

These decisions may be complicated, as clear guidelines for assessing the medical severity of NSSI injuries are lacking (Lloyd-Richardson et al., 2015). In addition, mental health practitioners may not have the medical training necessary to make an assessment about NSSI injuries (Lloyd-Richardson et al., 2015). Detailed information on NSSI assessment is presented in Chapter 4.

When balancing the client's rights to autonomy and treatment in the least restrictive setting, the following NSSI risk considerations should be considered:

Physical health risks—may include sharing blades, wound severity, unsafe wound care practices (seek medical consultation to assess)
Impulsivity—substance abuse, impulsive thoughts, impulsive actions
Distress tolerance—client is not able to handle increased stress and strain
Numbing—increased NSSI may produce an effect of greater NSSI needed to feel "something" (e.g., tolerance); dissociation
Suicidality—risk, history of prior attempts, most recent attempt/s, ideation, plans, means

Suicidality

Perhaps the greatest risk management assessment that needs to occur related to NSSI is that of suicidality. Counselors are cautioned not to make assumptions about the connection between NSSI and suicide and to evaluate each behavior separately as well as to look for the potential of interconnected relationships between the two. The relation between suicide and NSSI is covered in detail in Chapter 3. However, a review of the differences between NSSI and suicide is presented in Table 6.1 to highlight risk management concerns. As noted in the table, clinicians should consider the various contextual aspects associated with both NSSI and suicide for the sake of risk management, client safety, and client empowerment (Hoffman & Kress, 2010).

Hoffman and Kress (2010, p. 347) suggest that mental health practitioners assess both NSSI and suicide thoroughly and continuously. In addition, they recommend that clinicians work through a decision tree to interpret NSSI risk management factors. For example, clients who self-injure and also present with current suicidal ideation and a past history of suicide attempts should be considered high risk, requiring further intervention (e.g., connection to support resources, possible hospitalization). Clients who self-injure yet do not present with current suicidal ideation or a history of past attempts should be considered lower risk. They should be continuously assessed regarding both NSSI and suicide. Considerations for NSSI ongoing assessment include frequency, severity, dissociation, concurrent substance abuse, and the presence of psychological repercussions such as shame/guilt (Hoffman & Kress, 2010, p. 347). If the necessity warrants, these clients may also be considered high risk and require the further interventions listed above.

TABLE 6.1. Differences Between NSSI and Suicide

Behavior	NSSI	Suicide
Intent	Temporary end to distress; not intending to cause death	Permanent end to distress; intending to cause death
Severity/lethality of methods	Less lethal methods, although can be severe	More lethal methods
Number of methods	More varied	Fewer or same method
Frequency	More frequent	Less frequent
Cognitive state	Hope to seek temporary relief	Less hope; more helpless
Repercussions	Lack of success = try another method	Lack of success = more distress

Summarized from Muehlenkamp and Kerr (2010)

Legal Concerns

Most state laws (and codes of ethics) require mental health professionals to intervene when clients are a risk to themselves (suicide) or others (homicide). However, laws do not address NSSI behaviors as specifically as they do suicidal behaviors. Hoffman and Kress (2010) propose that counselors consider both the use of no harm contracts (e.g., those that specify parameters around self-harming behaviors) and commitment to treatment statements (e.g., those that focus on more positive alternatives to NSSI or positive participation in counseling), as there can be benefits and limitations associated with each (Range et al., 2002; Rudd, Mandrusiak, & Joiner, 2006). Clinicians, regardless of setting, must remain diligent in their assessment, evaluation, and documentation procedures should their professional judgment ever be called into question.

Informed Consent

Informed consent is a very important component of a successful therapeutic relationship. Informed consent is the client's informed ability to consent to treatment. It is an important ongoing process where clients are given a full picture of both the risks and benefits of treatment. They are also provided information on the clinician and their background and training, as well as given the choice to decide whether or not they want to enter into treatment. Informed consent is also a time when clients are provided with enough information and can decide what they want to disclose to their clinician versus what they do not want to disclose.

Ethical Issue—Informed Consent

> **American Association for Marriage and Family Therapy (2015) Code of Ethics 1.2**
>
> "The content of informed consent may vary depending upon the client and treatment plan; however, informed consent generally necessitates that the client: (a) has the capacity to consent; (b) has been adequately informed of significant information concerning treatment processes and procedures; (c) has been adequately informed of potential risks and benefits of treatments for which generally recognized standards do not yet exist; (d) has freely and without undue influence expressed consent; and (e) has provided consent that is appropriately documented."

American Counseling Association (2014) Code of Ethics A.2.a.

"Clients have the freedom to choose whether to enter into or remain in a counseling relationship and need adequate information about the counseling process and the counselor."

American Psychological Association (2010) Ethical Principles of Psychologists and Code of Conduct 10.01 (a)

"When obtaining informed consent to therapy as required in Standard 3.10, Informed Consent, psychologists inform clients/patients as early as is feasible in the therapeutic relationship about the nature and anticipated course of therapy, fees, involvement of third parties, and limits of confidentiality and provide sufficient opportunity for the client/patient to ask questions and receive answers."

National Association of Social Workers (2008) Code of Ethics 1.03

"(a) Social workers should provide services to clients only in the context of a professional relationship based, when appropriate, on valid informed consent. Social workers should use clear and understandable language to inform clients of the purpose of the services, risks related to the services, limits to services because of the requirements of a third-party payer, relevant costs, reasonable alternatives, clients' right to refuse or withdraw consent, and the time frame covered by the consent. Social workers should provide clients with an opportunity to ask questions."

Confidentiality

Confidentiality is another important concept. In graduate school, mental health practitioners-in-training are taught that confidentiality means, "What is said in the room stays in the room." Clinicians who work with clients who self-injure may face ethical dilemmas involving confidentiality and risk management.

Box 6.2 Client Case Example: Enrique, continued

During intake and informed consent, the counselor outlines the topic of informed consent, including the risks and benefits that can be expected. In this situation, the counselor talks with Enrique about the fact that talking about his concerns may make his NSSI worse (increasing frequency and duration). The counselor also discusses their background and qualifications in treating people who self-injure.

Ethical Issue—Confidentiality

American Association for Marriage and Family Therapy (2015) Code of Ethics 2.1

"Marriage and family therapists disclose to clients and other interested parties at the outset of services the nature of confidentiality and possible limitations of the clients' right to confidentiality. Therapists review with clients the circumstances where confidential information may be requested and where disclosure of confidential information may be legally required. Circumstances may necessitate repeated disclosures."

American Counseling Association (2014) Code of Ethics B.1.d., B.2.a.

Code B.1.d.

"At initiation and throughout the counseling process, counselors inform clients of the limitations of confidentiality and seek to identify situations in which confidentiality must be breached."

Code B.2.a

"The general requirement that counselors keep information confidential does not apply when disclosure is required to protect clients or identified others from serious and foreseeable harm or when legal requirements demand that confidential information must be revealed."

American Psychological Association (2010) Ethical Principles of Psychologists and Code of Conduct 4.02 (a)

"Psychologists discuss with persons (including, to the extent feasible, persons who are legally incapable of giving informed consent and their legal representatives) and organizations with whom they establish a scientific or professional relationship (1) the relevant limits of confidentiality and (2) the foreseeable uses of the information generated through their psychological activities."

National Association of Social Workers (2008) Code of Ethics 1.07 (c)

"Social workers should protect the confidentiality of all information obtained in the course of professional service, except for compelling professional reasons. The general expectation that social workers will keep information confidential does not apply when disclosure is necessary to prevent serious, foreseeable, and imminent harm to a client or other identifiable person."

One possible strategy is for clinicians to clarify in advance the times when they might need to break the client's confidentiality related to NSSI behaviors. This way, clients can have an advanced warning for what they might expect if confidentiality were to have to be breached. For example, a clinician could tell the client during intake/informed consent that if the client were to tell them that they were self-harming, then the clinician would have to break their confidentiality and talk with their parents. If the client is a minor, the clinician could also clarify that they would involve the client in the conversation with their parents to every extent possible. Given that NSSI behaviors are grayer than suicidal and homicidal behaviors, informed consent is also a time when the clinician can determine what boundaries they need to put around NSSI specifically. Thus when considering risk management, what behaviors would require reporting versus what NSSI behaviors may not require reporting? This may connect to risk management and severe forms of NSSI that result in major tissue damage, or NSSI behaviors that are a result of high-risk behaviors and circumstances (e.g., substance abuse, dissociation, impulsivity).

The concept of confidentiality in different settings (e.g., schools, treatment centers) can be very complex, as multiple stakeholders are involved. For example, the American School Counselor Association's *Ethical Standards for School Counselors* (ASCA, 2010) address this topic in standard **A.2.c. Confidentiality**:

> "Recognize the complicated nature of confidentiality in schools and consider each case in context. Keep information confidential unless legal requirements demand that confidential information be revealed or a breach is required to prevent serious and foreseeable harm to the student. Serious and foreseeable harm is different for each minor in schools and is defined by students' developmental and chronological age, the setting, parental rights and the nature of the harm. School counselors consult with appropriate professionals when in doubt as to the validity of an exception."
> (p.2)

Box 6.3 Client Case Example: Mason

Mason is 10 years old and in 5th grade in elementary school. He is referred to his school counselor due to a teacher discovering some raw-looking marks on his arms in class. The teacher has noticed that his grades seem to be slipping and that he has become more quiet than usual. Mason tells the school counselor that he wants to tell her a "secret." He then tells her about his NSSI. The school counselor has to consider Mason's case in context:

Stage of development/chronological age: Pre-adolescent, age 10
Parental rights: Parents have the right to be informed regarding their child's well-being
Nature of the harm: Unknown, needs to be assessed
Consultation: Referring teacher, principal, school nurse, other administrators, school policies

See Chapter 9 for more information on nuances of working with NSSI in different settings.

Working with Minors

Ethical Issue—Working with Minors

Mental health practitioners may also face ethical dilemmas related to both informed consent and confidentiality if they are working with minors (those under 18 years of age). Although all of the major mental health professions' codes of ethics (e.g., AAMFT, ACA, APA, NASW) address working with those who are unable to give consent, including minors, the American Counseling Association (2014) Code of Ethics B.5.b. provides specific ethical recommendations:

> "Counselors inform parents and legal guardians about the role of counselors and the confidential nature of the counseling relationship, consistent with current legal and custodial arrangements. Counselors are sensitive to the cultural diversity of families and respect the inherent rights and responsibilities of parents/guardians regarding the welfare of their children/charges according to law. Counselors work to establish, as appropriate, collaborative relationships with parents/guardians to best serve clients."

Clinicians who work with minors face additional challenges when considering the rights and autonomy of these clients alongside the rights of parents/caregivers to be informed and involved in their child's treatment (White et al., 2003). Breaking the minor child's confidentiality may cause a rupture in the relationship between the client and the counselor or place additional stress on the client's family dynamics at home.

Once again, clinicians should remain mindful of the ethical mandates for the various settings in which they work. For example, the American School Counselor Association's *Ethical Standards for School Counselors* (ASCA, 2010) dictate that school counselors are aware of this topic in standard **A.2.d. Confidentiality**:

> "Recognize their primary obligation for confidentiality is to the students but balance that obligation with an understanding of parents'/guardians' legal and inherent rights to be the guiding voice in their children's lives, especially in value-laden issues. Understand the need to balance students' ethical rights to make choices, their capacity to give consent or assent and parental or familial legal rights and responsibilities to protect these students and make decisions on their behalf."
>
> (p.2)

In this instance, school counselors have responsibilities to the student, the parent/guardian, and the school system. In other settings where clinicians work with minor clients (e.g., residential treatment), there are both client and systemic responsibilities to consider.

White et al. (2003) offer the following suggestions for breaking confidentiality when working with NSSI and minors:

- Involve the minor client, as much as possible
- Provide information about NSSI in a way that is respectful to the client
- If possible, and if the NSSI is not life-threatening, work with the client to disclose the information to the parent/caregiver
- Involve the parent/family in the minor's treatment, to the extent possible.

In the example in Box 6.4, the school counselor both respects the limits of confidentiality (the information that she can and can't keep between herself and the minor client) and the client's rights to informed consent and autonomy (the ability to make choices about his treatment and the right to know what's going to happen). The school counselor sought out Mason's level of understanding about confidentiality and gave him a choice about how he wanted to move forward regarding talking with his parents about his NSSI. Notice the choice was not whether his parents were told, but how his parents were told (e.g., who provided the information).

Box 6.4 Client Case Example: Mason (Disclosing NSSI to Mason's Parents)

In the case above, the school counselor had to weigh some difficult dynamics. After talking with Mason, she discovered that his NSSI was severe. The school counselor completed a suicide assessment, and, although she didn't feel that the NSSI was life-threatening, she did feel the need to disclose the behavior to Mason's parents for the purposes of referral.

School Counselor: Mason, do you remember when you told me that you wanted to tell me about your secret and I talked with you about confidentiality? Can you tell me what you remember that means?

Mason: Yes, it's kind of like when you are dealing with the student and you can't give any other information to another person. You said there were times you might need to talk to the person's parents.

School Counselor: Yes, exactly. After we've been talking, I think it would be the best idea for you and I to share some information about your cutting with your parents. I know that this has been something that you've been thinking about a lot lately and I am really glad that you shared it with me. What do you think about us telling them together?

Mason: O.K., I was hoping that you weren't going to say that. I want you to tell them. I can be there but I don't want to say it.

Clinician Competence and Reactions

Clinician competence is another vital area that most ethical codes address. Some clinicians may be concerned that they are ill prepared to work with clients who self-injure. Given the complex relationship between NSSI and suicide, and the risks inherent therein, mental health practitioners who work with this client population must also be skilled in assessment and evaluation. Clinician's feelings of incompetence may become especially exasperated if clients are continually in crisis or if the self-harming behaviors are particularly severe. In addition, clinicians who work with clients who self-injure should also be aware of diagnostic comorbidity (clients who struggle with NSSI may also struggle with anxiety, depression, and eating disorders, among other conditions. See Chapter 5 for more information on NSSI and diagnosis).

So, how do mental health practitioners become more competent? As with working with any client population, clinicians seek out educational and training experiences that are commensurate with their level of development. This means that clinicians must practice within their level of competence. If they are not competent with a client population or concern, they should consider whether or not to accept the client/referral. If they do decide to see the client for treatment, they should seek out more education, regularly consult with colleagues, or seek additional supervision regarding these issues. Clinicians who are not experienced in working with clients who self-harm are encouraged to seek appropriate supervision and consultation and to document their work appropriately. For more information about supervision and NSSI, see Chapter 11.

Ethical Issue—Competence

American Association for Marriage and Family Therapy (2015) Code of Ethics 3.10

"Marriage and family therapists do not diagnose, treat, or advise on problems outside the recognized boundaries of their competencies."

American Counseling Association (2014) Code of Ethics C.2.a.

"Counselors practice only within the boundaries of their competence, based on their education, training, supervised experience, state and national professional credentials, and appropriate professional experience"

American Psychological Association (2010) Ethical Principles of Psychologists and Code of Conduct 2.01 (a)

"Psychologists provide services, teach, and conduct research with populations and in areas only within the boundaries of their competence, based on their education, training, supervised experience, consultation, study, or professional experience."

National Association of Social Workers (2008) Code of Ethics 1.04 (a)

> "Social workers should provide services and represent themselves as competent only within the boundaries of their education, training, license, certification, consultation received, supervised experience, or other relevant professional experience."

Clinician Reactions

One particular concern for mental health professionals who work with clients who self-injure is the topic of clinician reactions. According to Cresswell and Karimova (2010), these reactions may indicate a type of negative moral judgment (p. 159). In addition, these reactions can influence how clinicians approach their clients as well as how they proceed with treatment. Chapter 11 (Supervision) provides further information on examining clinician reactions to NSSI.

The literature describes various reactions that may be common for clinicians to have to NSSI, including:

- Seeing the behaviors as attention-seeking or manipulative
- Sensing that NSSI is a "cry for help"
- Feeling a sense of revulsion
- Feeling overwhelmed or hopeless
- Feeling frustrated
- Attempting to control the client's behavior
- Feeling a pressure to fix or reduce NSSI
- Experiencing a lack of competence

The research literature also describes how clients are aware of and respond to health professionals' reactions. Clients do perceive negative reactions and that

Box 6.5 Client Case Example: Mike

Mike is a counselor working in private practice. Recently, he began to see a client named Julie. As he has been further assessing Julie's NSSI, Mike has learned that she has been practicing multiple methods including burning herself with an iron on her stomach. For some reason, this really bothers Mike. He has noticed that he is increasingly uncomfortable talking about the episodes with the iron in their sessions and wonders if his discomfort is apparent to Julie or affecting their work together.

influences future treatment decisions (McHale & Felton, 2010). Finally, Hoffman and Kress remind clinicians that "constant monitoring of countertransference reactions and accepting that one cannot control a client's decision to SI are important" (2010, p. 348).

Ethical Decision Making

According to Barnett and Molzon (2014), mental health professionals need to develop a sophisticated approach to addressing ethical challenges and dilemmas that involves the application of a process of ethical decision making rather than looking for "the right answer" (p. 1056). Given that ethical dilemmas present frequently in counseling sessions, this is good advice. The importance of seeking consultation with others cannot be underestimated. There are many different models of ethical decision making for mental health practitioners (see Cottone & Claus, 2000, for a review of ethical decision-making models). For the purposes of this chapter, we will introduce the Forester-Miller and Davis (1996) *Practitioner's Guide to Ethical Decision Making* Model. This model is based on Kitchener's principles of ethical decision making and is endorsed by the American Counseling Association (ACA).

Components of the model include:

I. Determine whether a problem exists
II. Consult the American Counseling Association [or your profession's] *Code of Ethics*
III. Examine the context (nature and dimensions) of the ethical dilemma
IV. Generate all possible courses of action (include consultation)
V. Consider the potential consequences. Make the decision
VI. Evaluate the decision
VII. Implement the decision/course of action (Forester-Miller & Davis, 1996, p. 4)

Box 6.6 Sample Questions to Ask When Weighing an Ethical Dilemma

Will engaging in this behavior be in my client's best interest?
Will acting in this way be consistent with my obligations to my client?
Could this action result in harm to my client?
Have I consulted with my peers and supervisors regarding this issue?
Could I stand in a well-lit room and face my peers to explain my decision?

Case: Ethical Decision-Making Model in Practice

Let's return to the case of Enrique discussed earlier in the chapter (Box 6.1 and 6.2). We are going to explore this case using an ethical decision-making model based on Forester-Miller and Davis's ethical decision-making model noted above. Remember, Enrique is 19 years old and has come to counseling related to stress caused by a recent breakup of a romantic relationship. During the intake process, Enrique disclosed his NSSI to the counselor; he also reported that he did not want to address his self-injury in session, as he did not consider it an issue. During the course of routine NSSI risk assessment, the counselor discovers that Enrique's self-reported NSSI has become both more frequent and more severe after his recent breakup. The counselor is having conflicted feelings regarding the NSSI and Enrique's safety.

I. Determine Whether a Problem Exists

In this case, the clinician must first determine whether any ethical or legal dilemmas exist. The counselor feels torn between the fact that Enrique is an autonomous human being and should have the right to make decisions about his own treatment. However, the counselor also upholds the ethical principle of *do no harm*. He feels as though Enrique would benefit from discussing his NSSI in treatment and has concerns about his safety, as there has been a change in the NSSI.

II. Consult the American Counseling Association *Code of Ethics* [or Your Profession's Code of Ethics]

The next step in the model directs the counselor to the *Code of Ethics* to pinpoint the specific ethical code/s that may play a role in the dilemma. American Counseling Association (ACA) Codes A.1.c. and A.2.a. (referenced earlier in this chapter) directly relate to this dilemma. In addition, the counselor's potential reaction to NSSI relates to both the foundational ethical principles of *Autonomy* and *Nonmaleficence*.

III. Examine the Context (Nature and Dimensions) of the Ethical Dilemma

Now having more information about the specific ethical code/s, the counselor can consider other relevant contextual information about the dilemma. In this case, the clinician has to consider the client's age (19; no longer a minor), risk management concerns (a suicide assessment was performed and the client was not determined to be suicidal), the NSSI risk assessment (the NSSI had increased in frequency and severity and was on an upward trend; however, it was not life-threatening and the assessment did not result in any heightened risk management concerns).

IV. Generate all Possible Courses of Action (Include Consultation)

During this step of the model, the clinician generates a list of all possible courses of action, including doing nothing. The clinician also seeks consultation with others.

Possible courses of action considered:

1. Do nothing (allow Enrique's counseling to progress not addressing the NSSI)
2. Refer Enrique to another mental health professional
3. Revisit informed consent with Enrique and share the results of the risk assessment and desire to work with the NSSI during treatment
4. Revisit the informed consent with Enrique and share the results of the risk assessment and the need to continue to monitor the NSSI; seek ongoing supervision regarding monitoring the clinician's own reactions.

The clinician also consults with other mental health staff at the agency and seeks their opinions on other courses of action.

V. Consider the Potential Consequences. Make the Decision

The clinician must now consider the potential consequences of making the range of decisions listed in step IV.

1. Do nothing. Consequence: the client will continue in treatment; the NSSI may or may not get worse (or better); the need for assessment will continue
2. Refer Enrique to another mental health professional. Consequence: Enrique may or may not accept the referral
3. Revisit informed consent with Enrique and discuss working with NSSI during treatment. Consequence: Enrique may decide to not continue with treatment if he feels strongly about not addressing the NSSI; the need for assessment will continue
4. Revisit informed consent with Enrique and discuss continuous monitoring of NSSI during treatment. Seek supervision to monitor clinician's reactions. Consequence: Enrique may or may not decide to continue with treatment. His decision to not focus on the NSSI is honored; however, the clinician is honest about the need to continue to monitor the behaviors closely. The clinician may or may not have a personal reaction to the NSSI.

After weighing these three options, the clinician decides to revisit informed consent with Enrique and let him know that the NSSI will need to be continuously monitored given the initial evaluation. This is an example of collaboration and compromising discussed in Chapter 4 (on intake and NSSI assessment). The clinician also decides to arrange for supervision regarding his/her own reactions to this client and the NSSI to safeguard against over- or under-reactive approach to treatment.

VI. Evaluate the Decision

After making the decision, the clinician must now evaluate how they feel about their decision, as well as the process in which the decision was made.

VII. Implement the Decision/Course of Action

The clinician now meets with Enrique to revisit informed consent and share the results of the risk assessment. The clinician simultaneously begins the process of supervision regarding their interpersonal reactions to the NSSI.

Conclusion

Ethical concerns are among the most stressful for mental health professionals. This chapter addressed ethical concerns related to NSSI. Common ethical concerns involving informed consent, confidentiality, special concerns related to working with minors, and clinician's reactions were also covered. Risk management was also explored. Finally, the need for mental health practitioners to work with ethical decision-making models was explained and one model was presented. The importance of consultation regarding ethical dilemmas is stressed.

Resources

American Association of Marriage and Family Therapists Code of Ethics: https://www.aamft.org/imis15/AAMFT/Content/Legal_Ethics/Code_of_Ethics.aspx

American Counseling Association Code of Ethics: https://www.counseling.org/resources/aca-code-of-ethics.pdf

American Psychological Association Code of Ethics: http://www.apa.org/ethics/code/principles.pdf

National Association of Social Workers Code of Ethics: https://www.socialworkers.org/pubs/code/code.asp?print=1&

References

American Association for Marriage and Family Therapy. (2015). *Code of ethics*. Washington, DC: Author.

American Counseling Association. (2014). *ACA code of ethics*. Alexandria, VA: Author.

American Psychological Association. (2002, as amended in 2010). American Psychological Association ethical principles of psychologists and code of conduct. *American Psychologist, 57*, 1060–1073.

American School Counselor Association. (2010). *Ethical standards for school counselors*. Alexandria, VA: Author.

Barnett, J. E., & Molzon, C. H. (2014). Clinical supervision of psychotherapy: Essential ethics issues for supervisors and supervisees. *Journal of Clinical Psychology: In Session, 70*, 1051–1061.

Cottone, R., & Claus, R. (2000). Ethical decision-making models: A review of the literature. *Journal of Counseling & Development, 78*(3), 275–283.

Cresswell, M., & Karimova, Z. (2010). Self-harm and medicine's moral code: A historical perspective, 1950–2000. *Ethical Human Psychology and Psychiatry, 2*(2), 158–175.

Forester-Miller, H., & Davis, T. (1996). A practitioner's guide to ethical decision making [White Paper]. Retrieved from http://www.counseling.org/docs/ethics/practitioners_guide.pdf?sfvrsn=2

Hoffman, R., & Kress, V. (2010). Adolescent nonsuicidal self-injury: Minimizing client and counselor risk and enhancing client care. *Journal of Mental Health Counseling, 32*(4), 342–347.

Kitchener, K. S. (1984). Intuition, critical evaluation and ethical principles: The foundation for ethical decisions in counseling psychology. *Counseling Psychologist, 12*(3), 43–55.

Kress, V. E., & Hoffman, R. (2008). Non-suicidal self-injury and motivational interviewing: Enhancing readiness for change. *Journal of Mental Health Counseling, 30*, 311–329.

Lloyd-Richardson, E. E., Lewis, S. P., Whitlock, J. L., Rodham, K., & Schatten, H. T. (2015). Research with adolescents who engage in non-suicidal self-injury: Ethical considerations and challenges. *Child and Adolescent Psychiatry and Mental Health, 9*(37). doi: 10.1186/s13034-015-0071-6

McHale, J., & Felton, A. (2010). Self-harm: What's the problem? A literature review of the factors affecting attitudes towards self-harm. *Journal of Psychiatric and Mental Health Nursing, 17*, 732–740.

Muehlenkamp, J. J., & Kerr, P. L. (2010). Untangling a complex web: How non-suicidal self injury and suicide attempts differ. *The Prevention Researcher, 17*, 8–10.

National Association of Social Workers (NASW). (2008). *Code of ethics of the national association of social workers*. Washington, DC: Author.

Range, L. M., Campbell, C., Kovac, S. H., Marion-Jones, M., Aldridge, H., Kogos, S., & Crump, Y. (2002). No-suicide contracts: An overview and recommendations. *Death Studies, 26*, 51–74.

Rudd, M. D., Mandrusiak, M., & Joiner, T. (2006). The case against no-suicide contracts: The commitment to treatment statement as a practice alternative. *Journal of Clinical Psychology, 62*, 243–251.

White, V. E., McCormick, L. J., & Kelly, B. L. (2003). Counseling self-injurious clients: Ethical considerations. *Counseling and Values, 47*, 220–229.

Section III
Treatment Considerations

seven
Evidence-Based Treatments

While non-suicidal self-injury (NSSI) is growing in prevalence among teens and young adults, very little is known about treating self-injury specifically. Various evidence-based treatments have been implemented and found to work in decreasing NSSI; however, changes in NSSI have been a secondary benefit to a treatment originally developed to treat another pervasive disorder, such as Borderline Personality Disorder or depression. Additionally, most researchers have conducted these studies with individuals diagnosed with Borderline Personality Disorder, potentially complicating what treatments may look like in populations without this diagnosis or symptomology. To complicate matters further, while the majority of the treatments listed in this chapter have been found to effectively reduce NSSI, there is conflicting evidence. For example, most dialectical behavioral treatments (DBT) have been found to reduce NSSI and other suicidal behaviors; however, usually not more than treatment as usual. What this means is that DBT decreases or extinguishes NSSI behaviors, yet other treatments as usual (i.e., individual therapy, medication) have also decreased NSSI at similar rates, indicating there is truly no significant difference between how you might typically work with a client and the implementation of a manualized treatment in working with clients who self-injure.

There are many possible reasons for this lack of difference: (a) most of these studies have been conducted with individuals with more severe and pervasive diagnoses such as Borderline Personality Disorder, (b) most of the treatments have been conducted with smaller sample sizes, thus the results may not hold up consistently across different populations or reveal a true difference in a study due to the small number of people who received the treatment, (c) individuals who self-injure look very different, some with and some without severe diagnoses, thus one treatment may not work for every person, (d) high dropout rates for the majority of the treatments tested (ranging from 20% to over 50% of clients drop out prior to the end of treatment), and (e) researchers have not controlled for the reasons why an individual self-injures prior to treatment (e.g., social, emotion regulation, family conflict). Therefore, it is important that you take into consideration the whole context of the person, more specifically the client's diagnosis or comorbidity of symptoms as well as the reasons or functions of his/her self-injury. Going back to Chapter 2 on the theories of NSSI, as an example, it is imperative to understand if self-injury serves as an emotion regulation tool, or whether its purpose is socially reinforced. Additionally, it would be important to understand if your client's NSSI had an addictive quality for them, as this could impact treatment decisions.

Historically, the standard treatment for NSSI has been hospitalization, but this has been found to be an expensive option that has not demonstrated reliable effectiveness (Linehan, 2000). Hospitalization may have historically been selected as a treatment method given the misunderstanding and representation of NSSI as a form of suicidal behavior. While NSSI and suicide are related, they remain distinct behaviors. Due to the purpose of NSSI to maintain life and functioning, a brief hospitalization stay along with medication has shown little to no assistance in decreasing NSSI specifically.

As mentioned, very little research has been conducted on effective treatments of NSSI, with even less being conducted on NSSI alone outside of exploring other mental health disorders and symptoms. Yet, we can take information from each of the studies conducted with various disorders and glean not only potential manualized treatments, but also forms of treatment that appear to consistently be working in both inpatient and outpatient settings. We can still learn from all of these treatments and determine the treatment that is best fit for the student or client we are working with. This chapter will provide information on manualized, evidence-based treatments, and the following chapter will provide additional suggestions, interventions, and treatment recommendations.

The most commonly supported treatments have been versions of Cognitive Behavioral Therapy (CBT) and Dialectical Behavior Therapy (DBT). Both of these therapies aim to increase problem solving skills among clients. Each of these, along with other forms of treatment with empirical evidence, is discussed in this chapter.

Cognitive Behavioral Therapy (CBT)

General CBT

Most CBT programs aim to reduce NSSI behaviors by exploring possible cognitive distortions and enhancing one's ability to cope adaptively through problem solving methods rather than avoidance. When explored alone, CBT has indeed decreased self-harm behaviors; however, rarely did CBT decrease self-harm more than treatment as usual (e.g., Donaldson et al., 2005; Taylor et al., 2011). CBT seems most effective when paired with another form of treatment. Specifically, Slee, Spinhoven, Garnefski, and Arensman (2008) paired a 12-session CBT model with treatment as usual (TAU) for 15- to 35-year-olds who self-injured. This means that the CBT provided was in addition to the TAU for these clients, which included anything from individual therapy to medication. Slee and colleagues found that clients in the CBT+TAU group decreased in both self-harm behaviors (defined as self-injury with and without intention to die as well as self-poisoning, so behaviors beyond that of just NSSI), as well as increased their ability to regulate emotions. These changes were maintained at a 9-month follow up of clients.

The central feature of Slee and colleagues' intervention was to identify and modify the cognitions or emotions that were maintaining the desire and need to self-harm. The first step in their treatment was to assess and explore the most recent self-harm event to help understand and specify the emotional, cognitive, and behavioral factors related to self-harm. Once this concrete event was explored in detail, the goal then was to modify dysfunctional cognitions, implement emotion regulation strategies such as mindfulness and acceptance of emotions, followed by implementing problem solving techniques. Figure 7.1 contains an example of the order in which Slee and colleagues implemented their CBT protocol. The figure does not contain the exact interventions they implemented but provides examples.

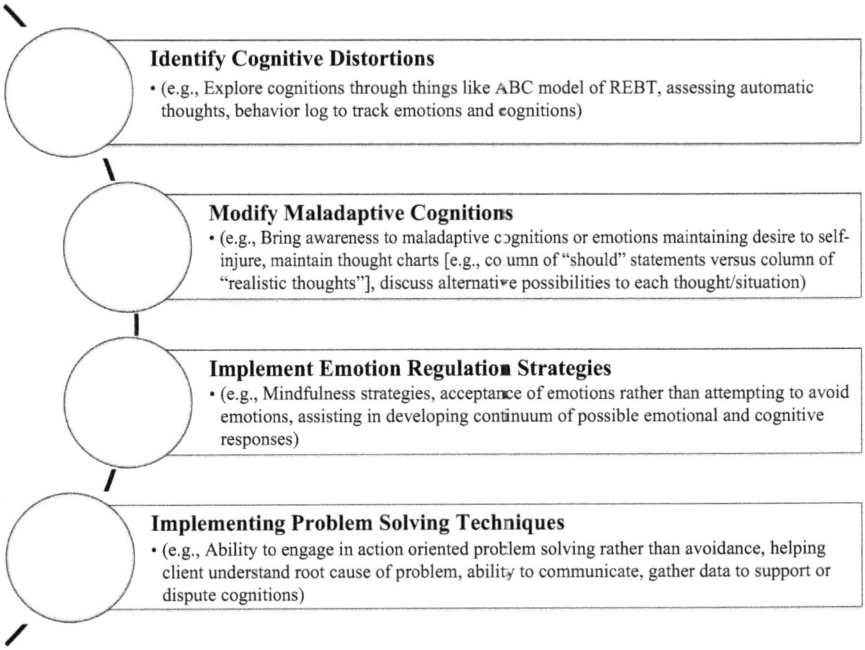

FIGURE 7.1. Example of cutting down or CBT process for working with NSSI.

What is unclear in the study conducted by Slee and colleagues was whether it was the addition of CBT specifically that enhanced emotion regulation strategies of clients, leading to a decrease in self-harm behaviors, or whether it was that the clients in this CBT treatment group received double the therapy (i.e., medication + CBT; or TAU individual sessions + CBT session) weekly for a minimum of 10 weeks. Regardless, there seem to be components of CBT that work to alter cognitions around self-harm, thus decreasing the behaviors.

Manual-Assisted CBT

Manual-assisted cognitive behavioral therapy (MACT) has been used to treat self-injurious behavior. Evans and colleagues (1999) found both lower rates of engagement in self-injury as well as an increase in time delay from desire to engagement in self-injury among clients who received MACT versus TAU. MACT is designed to be a short-term treatment program of 6 sessions that includes teaching skills to manage emotions and negative thinking while increasing problem solving skills among clients. Clients were provided each chapter of the manual for each session in which they could read the content as well as work through various worksheets. See Table 7.1 for an example of the 6 sessions of MACT discussed by Evans and colleagues (1999).

Taylor and colleagues developed (2015) another CBT manualized treatment specific to adolescents. They developed an 8- to 12-week CBT protocol for youth that incorporates aspects of acceptance of emotions and motivational interviewing strategies to increase willingness and motivation to participate in therapy. In their one study of the treatment (Taylor et al., 2011) they found

TABLE 7.1. Manual-Assisted Cognitive Theory (MACT)

1	Explore and analyze most recent episode of self-harm, including response from others and whether others know about self-harm
	Discuss/list advantages and disadvantages of self-harm
2	Provide problem solving techniques
3	Train and assist clients in self-monitoring thoughts and feelings
4	Distress coping strategies
5	Education regarding dangers of substance use and abuse
6	Revisit attempts or episodes of self-harm
	Skill deficits identified
	Coping strategies for future identified

*Table description adapted from Evans and colleagues (1999)

that self-harm behaviors (including NSSI and suicidal behaviors) decreased among the 25 youth by treatment completion, with reductions in self-harm maintained at a 3-month follow up. They did not compare this treatment to a control group or treatment as usual; therefore, the effectiveness of this treatment above therapy as usual is unknown. Their program contains four modules:

1. Getting Started, which entails determining client motivation, conducting motivational interviewing (if necessary), setting goals, providing psychoeducation about self-harm behaviors, and gaining an understanding of the function of self-harm for the client;
2. Feelings, Thoughts, and Behaviors to better understand and examine cognitive distortions, explore automatic thoughts, and engage in thought challenging;
3. Coping, which walks clients through gaining new problem solving skills; and finally,
4. On You Go, which reviews goals, identifying triggers and providing tools for post treatment.

While this treatment has limited empirical evidence demonstrating its effectiveness, Taylor and colleagues (2015) have provided a manual that can be purchased, titled *The Cutting Down Program*, at most online bookstores.

CBT and Family

Finally, another form of CBT that has shown promise, but with limited empirical evidence, is a CBT program that incorporates a combination of CBT individual sessions, CBT family sessions, and parent training. Esposito-Smythers and colleagues (2011) created what they call "Integrative CBT (I-CBT)," which includes a variety of individual sessions of CBT (such as those described in the multiple programs above), family CBT, which includes behavioral contracting, along with parent training sessions (e.g., about self-harm as well as how parents can monitor behaviors) over a 12-month time frame. They indicated that this 12-month program includes 6 months of active weekly sessions, 3 months of biweekly sessions, and 3 months of maintenance sessions, as needed. Again, similar to previous studies, their exploration of I-CBT's effectiveness included clients who engaged in NSSI along with suicidal behaviors. Regardless, they did find that youth who received I-CBT had fewer suicide attempts over 18 months compared to youth in the treatment-as-usual group. While they explored more of the suicidal behaviors in treatment, this may show some effectiveness for working with NSSI specifically, given the high correlation between the two behaviors.

Summary of CBT

Based on these studies, it can be seen that CBT does have a positive effect in reducing NSSI or deliberate self-harm behaviors. Some of the difficulties in truly understanding the impact of CBT on NSSI is that most of these studies have been conducted exploring general self-harm behaviors that include behaviors with and without suicidal ideation, and also that most participants in the studies included clients diagnosed with Borderline Personality Disorder (BPD). While self-harm is one of the criteria for BPD, there is a large proportion of individuals who engage in NSSI who do not meet criteria for BPD.

Even if CBT does not reduce self-harm behaviors more than TAU, it still can provide some helpful strategies in working with clients who engage in NSSI. More specifically, one of the goals of CBT is to examine how thoughts lead to behaviors and emotions. As mentioned in Chapter 2, there are many reasons why an individual may self-harm, including affective or social reasons. Therefore, exploring the how or why an individual self-harms is important (for more specific questions on assessment and intake, see Chapter 4).

A typical exercise in CBT is to conduct a cognitive behavioral analysis, or explore the antecedents, behaviors, and consequences, of situations for the client (see Worksheet 7.A for an example). In this case, NSSI behaviors or urges would be listed in the behavior box of the worksheet; then the client would explore the antecedent or precipitating event as well as the consequence to engaging in NSSI (see Row A of Worksheet 7.A). Taking this analysis further, asking the client to continue to explore the automatic thoughts to the specific situation as well as the resulting emotions that led to the behavior of NSSI can help the client and the clinician gain further depth in understanding the situations and reasons that might lead a client to engage in NSSI.

The next step of CBT is typically disputing or restructuring cognitions. This asks a client to help identify the facts behind their existing thought in the situation, or asks the client for the evidence to support that thought. Ask the clients questions such as "What support do you have for that belief?" or "What helps to prove that specific thought is true?" But also ask clients the alternative perspective, such as "Is there anything that does not support that belief? Anything that happened, including behavior, what someone else may have said, or anything in the context?" "Are there any other possible explanations for what happened? And is there anything that supports those other explanations?" Using a thought record can be helpful in putting concrete evidence down on paper. Helping clients in session using a thought record (see Worksheet 7.B), as well as asking them to record thoughts in between sessions as homework, can be helpful in clarifying and disputing cognitions and clearly understanding precipitating events to beliefs and behaviors.

COGNITIVE BEHAVIORAL ANALYSIS

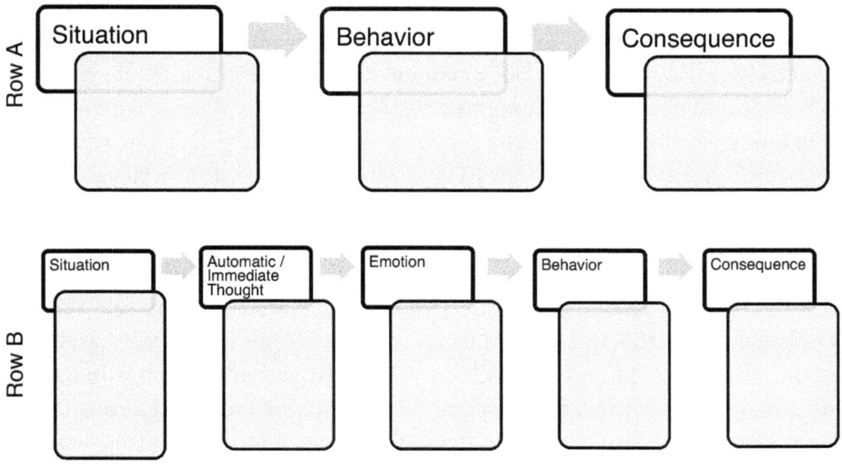

COGNITIVE BEHAVIORAL THOUGHT RECORD

Situation (e.g., place, people, events)	Immediate or Automatic Thought	Evidence to support the thought	Evidence that does not support the thought	Possible alternative thoughts

Dialectical Behavior Therapy (DBT)

Along with CBT, DBT has been one of the forms of treatment that has been found to be most effective when working with NSSI. Yet, similar to CBT, while DBT has been found to reduce NSSI and other self-harm behaviors, it really has not been found to be more efficacious than treatment as usual in most cases. Regardless, it has been found to reduce or extinguish NSSI behaviors.

DBT was developed by Marsha Linehan, who suggested that one of the reasons for self-harm behavior is due to emotion dysregulation, as well as a poor fit between one's emotion regulation strategies and environment. DBT was one of the first treatments to specifically target self-harm behaviors, as DBT was originally designed to treat adult female clients with borderline personality disorders (BPD), of which one diagnostic criteria is deliberate harm to self. While in its original form DBT was created as an intensive, adult inpatient treatment, it has since been altered and adapted for outpatient and adolescent populations. However, given the intensive nature of DBT, which includes a rigorous combination of group skills training, individual therapy, and phone skills coaching, as needed, for a full year, this has been difficult to incorporate and ensure treatment adherence in outpatient settings for adults, as well as for youth and their families. DBT requires a large time and expense commitment for most individuals. However, it has been found to be effective at reducing self-harm behaviors, and some researchers have adapted DBT to smaller time frames (e.g., Stanley et al., 2007; Tørmoen et al., 2014) without compromising effectiveness in reducing self-harm behaviors.

The overall goal of DBT is to help individuals regulate their emotions, as well as enhance their interpersonal relationships and communication patterns, instead of resorting to avoidant methods and harmful strategies to cope and communicate, such as NSSI. This goal is typically broken down into specific target behaviors, which include: (a) decrease life-threatening and NSSI behaviors, (b) decrease treatment-interfering behaviors such as noncompliance, (c) decrease behaviors that have adverse effect on quality of life (e.g., truancy, high-risk behaviors, substance use, eating disorders, depression, anxiety), and (d) increase behavioral skills. Behavioral skills are typically increased through the skills training groups where individuals learn emotion regulation strategies, distress tolerance, mindfulness, dialectics, self-validating compassion, and interpersonal effectiveness (see Figure 7.2 for example skills training protocol). Training and education of these skills occurs in group therapy, while the goal of individual therapy is to work on the unique situation and application of these skills with each individual client. Group therapy itself should not be used to discuss unique and individual aspects of NSSI behaviors, as this can lead to contagion effects, along with sharing of methods. Group therapy should specifically be used for behavioral and prosocial skill development and modification.

While the majority of DBT programs offered are 52 to 54 weeks in length, a few clinicians have shortened this time frame with success. Stanley and colleagues

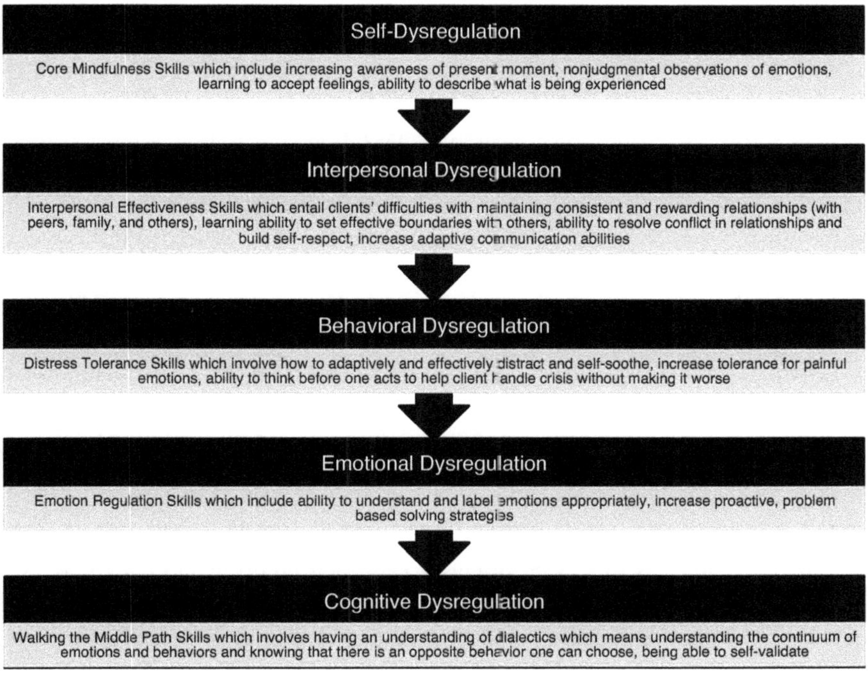

FIGURE 7.2. Typical order of DBT skills training

(2007) implemented a six-month program for 20 adult women diagnosed with BPD. They found a significant reduction in NSSI urges, behaviors, suicidal ideation, distress, depression, and hopelessness at treatment completion; however, they did not assess any long-term follow up, nor did they have a control group to determine effectiveness of this six-month DBT program over treatment as usual. However, this is similar to what van Goethem and colleagues (2012) found in their implementation of a six-month DBT protocol for adults diagnosed with BPD. In their treatment program, self-harm behaviors decreased along with an increase in active coping strategies. Interestingly, clients made more changes in the first 3 months of treatment than the latter 3 months. Neither of these authors provided details about their DBT protocols other than the time frame of implementation.

The shortest DBT treatment protocol found to date was that developed by Tørmoen and colleagues (2014). They developed a 16-week DBT outpatient protocol for adolescents diagnosed with BPD. They followed the typical DBT protocol of skills training by providing one hour of individual therapy per week, two hours of multi-family skills training group per week, family therapy as needed, and phone skills coaching as needed. Both urges to and actual engagement in self-harm (including suicidal behaviors and NSSI) decreased by the end of the 16-week program, and appeared to extinguish by the 1-year follow up among all 27 clients, thus revealing continued treatment effectiveness post treatment.

Summary of DBT

While DBT has been found to be effective, rarely has it been explored in non-BPD clients in any setting. Therefore, the impact of DBT among non-BPD clients is unclear at this point. Additionally, no study has found DBT to function better than treatment as usual when it has been explored as a comparison treatment. Thus, the length, expense, and treatment adherence difficulties of DBT are unclear in relation to the outcomes when compared to treatment as usual. What is needed at this point is to decipher which aspect(s) of DBT is the most helpful in working with clients who self-injure without BPD diagnosis (e.g., mindfulness, interpersonal skills, distress tolerance skills).

Regardless of these limitations, what sets DBT apart from other treatment protocols is the focus on mindfulness, acceptance of emotions, understanding the dialectical nature of behavior choices for any given emotion, as well as gaining tolerance for negative emotions. Typically, as noted in Figure 7.2 (the typical order of DBT), DBT starts with helping the client gain a basic understanding of mindfulness. This includes teaching clients to be in the moment and become aware of their surroundings and emotions, as well as eventually accept their emotions nonjudgmentally. The first step to this, as represented in most DBT protocols or treatment manuals, is to begin by having the client be in the moment and *observe*, *describe*, and *participate* (see Worksheet 7.C).

Observing is simply having the client notice or pay attention. This includes observing both the external events and situations using the five senses (i.e., sight, taste, sound, touch, and smell) as well as internal events in their mind and body (i.e., thoughts, physical sensations, emotions, urges, and desires). Describing is to give words to what the client notices, labeling the facts of the external and internal situation. While this may seem simple, clients may have difficulty with this step given that most of the time they run or avoid the external and internal situation through the use of NSSI. This activity may be uncomfortable and foreign to individuals who self-injure; therefore, being able to spend time on this is important. During this activity, it is important to train clients to keep a thought a thought, and an emotion an emotion rather than creating labels of oneself. Instead of saying "I am so stupid," have the client make a factual statement, such as "I had the thought 'I am so stupid.' " After a client has gathered and shared information in the observing and describing steps, they use this information to make an informed decision in the participating step. Typically clients who self-injure already participate, or make a decision to act, without observing or describing, and thus they are making a decision without truly understanding what is occurring internally and externally in the situation.

Distress tolerance is another skill learned in DBT. One of the main components of distress tolerance, other than learning to accept one's emotion, is learning to delay time from the urge to self-harm to the actual engagement in the behavior. Thus, instead of immediately avoiding the emotion or the painful distress he or she is experiencing, the goal in therapy is to learn to tolerate the emotion. The goal

DBT: MINDFULNESS OBSERVE, DESCRIBE, PARTICIPATE

Observe (External)

- ☐ What do/did you see?
- ☐ What do/did you hear?
- ☐ What do/did you taste?
- ☐ What do/did you smell?
- ☐ What do/did you feel?

Observe (Internal)

- ☐ What did you notice about your thoughts?
- ☐ What did you experience in your body?
- ☐ What did you notice about your emotions?
- ☐ What did you want to do?

Describe

Take a moment to write or discuss each of the observations listed above

Participate

Based on what you observed and described, what could you do now? What would be a good action?

If you already responded, what was the action? What did you do? Did this work? Did it get the response you wanted?

is not to eliminate the emotion altogether (which is what NSSI typically does in the immediate moment) but to moderate the emotion, to regulate it into a manageable level so that the client can cope with it appropriately. One way to do this is to not make the crisis or the emotion worse, which occurs by avoiding the emotion (or engaging in NSSI), but instead to gain tolerance for the uncomfortable emotion. Avoidance can escalate a feeling due to it never being resolved or regulated. In DBT, distress tolerance begins by immediately providing a distraction from the urge to self-injure (see Worksheet 7.D). Clients can do this through the ACCEPTS acronym, which indicates that they can use activities, contribute to others, compare the current circumstance or emotion with other people, emotions, or previous situations, select the opposite behavior to the emotion, push away the current emotions until they can be handled another time, change immediate thoughts that might be ruminating about self-harm, and experience different physical sensations. Once the client learns to distract, resulting in a time delay between the urge or desire to self-injure and the actual engagement in self-harm, they can learn to self-soothe or implement other adaptive, problem solving–focused strategies.

Another example of a DBT activity is the chain analysis technique (Kinch & Kress, 2012; Miller & Smith, 2008). The chain analysis is a way in which the clinician and the client can explore NSSI step by step, including environmental and behavioral events and antecedents and consequences of the self-harm behavior. This is similar to the CBT behavioral analysis activity, but instead of just using a worksheet, the chain can be created by using paper chain links, creating a movie or storyboard, along with other possible connecting metaphors. When completed, discussion or exploration questions can include "which link in this chain could you expand upon with more details?" as well as "which link in this chain could you have done something differently that would change the entire chain of events (i.e., avoid self-injury)?"

Problem Solving Therapy (PST)

PST is another form of treatment that has had mixed results, yet seems to have a positive impact on decreasing self-harm behaviors. Most of the studies that have explored PST have focused on the larger spectrum of self-harm behaviors, including suicidal behaviors and self-poisoning, while NSSI has not been explored in isolation. Interestingly, most of the studies conducted on PST and self-harm were completed one to three decades ago, ranging from 1978 to 1994. Hawton and colleagues (1998) conducted a summary of 20 different forms of treatment, and while they concluded that there was no consensus on which treatment was the most effective, PST showed the most promise in reducing self-harm behaviors. More recently a meta-analysis was conducted on six problem solving treatments, finding that PST has shown some promise in decreasing suicidal behaviors along with other symptoms such as depression and hopelessness better than clients in a treatment-as-usual control group (Townsend et al., 2001). This could be

DBT: DISTRESS TOLERANCE ACTIVITY

Distraction can help you tolerate the immediate crisis or emotion

Remember to **ACCEPTS**

Select something in one or more category below that may help you distract. Or come up with an idea of your own not on this list.

Activities →
- Sports or exercise
- Watch a movie
- Go to beach, park, zoo
- Hang out with other people
- Engage in a hobby

Contributing →
- Volunteer
- Write someone an email or letter
- Bake or cook for another
- Help someone else

Comparisons →
- Consider another's situation that may be worse than yours
- Consider another time in your life when you were doing worse

Opposite **E**motions →
- Consider the possible behavior to this emotion, pick the opposite behavior
- If angry, watch a comedy movie or laugh
- If sad, exercise or listen to upbeat music

Pushing Away →
- Pushing away the emotion until it can be dealt with later
- Put "on a shelf"
- Put "in a box"
- "Turn down the volume"

Thoughts →
- Change thoughts by singing song lyrics
- Multiplication
- Planning a grocery list
- Directions to your next vacation

Sensations →
- Take a cold shower
- Hold ice
- Hug someone
- Change into comfortable clothes
- Comfort or hold a pet

important, given that depression and suicidal behaviors have been highly correlated with NSSI behaviors.

Given that individuals who self-harm tend to avoid negative, painful emotions, with NSSI being one avoidance method, it is assumed that most of these individuals have difficulty finding adaptive solutions to their problems. This is the main goal of PST, to identify and resolve a problem through teaching clients general coping skills so they can deal with the current, and future, problems they encounter. Counselors achieve this by teaching clients the various steps in problem solving (see Table 7.2). The major assumption behind PST is that clients engage in self-harm behaviors due to dysfunctional coping behaviors that result from cognitive and behavioral deficiencies or breakdowns in how they analyze and engage in the problem solving process (D'Zurilla & Nezu, 2001).

In New Zealand, the Department of Psychological Medicine at the University of Auckland provides a website (http://www.problemsolvingtherapy.ac.nz/index.html) designed to provide basic information on PST, as well as supplemental tools for clinicians who have been trained in PST. They do indicate that the website should not serve as a training, but be a supplement or support to training programs. On the website, they delineate seven steps (Table 7.2) of PST, and provide worksheets as well as short video and audio clips showing what various steps may look like in therapy sessions. They describe that PST is typically provided across 4 to 8 sessions where the client and clinician collaborate to identify problems in the client's life and help to focus and develop solutions to one or more of these problems.

The steps in PST include Problem Orientation, where the goal is to understand a client's thoughts and feelings about problems, as well as their perceived ability to resolve their problems. A client can have a negative or positive problem orientation. Negative problem orientation is typically what someone who self-injures has, as they tend to use NSSI to avoid solving their problems or any of the negative emotions attached to their existing and past problems. A positive problem orientation is when a person believes they have the ability to solve their problems, and their approach to doing so is rational and effective. Typically this first step in PST includes education to better understand specific problems, and attitudes toward these problems and solving problems in general. Step 2 in PST entails Recognizing

TABLE 7.2 7. Steps in PST

Step 1	Problem Orientation
Step 2	Recognizing and Identifying Problems
Step 3	Selecting and Defining a Clear Problem
Step 4	Generating Solutions
Step 5	Decision Making
Step 6	Creating and Implementing a SMART Action Plan
Step 7	Reviewing and Evaluating

and Identifying Problems, which may include a behavioral analysis to help create a list of existing problems, and tracking problems across time and situations. This helps clients determine a few concrete problems that they may decide to work on in therapy while learning new problem solving skills.

Step 3 is to have the client select one problem and clearly define it, thus Problem Selection and Defining. As mentioned on the Problem Solving Therapy website, this step seems like it would be simple; however, many of these clients have avoided the problems for a long period of time through using behaviors such as NSSI or other avoidant coping strategies (e.g., substance use), that actually defining the problem clearly is not something that has historically occurred for most of these individuals. However, taking time to define a problem clearly can help a client come up with a more effective, adaptive problem solving solution. Step 4 is Generating Solutions where clients are asked to generate multiple possible solutions to the problem without evaluating the usefulness. Step 5 is Decision Making, where clients are asked to walk through the pros and cons of each possible solution they generated in Step 4, including assessing the possible outcomes and consequences of each. The goal by the end of this step is for the client to select a few solutions to try in resolving their problem. Step 6 is Creating and Implementing a SMART Action Plan. This entails taking the selected solutions from Step 5 and creating action plans that follow the SMART outline (i.e., Specific, Measureable, Achievable, Relevant, and Time-bound). Once SMART is determined, clients are asked to carry out the selected solutions. The final step of PST, Reviewing Progress, is to help evaluate their solutions, whether one or more of the solutions selected had its desired impact, and whether any more needs to be done in relation to this specific problem as well as to the client's overall problem solving skills.

Summary of PST

As mentioned, PST has been found to have lasting results with symptoms such as depression or hopelessness, with mixed results regarding self-harm behaviors. However, PST has shown the best promise when it has incorporated other cognitive, interpersonal, and behavioral elements to be more comprehensive (Muehlenkamp, 2006). One example of this was the CBT protocol known as MACT, discussed earlier in this chapter. Additionally Crowe and Bunclark (2000) developed PST for inpatient clients and combined it with cognitive restructuring, medication, and group and family counseling to suicidal clients. They found that post treatment about half of those who received this treatment had no additional suicidal behaviors, while clients who had not received PST maintained their existing self-harming behaviors. Thus, PST may be effective in increasing problem solving skills among those who self-injure, but may be more effective when combined with additional aspects of treatment, such as emotional, cognitive, and interpersonal.

Other Possible Efficacious Treatments

Possibly efficacious treatments are those that have empirical support, but this support is limited. In each of the cases below, typically only one study has been conducted that shows the reduction in NSSI or other self-harm behaviors, and most have shown retention of these improvements in post-therapy follow up. However, caution needs it to be noted here that each of these improvements has been found in only one study, and thus these findings may not be transferrable to all clients or treatment settings. Additionally, limited information is known on some of the treatments implemented below. Finally, not all of the studies explored NSSI specifically, with most exploring general deliberate self-harm behaviors or suicidal ideation. However, due to the limited knowledge of effective treatments, as well as the high correlation of suicidal behaviors and NSSI, these treatments are provided for mental health professionals to determine if they are deemed appropriate in working with their specific clients.

The first treatment was created by Gratz and Gunderson (2006) and incorporated components of Acceptance and Commitment Therapy (ACT) and DBT to create a 14-week group intervention that is to be combined with TAU. They indicated that emotion regulation is needed for individuals who engage in self-harm behaviors. They defined emotion regulation not as the controlling of emotions but more so the controlling of behaviors when emotion is present. More specifically, they defined emotion as (a) the awareness, understanding, and acceptance of emotion, (b) the ability to engage in goal-directed behavior and restrain impulsive behaviors, (c) the use of situationally appropriate strategies to moderate the intensity and duration of emotional responses to specific stimuli, without a focus on eliminating emotions, and (d) the willingness to experience emotions. To test whether this ACT+DBT group intervention worked, they enrolled 12 adult

TABLE 7.3. Summary of Gratz and Gunderson (2006) ACT+DBT 14-Week Group Topics

Week	Topic Covered
Week 1	Identify the function of self-harm
Weeks 2–6	Emotional awareness
	Primary vs. secondary emotions
	Clear vs. cloudy emotions
	Function of emotions
Weeks 7–8	Emotional avoidance vs. acceptance
Weeks 9–10	Behavioral change (non-avoidance emotion regulation strategies and impulse control)
Weeks 11–12	Valued directions (behavioral modification)
Weeks 13–14	Commitment to values

females diagnosed with BPD who were receiving TAU services in addition to the group, and compared them to 10 adult females diagnosed with BPD who only received TAU. The 14-week group protocol (see Table 7.3) provides education and experiential activities for clients to be able to identify and label emotional states, gain a better understanding of the function of emotions which in turn is expected to lead to emotional acceptance, gain an understanding that emotional avoidance can actually amplify the experience of painful emotions, and increase knowledge and skill in coping methods that are problem focused and not avoidant in nature. They found that individuals who received TAU and group intervention were more likely to decrease in depression, anxiety, stress, BPD symptoms, self-harm, and emotion dysregulation compared to the TAU-only group. Thus, the added education and practice provided in the ACT+DBT group seems to be effective in decreasing NSSI behaviors.

Furthering what Gratz and Gunderson (2006) did with ACT, Tapolaa, Lappalainen, and Wahlstrom (2010) added ACT and Solution Focused Brief Therapy (SFBT) to develop a 4-week intervention to prevent deliberate self-harm in adults. They felt that due to low treatment adherence to other forms of therapy (e.g., CBT, DBT) it was important to develop a time-limited, lower cost approach that also addressed the experiential avoidance typical of individuals who self-harm. Thus, similar to Gratz and Gunderson, they selected ACT to assist clients in accepting their emotions rather than avoiding emotions. They also determined that due to the lack of hopeful future-oriented thinking among individuals who self-harm, specifically individuals who are suicidal, they needed to incorporate the positive future-oriented thinking that is found in SFBT. They created a 4-session ACT+SFBT to be combined with TAU, and compared it to TAU. Their article contains the larger scripted 4-week protocol; however, the summary of these 4 weeks includes:

1. using the miracle question to determine treatment goals, introduction to treatment, mindfulness exercise;
2. mindfulness exercise revisited, SFBT scaling the problem, exceptions finding question, expectations for future questions, and a low frustration tolerance exercise;
3. mindfulness exercise revisited, and positive metaphorical story to help with identification of self solutions, emotions, and thoughts; and
4. mindfulness exercise, avoidance versus action discussion, review of overall treatment, and motivation for further change questions.

Tapolaa and colleagues found that both groups (i.e., the treatment group and the TAU group) decreased DSH behaviors; however, the treatment group (who received the ACT+SFBT along with TAU) decreased in depression and increased in their ability to regulate emotions above and beyond that of the TAU-only group. Thus, DSH did decrease, along with additional positive benefits that may lead to further maintenance of improvements; however, they did not do a longer-term follow up of their clients.

Family-Based Therapies for NSSI

Finally, various family therapies have been shown to have some promise in decreasing self-harm behaviors. More specifically, multisystemic therapy, which was originally developed for antisocial and incarcerated youth, is a family based treatment that focuses interventions on multiple systems that maintain youth problematic behavior. This could include the individual youth, the family system, as well as additional systems (e.g., school) that the youth may be a part of. Not much has been explored on multisystemic therapy in relation to self-harm; however, in one study, multisystemic therapy demonstrated superiority compared to hospitalization in decreasing DSH (Huey et al., 2004). What is unclear is the effectiveness of multisystemic therapy in comparison to TAU or other outpatient forms of treatment.

Family based attachment therapy (FBAT) has also been found to be effective (Diamond et al., 2010). The goal of this treatment is to increase family relationships through process oriented, emotion focused, and cognitive behavioral strategies aimed to enhance attachment bonds through 3 months of weekly family sessions. Diamond and colleagues found a significant decrease and a more rapid reduction in suicidal ideation among individuals in FBAT compared to those in TAU, and this change was maintained 12 weeks post treatment. While FBAT has been found to be effective in decreasing suicidal ideation, it has not been explored with NSSI specifically. Further exploration needs to be done to assess the impact of this treatment on individuals and families who self-injure specifically.

Another family based treatment found to be effective was parent training. Pineda and Dadds (2013) created a 4-session parent education program specific to suicidal ideation, entitled the Resourceful Adolescent Parent Program (RAP-P). The RAP-P was designed for parents only, and is to be used in succession to additional treatment. The goal in this education program is to teach parents about suicidal behaviors, enhance effective parenting, and decrease family conflict and stress. This 4-session training program for parents was found to decrease suicidal ideation in the adolescent, which was maintained at a 6-month follow up. What is less clear from this program is what the additional treatment was for each youth and the impact of the specific treatment.

T-SIB

One final treatment specifically developed for NSSI has been more recently developed. This is the Treatment for NSSI in Young Adults (T-SIB) by Andover, Schatten, and Morris (2014). T-SIB was developed as a short-term outpatient therapy, 9 sessions, solely for the purpose of reducing the frequency and severity of NSSI among young adults 18 to 29 years of age. T-SIB includes motivational enhancement strategies prior to treatment beginning, functional analysis of NSSI, skill training for problem solving strategies, distress tolerance, cognitive distortions, and interpersonal skills. While the results of the larger clinical trial (www.clinicaltrials.gov/ct2/show/NCT01018433) have not been published yet, T-SIB has been found to be efficacious in treating NSSI behaviors (Andover et al., 2014;

Muehlenkamp, 2006). Andover and colleagues reported that NSSI behaviors and urges decreased by 50% in the 9 weeks of the T-SIB treatment protocol, and the number of NSSI episodes continued to decrease at the 3-month follow up.

Andover and colleagues provide a general description of their T-SIB 9-session treatment protocol. While they do not state it directly, they appear to draw from various components of DBT, CBT, and PST. What they do report is that T-SIB "Integrates theoretically appropriate and empirically supported strategies to reduce NSSI behaviors and urges through functional assessment, which allows for the identification of the functions and reinforcers of an individual's NSSI, and the differential reinforcement of more adaptive coping strategies." (p. 492). The breakdown of the T-SIB treatment protocol, provided by Andover and colleagues, is provided in Table 7.4.

TABLE 7.4. Summarized T-SIB 9-Session Treatment Protocol (summarized from Andover et al., 2014)

Session	Overview	Description
1	Psychoeducation and Addressing Ambivalence	▪ Provide psychoeducation regarding NSSI, orient client to the treatment, and use motivational interviewing or enhancement strategies to decrease ambivalence toward treatment
2	Functional Assessment	▪ Conduct an initial functional analysis on a current or recent NSSI behavior or urge to NSSI (if behavior not recent). This is similar to a CBT behavioral analysis or a DBT chain analysis. ▪ Provide immediate alternative strategies if appropriate (e.g., if NSSI in room, limit time in room; if use scissors find a way to make scissors less easily accessible to delay time to behavior) ▪ Provide homework to complete functional assessment for each NSSI urge or behavior
3	Functional Assessment	▪ Continue functional assessment, but expand to find an exception situation (i.e., time when NSSI was not selected)
4	Functional Assessment and Differential Reinforcement of Alternative Behaviors	▪ Identify alternative behaviors that serve a similar function for client's NSSI, such as coping skills that have been successfully used in the past or behaviors that can be used to distract ▪ Provide homework for client to use this list of alternative strategies when experiencing mild negative affect. Andover and colleagues specifically state to not ask client to replace NSSI with these alternatives at this stage in therapy

(Continued)

TABLE 7.4. (Continued)

Session	Overview	Description
5	Differential Reinforcement of Alternative Behaviors	▪ Evaluate the impact of the alternative strategies used during the homework ▪ Revise the list of alternative behaviors if needed ▪ Provide homework for the client to use the alternative behaviors in lieu of NSSI
6	Differential Reinforcement of Alternative Behaviors	▪ Evaluate and revise list of alternative behaviors again based on client experience ▪ Conduct functional assessment on the alternative behaviors to reinforce behaviors if they were effective
7 and 8	Individual Modules	▪ These sessions are individually determined for each client depending on the purpose or preceding events of their NSSI. More specifically, these two sessions consist of one of three possible modules: ▪ Distress Tolerance ▪ Interpersonal Communication ▪ Cognitive Distortions
9	Termination	▪ Review gains made during treatment ▪ Address obstacles to maintaining gains in future, post treatment

Conclusion

While few evidence-based treatments have been found that are specifically designed for NSSI behaviors, trends exist across treatments that have been found to be effective in reducing NSSI or other self-harm behaviors. More specifically, each treatment that has been effective seems to incorporate a combination of emotion regulation awareness, problem solving skills training, and cognitive restructuring. This seems to be able to occur at almost any level, with most of the treatments focusing on the individual, while others incorporate some aspect of the client's family, whether that be in group skills training, family therapy, or parent training.

Regardless, it appears that the majority of treatments found to be efficacious incorporate aspects of functional behavioral analysis, behavioral interventions, and cognitive restructuring (Muehlenkamp, 2006). As mentioned above, functional behavioral analysis, which is used in CBT, DBT, as well as T-SIB, is used to explore at least one—but hopefully more than one—episode of NSSI, with the goal of understanding the function (e.g., affective or social), purpose (e.g., emotion regulation, grounding, isolation, attention), the precipitating and maintaining events (e.g., cognitive, emotional, relational, environmental), and skill deficits (e.g., distress tolerance, lack of coping skills, inability to communicate, difficulty maintaining relationships). If clinicians have a better understanding of the function behind NSSI, the more focused treatment can become. After understanding the function through functional behavioral analysis, mental health professionals can collaborate with clients in providing behavioral interventions. These would depend on the actual purpose or function of NSSI, but might include alternative ways to express emotions, such as in T-SIB and DBT; enhancing the ability to identify emotions, as explored in the mindfulness activity of DBT of observe and describe; enhancing communication skills or the ability to verbalize emotions or thoughts to others; and increasing effective and positive problem solving skills, as explored in PST and T-SIB. Finally, cognitive restructuring entails empathizing with the client about the need for NSSI as a survival mechanism up to this point, but to begin determining alternative ways to think about events and situations, and disputing current cognitive distortions. Therefore, the treatments listed above (along with TAU) have been found to reduce NSSI and DSH behaviors for a variety of clients in inpatient and outpatient settings.

References

Andover, M. S., Schatten, H. T., Morris, B. W., & Miller, I. W. (2014). Development of an intervention for nonsuicidal self-injury in young adults: An open pilot trial. *Cognitive and Behavioral Practice, 22*, 491–503.

Crowe, M., & Bunclark, J. (2000). Repeated self-injury and its management. *International Review of Psychiatry, 12*, 48–54.

Diamond, G. S., Wintersteen, M. B., Brown, G. K., Diamond, G. M., Gallop, R., Shelef, K., & Levy, S. (2010). Attachment based family therapy for adolescents with suicidal ideation: A randomized controlled trial. *Journal of the American Academy of Child & Adolescent Psychiatry, 41*, 1190–1196.

Donaldson, D., Spirito, A., & Esposito-Smythers, C. (2005). Treatment for adolescents following a suicide attempt: Results of a pilot trial. *Journal of the American Academy of Child & Adolescent Psychiatry, 44*(2), 113–120.

D'Zurilla, T. J., & Nezu, A. M. (2001). Problem solving therapies. In K. Dobson (Ed.), *Handbook of cognitive-behavioral therapies* (2nd edition) (pp. 211–245). New York: Guilford Press.

Esposito-Smythers, C., Spirito, A., Kahler, C. W., Hunt, J., & Monti, P. (2011). Treatment of co-occurring substance abuse and suicidality among adolescents: A randomized trial. *Journal of Consulting and Clinical Psychology, 79*, 728–739.

Evans, K., Tyrer, P., Catalan, J., Schmidt, U., Davidson, K., Dent, J., Tata, P., Thornton, S., Barber, J., & Thompson, S. (1999). Manual-assisted cognitive behavior therapy (MACT): A randomized controlled trial of a brief intervention with bibliotherapy in the treatment of recurrent deliberate self-harm. *Psychological Medicine, 29*, 19–25.

Gratz, K. L., & Gunderson, J. G. (2006). Preliminary data on acceptance-based emotion regulation group intervention for deliberate self-harm among women with borderline personality disorder. *Behavior Therapy, 37*, 25–35.

Hawton, K., Arensman, E., Townsend, E., Bremner, S., Feldman, E., Goldney, R., Gunnell, D., Hazell, P., van Heeringen, K., House, A., Owens, D., Sakinofsky, I., & Träskman-Bendz,

L. (1998). Deliberate self-harm: Systematic review of efficacy of psychosocial and pharmacological treatments in preventing repetition. *British Medical Journal, 317*, 441–447.

Huey, S. J., Henggeler, S. W., Rowland, M. D., Halliday-Boykins, C. A., Cunningham, P. B., Pickerel, S. G., & Edwards, J. (2004). Multisystemic therapy effects on attempted suicide by youths presenting psychiatric emergencies. *Journal of the American Academy of Child & Adolescent Psychiatry, 43*, 183–190.

Kinch, S., & Kress, V. E. (2012). The creative use of chain analysis techniques in counseling clients who engage in nonsuicidal self-injury. *Journal of Creativity in Mental Health, 7*, 343–354.

Linehan, M. M. (2000). Behavioral treatments of suicidal behaviors: Definitional obfuscation and treatment outcomes. In R. W. Maris, S. S. Cannetto, J. L. McIntosh, & M. M. Silverman (Eds.), *Review of suicidology* (pp. 84–111). New York, NY: Guilford Press.

Miller, A. L., & Smith, H. L. (2008). Adolescent non-suicidal self-injurious behavior: The latest epidemic to assess and treat. *Applied and Preventative Psychology, 12*, 178–188.

Muehlenkamp, J. J. (2006). Empirically supported treatments and general therapy guidelines for non-suicidal self-injury. *Journal of Mental Health Counseling, 28*, 166–185.

Pineda, J., & Dadds, M. R. (2013). Family intervention for adolescents with suicidal behavior: A randomized controlled trial and mediation analysis. *Journal of the American Academy of Child and Adolescent Psychiatry, 52*, 851–862.

Slee, N., Spinhoven, P., Garnefski, N., & Arensman, E. (2008). Emotion regulation as mediator of treatment outcome in therapy for deliberate self-harm. *Clinical Psychology and Psychotherapy, 15*, 205–216.

Stanley, B., Brodsky, B., Nelson, J. D., & Dulit, R. (2007). Brief Dialectical Behavior Therapy (DBT-B) for suicidal behavior and non-suicidal self-injury. *Archives of Suicide Research, 11*(4), 337–341.

Tapolaa, V., Lappalainen, T., & Wahlstrom, J. (2010). Brief intervention for deliberate self-harm: An exploratory study. *Suicidology Online, 1*, 95–108.

Taylor, L., Oldershaw, A., Richards, C., Davidson, K., Schmidt, U., & Simic, M. (2011). Development and pilot evaluation of a manualized cognitive-behavioural treatment package for adolescent self-harm. *Behavioural and Cognitive Psychotherapy, 39*, 619–625.

Taylor, L., Simi, M., & Schmidt, U. (2015). *Cutting down: A CBT workbook for treating young people who self-harm*. New York: Routledge.

Tørmoen, A. J., Groholt, B., Haga, E., Brager-Larsen, A., Miller, A., Walby, F., Stanley, B., & Mehlum, L. (2014). Feasibility of dialectical behavior therapy with suicidal and self-harming adolescents with multi-problems: Training, adherence, and retention. *Archives of Suicide Research, 18*, 432–444.

Townsend, E., Hawton, K., Altman, D. G., Arensman, E., Gunnell, D., Hazell, P., House, A., & Van Herringen, K. (2001). The efficacy of problem solving treatments after deliberate self-harm: Meta-analysis of randomized controlled trials with respect to depression, hopelessness and improvement in problems. *Psychological Medicine, 31*, 979–988.

van Goethem, A., Mulders, D., Muris, M., Arntz, A., & Egger, J. (2012). Reduction of self-injury and improvement of coping behavior during Dialectical Behaviour Therapy (DBT) of patients with Borderline Personality Disorder. *International Journal of Psychology and Psychological Therapy, 12*, 21–34.

eight
Specific Clinical Interventions

Results of evidence-based treatments tend to be mixed; yet much can still be learned concerning effective treatment in reducing or extinguishing NSSI behaviors. Across the various treatments that have been found to be efficacious with NSSI or other deliberate self-harming (DSH) behaviors, consistent components include emotion regulation strategies, cognitive restructuring, enhancing problem solving treatment strategies, and interpersonal communication and relations. There are times, however, that these manualized treatments may not be the best treatment for a particular client. More specifically, if the client or family will not adhere to the entire treatment, if the cost is too expensive for a client, or if the clinician does not specifically believe in the treatment. Another approach, which is not evidence-based or manualized but has been used in therapy, is to utilize specific cognitive, emotive, and problem solving–focused interventions and can be used to complement most any theoretical orientation.

It makes sense for mental health professionals to use the theoretical lens they are most comfortable with to conceptualize and work with their clients, as their buy-in and belief of a theoretical treatment is an influential factor for client change and outcome. The interventions provided in this chapter include those that match up with the emotive, cognitive, and relational components found in most of the treatments listed in Chapter 7. These include cognitive and behavioral interventions, expressive interventions, along with a brief discussion of psychopharmacology interventions. Each of the interventions listed below either has been used in therapy by the current authors, has empirically based evidence behind the intervention, or has been suggested by other researchers and clinicians as a method to work with clients who self-injure. Clinicians can explore the possibility of these interventions and techniques, but are urged to do so from the theoretical lens they use to formulate and implement treatment to their clients.

Prior to implementing any treatment, however, one important criterion is to ensure a strong, empathetic, and collaborative relationship (Muehlenkamp, 2006). Therapeutic alliance is one of the strongest predictors of client outcome. Carl Rogers discussed the core conditions of therapeutic change, most of which entailed having a strong therapeutic relationship. He highlighted the clinician being mindful and present in the session, empathizing with the client, and having unconditional positive regard as necessary for establishing a therapeutic relationship that is a strong working alliance. However, it is not enough for clinicians to exhibit empathy; Carl Rogers declared, rather, that the client has to *perceive* the empathy coming from the mental health professional.

In the case of NSSI behaviors, one way to show a client empathy in the session is to empathize with the pain the client may have experienced thus far, and to highlight how NSSI has been a viable and potentially helpful (albeit self-destructive) option up to this point. It can be helpful for the clinician to comment that NSSI may have been a coping tool for the client to help him or her survive intense or intolerable emotions, helped communicate pain and distress to others, or helped establish or isolate necessary relationships. Providing this understanding and empathy does not mean that you have to agree with the self-injurious behavior, but acknowledges that you can empathize with the necessity of it up to this point. One factor that keeps individuals who self-injure from seeking formal treatment services is the fear of judgment and prejudice by others (Long et al., 2015). This judgment has been experienced by individuals who self-injure from mental health professionals, medical professionals, teachers, and loved ones (Long et al., 2015; Wester & McKibben, 2016). Thus, making statements that empathize and show understanding about the need and purpose of the client's NSSI behaviors, along with suspending judgment, may increase the likelihood that the client will talk about NSSI and stay in treatment, as well as enhance the therapeutic relationship.

Another aspect of establishing a strong therapeutic relationship is to ensure the client has the autonomy to choose the course of action therapy may take; thus, if the client determines that he does not want to discuss or target NSSI as a goal in counseling, then the clinician needs to respect the client's autonomy regarding this decision (Hoffman & Kress, 2010; Kress & Hoffman, 2008). Another aspect that keeps clients from seeking formal treatment is the fear that they will be forced to cease NSSI behaviors (Long et al., 2015). More information is provided about the ethical responsibility around NSSI and autonomy in Chapter 6.

Client Desire to Change

Not all clients enter therapy wanting to be there or wanting to change NSSI behaviors. Consider the transtheoretical model (TTM; Prochaska & Norcross, 2001). The TTM suggests that mental health professionals' interactions and interventions used with clients need to match the stage of change a client is currently in, and thus not move too slow or too fast for a client. For example, in the case of NSSI, if the client does not believe NSSI is a problem in his life, then asking him to focus on it in therapy and change the behavior may make him feel as if you do not hear or understand him. He may become more defensive, which may result in increases in NSSI behaviors to gain more control, deciding to not share information about NSSI or any other behaviors that you may judge him on or force him to cease, or could even result in early termination from therapy. None of these are preferred outcomes in the therapy room. Behavioral interventions that have been applied prior to the client seeing a need or being ready to change (i.e., precontemplation stage in the TTM) have been deemed as unhelpful and perceived by clients as punitive (Long et al., 2015).

Understanding the Transtheoretical Model and Stages of Change

Prochaska and Norcross discussed each stage, as well as tasks needed to assist clients in moving to the next stage (see Figure 8.1). Therefore, it is important for mental health professionals to assess which stage the client may be in, specifically related to NSSI as well as generally regarding all other symptoms and presenting concerns. When clients are referred or forced to come in by others (e.g., court system, family members, teachers), they may not be aware they have a problem or may not deem NSSI or other symptoms to be a concern. An individual would fall into this stage of change if they indicate they have no desire to change the behavior (in this case NSSI, but this could relate to any other presenting concerns, as well). The Contemplation stage is one in which the individual sees that a problem exists. In this case, the client would acknowledge that NSSI was not a healthy behavior or that it was a behavior that needed to be changed, and they are seriously considering taking action to change the behavior. However, even though the client has this awareness and is considering action, no action has yet been taken. In the Preparation stage, individuals typically are ready to take action within the next few weeks, or may report small behavioral changes. In the case of NSSI, this may be an individual who indicates they are ready to try a different coping strategy, or may report that they successfully delayed NSSI the last time they experienced an urge.

The Action stage is when individuals are engaging in behaviors designed to modify or alter their behavior, emotions, experiences, or environment in order to address and overcome their presenting concerns, in this case to address or alter use of NSSI. While the actual NSSI might not extinguish in this stage, the client would be engaging in successful strategies to decrease the behavior and gain control over their urges. Prochaska and Norcross define this stage by saying that clients have successfully altered, or are continually working hard on altering, their behavior for a period of 1 day to 6 months. The Maintenance stage

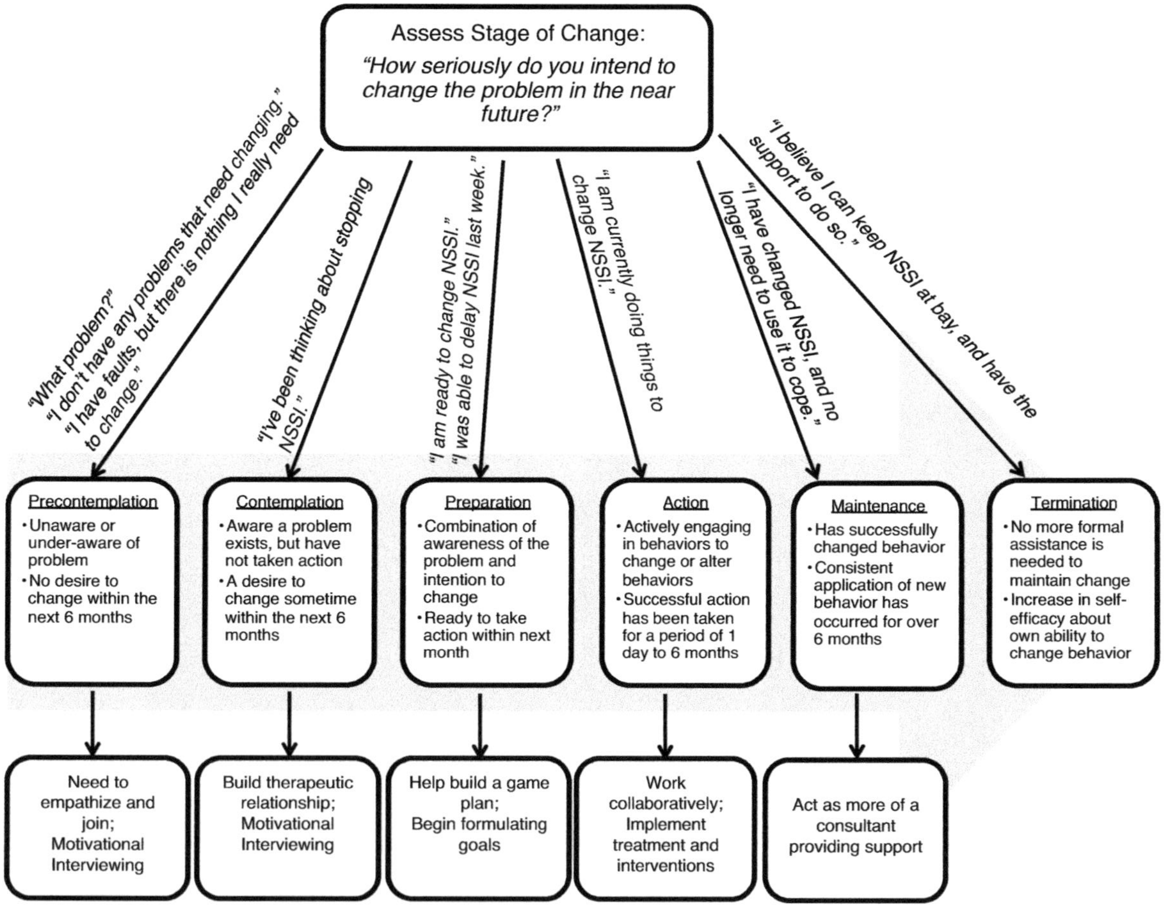

FIGURE 8.1. Transtheoretical Model Stages and assessment process

is when successful action has taken place and the client consistently engages in more adaptive, problem focused coping behaviors rather than NSSI. This stage is when a client has successfully implemented a new behavioral strategy for more than 6 months. Finally, the Termination stage is when clients have completed the change process and no longer have a need for formal assistance in changing or alleviating their NSSI behaviors. This is a stage where clients have complete self-efficacy and confidence in their ability to maintain this new behavioral change and avoid engagement in NSSI.

Using Motivational Interviewing (MI) to Help Clients Move through Stages of Change

In order to help a client move from Precontemplation and Contemplation, the clinician must first join collaboratively with the client by providing empathy and unconditional regard (as stated above). Additionally, motivational enhancement activities, such as Motivational Interviewing, have been found to be helpful in rousing a client to become aware of the existing problem and having a desire to do something to change. The idea behind Motivational Interviewing (MI) is that the client and the clinician join collaboratively together in treatment. Through conversation, the clinician helps to evoke an internal desire for the client to be motivated to change, and the clinician communicates that they value the client's autonomy to make the decision, or not, to change. These three foundational elements of MI are carried out through four main principles which include: (a) expressing empathy, which is used to build a strong relationship with the client; (b) developing discrepancy, which is when the clinician uncovers and magnifies awareness of the inconsistency between the client's current behavior and her desired values or goals; (c) rolling with resistance, in which the clinician reframes resistance into the stages of change, thus understanding where the client is in his motivation to alter his behaviors; and (d) supporting self-efficacy, which suggests that clinicians have confidence in their client's ability to understand when she is ready to change and when she can successfully do so, thus providing the client with the autonomy to make treatment decisions about her own care.

MI occurs in two phases (Miller & Rollnick, 2002): (1) building motivation and (2) commitment to change. Given that clients who self-injure may come with ambivalence, or no desire, to change or stop NSSI behaviors, the goal of the first phase is to explore this ambivalence with the client and clarify the reasons for wanting to maintain self-injuring versus changing or ceasing the behavior. During this phase, the clinician typically engages in **o**pen-ended questions, provides **a**ffirmation, **r**eflects content and feelings, and **s**ummarizes what he is hearing from the client. This helps the client feel understood and heard. The acronym typically used for this in MI is *OARS*. An example of how to use this is provided in the vignette in Box 8.1.

Box 8.1 The Case of Sally

Sally, a 16-year-old female, was asked to come to see you by her mother, who indicated that Sally has exhibited behavioral problems at home, her grades are slipping, and she has engaged in cutting for the past year. In coming into your office, Sally plops down on a chair, folds her arms, and glares at you.

Therapist:	*"Sally, what brings you in here today?"*	Open-ended question
Sally:	*(grumpily) "I don't want to be here, my mom said I had to come and she told me I can't hang out with my friends unless I came here."*	
Therapist:	*"So this is frustrating, to have to come here when you really don't want to. I wonder how we can make this time together helpful for you, so it doesn't feel like a waste of time?"*	Reflecting Open-ended question
Sally:	*"I don't know."*	
Therapist:	*"I know your mom had indicated a few things she was hoping you would talk about in here, including your grades at school, disregarding the rules at home, as well as cutting on your arms and legs. I wonder if we can talk about those and see what you think."*	Asking Permission Assessing Motivation
Sally:	*"I guess. I don't really see any of those as a problem, I see my mom as a problem."*	
Therapist:	*"I hear, and can see, the anger you have with your mom. I would like to hear your experience with grades, home rules, and cutting, and then we can focus on your annoyance at your mom. First, let's focus on the rules at home. I heard what your mom had said, but I am curious about your thoughts. What is occurring at home?"*	Reflecting Open-ended question
Sally:	*"The rules are stupid. Really, I am the only person who has to be home by 11:00 p.m. Do you know how that makes me look to my friends? I should be able to come home when I want to. My mom just doesn't get it, she is so strict." (rolling her eyes) "And I have to do so many chores! She doesn't do anything! I have to clean up my room, do the dishes, clean the laundry. That doesn't leave me any time for what I want to do."*	

Therapist:	*"So it feels too overwhelming, too busy. You don't feel heard or understood at home right now."*	Summarizing Reflecting
	More time passes in the therapy session . . .	
Therapist:	*"Let's talk about cutting. You have been cutting now for almost a year. What and when do you use cutting for?"*	Open-ended question
Sally:	*"I don't know. It makes me feel better."*	
Therapist:	*"I'm curious, when you cut, what doesn't feel good at the time? What is going on that you need to cut to feel better?"*	Open-ended questions
Sally:	*"I just get so pissed off and I don't feel like I have a say in anything. 'Do this . . . Do that . . .' is all I hear. I get so mad that I see red, and all I want to do is hit something . . . or someone. So I cut, and it makes me feel better. I don't see red anymore, I am not so pissed."*	
Therapist:	*"Being mad, particularly at mom it sounds like, makes you feel out of control. Cutting seems to be the solution, one thing that helps you feel in control. It sounds like cutting has worked when nothing else has."*	Summarizing Affirming
Sally:	*"Yeah . . . ."*	

In this case example, it can be seen how *OARS* may be used to empathize with a client and roll with her resistance. As presented, Sally is in the Precontemplation stage, and thus she doesn't see NSSI or any of her behaviors as a concern or a problem. She has externalized the problem to be her mom, not her decisions that have resulted in declining grades, unruly behavior at home, or her cutting. If the clinician would jump into goal setting at this point and indicate the goals to be what mom has reported, Sally would resist joining therapeutically with the clinician and more than likely would drop out of therapy or would not move into the Contemplation stage, or any other stage of change, for that matter. But using open-ended questions, reflections, affirmations, and summarization helps Sally feel heard by the clinician, thus rolling with her resistance to therapy and possibly removing some of the barriers she has erected.

The next step in MI would be to encourage momentum by pointing out the discrepancy between Sally's values and her own stated goals and her current behavior. This could be done within the first session, but more than likely would occur later on, although still within Phase 1 of MI, given that Sally was referred to treatment in the Precontemplation stage. The goal in pointing out discrepancy is to help the client see inconsistencies in what they are saying they want versus what they are doing. This can be done through pointing out contradictions the moment they occur in the counseling room, and can be highlighted by exploring pros and cons of behavior (see Worksheet 8.A Weighing Decisions). As can be seen in the case of Sally in Box 8.2, the clinician never did indicate that Sally *had* to work on her cutting or other problematic behaviors, as this would have increased resistance to therapy since Sally was not aware that these behaviors were problematic. Instead, the clinician rolls with Sally's resistance and is beginning to point out the discrepancies between what Sally wants (i.e., her mom to get off her back) and what she is currently doing (i.e., everything to have her mom 'on her back'). The goal here is to shift Sally from Precontemplation to Contemplation, and thus have her gain awareness that some of these behaviors are actually causing problems in her current life. This typically will not occur in one session, but can increase buy-in to therapy and willingness for the client to change or alter some behavior. While

Box 8.2 The Case of Sally, continued

Some time has passed in therapy with Sally. Sally indicated she would be willing to talk about grades, behaviors at home, and cutting; but indicated she did not feel those were the goals she needed to work on. Instead, she reported she wanted to get her mom "off her back." The therapist clarified that while neither she nor Sally could control mom's behavior, they could focus on the behaviors that bring mom "on her back." Sally agreed to this.

Therapist:	*"So you mention you want your mom 'off your back.' When does she tend to be 'on your back'?"*	Open-ended question
Sally:	*"All the time . . . ugh. Really when I don't do what she asked me to do around the house, like when the dishes are left in the sink. Or the laundry piles up. And really . . . she really flips out when she sees a new cut. I try to hide them, but sometimes my sleeve accidentally comes up too far."*	
Therapist:	*"So she's 'on your back' when you don't do your chores and when she sees new cuts."*	Summarizing
Sally:	*"Yep."*	
Therapist:	*"I'm curious if you would be willing to complete this worksheet with me . . ." (see Worksheet 8.A, "Weighing Decisions." Therapists can alter the behaviors listed on the form to match any behaviors needed for a client.)*	Asking Permission Pointing out Discrepancies

WEIGHING DECISIONS OF MY BEHAVIORS

<table>
<tr><td colspan="2">How might your life change if you choose to either continue or quit ________ behavior?</td></tr>
<tr><td colspan="2">If I continue or quit this behavior, my relationships with my family would . . .</td></tr>
<tr><td>If I continue this behavior:</td><td>If I quit this behavior:</td></tr>
<tr><td></td><td></td></tr>
<tr><td></td><td></td></tr>
<tr><td></td><td></td></tr>
<tr><td colspan="2">If I continue or quit this behavior, my relationships with my friends would . . .</td></tr>
<tr><td>If I continue this behavior:</td><td>If I quit this behavior:</td></tr>
<tr><td></td><td></td></tr>
<tr><td></td><td></td></tr>
<tr><td></td><td></td></tr>
<tr><td colspan="2">If I continue or quit this behavior, my relationship with myself would . . .</td></tr>
<tr><td>If I continue this behavior:</td><td>If I quit this behavior:</td></tr>
<tr><td></td><td></td></tr>
<tr><td></td><td></td></tr>
<tr><td></td><td></td></tr>
<tr><td colspan="2">If I continue or quit this behavior, my school or professional life would . . .</td></tr>
<tr><td>If I continue this behavior:</td><td>If I quit this behavior:</td></tr>
<tr><td></td><td></td></tr>
<tr><td></td><td></td></tr>
<tr><td></td><td></td></tr>
</table>

this may take many sessions, the ultimate goal is to slowly help the client gain intrinsic motivation to alter behavior and a commitment to change, thus moving into Phase 2 of MI, which entails the Preparation and Action stage of the TTM discussed above. Once in these stages, you can begin implementing manualized treatments (as discussed in Chapter 7) or interventions within your treatment plan (as discussed in this chapter).

It is important to note that MI has not yet been empirically tested to determine its effectiveness in working with clients who self-injure; however, it has been found to have success with many other indirect forms of self-harming behaviors such as substance abuse and eating disorders. Motivational enhancement strategies have also been used as part of the Manualized Cognitive Behavioral Therapy (MACT) evidenced-based practice for NSSI, discussed in Chapter 7. Therefore, it is believed that MI would be an effective method at helping clients, in the Precontemplation or Contemplation stages, who engage in NSSI behaviors to gain buy-in to therapeutic treatment. Additionally, MI may be useful in settings such as college campuses or schools where mental health professionals may seek to do outreach or active client/student recruitment for treatment, rather than waiting to provide reactive treatment for clients who are in crisis or who are referred to their office.

Various Interventions

As mentioned, very little is known regarding effective treatments for NSSI, specifically due to small sample sizes, few treatments exploring self-injury without the intention to die in isolation from other self-harm and suicidal behaviors, and an over-reliance on populations diagnosed with Borderline Personality Disorder (which is not the largest population of individuals who self-injure). What is known is that most treatments do decrease NSSI behaviors, but are not more effective than treatment as usual. This may be due to the fact that a myriad of presenting concerns exist among individuals who present with NSSI in treatment. These include, but are not limited to, depression, anxiety, antisocial behaviors, substance abuse, eating disorders, grief and loss, and perfectionistic behaviors. The treatments discussed below originated from a variety of sources, but have been suggested, tested, or used with individuals who self-injure. The goal of the interventions and techniques provided below are to provide creative ways for mental health professionals to assess and help clients gain awareness or movement with their emotions, cognitions, and behaviors related to NSSI. These techniques and interventions need to be incorporated within the clinician's theoretical and conceptual framework. They are sectioned into behavioral and cognitive interventions, expressive interventions, and psychopharmacological treatment. While the interventions are categorized this way, it is important to note that each intervention may have more than one effect (e.g., the mask activity discussed in the expressive section below may access and bring awareness to cognitions, emotions, and environmental factors for a client).

Behavioral and Cognitive Interventions

Given that individuals who self-injure tend to have low distress tolerance as well as rarely utilize or effectively engage in problem focused coping strategies successfully, behavioral interventions can serve two purposes. One is to delay time between the urge or desire to self-injure and the actual engagement in NSSI. This delay in behavior can provide small successes for individuals who originally believed they had no control over the behavior, as well as can provide moments of time where more adaptive strategies can be incorporated to alleviate intense emotions or situations.

Removing Methods of Self-Injury or Engaging in Physical Exercise

Other coping strategies to resist urges to self-injure or to regulate emotions have typically been tried by individuals who self-injure (Klonsky & Glenn, 2008; Wester & McKibben, 2016). These include going for walks, watching television, listening to music, and taking a shower. In a study conducted by the first author and a colleague, Bradley McKibben (2016), the most helpful coping strategies 89 young adults indicated they used to try to resist NSSI urges included "removing the instruments typically used to self-harm from the home" and "doing sports or exercise." Therefore, one of the ways to help clients resist or delay urges to self-injure is to ask them to make access to their means of self-harm more difficult. This may include removing the item(s) completely from the home, throwing them away, bringing the instruments in to the mental health professional's office to have the clinician store them or throw them away with the client, or if even that feels too drastic for the client, then to help the client determine how to put barriers up between themselves and the instrument used to self-harm. For example, have the client wrap tape around a blade so that getting to the blade to use it to cut may be more difficult, or to put an instrument in a locked box with the key in a different location in the house. This can create a delay from the desire to self-injure and the actual ability to engage in the behavior since it would require gaining access to the instrument, or purchasing an entirely new instrument. By the time the instrument is purchased, or usable, the need to self-injure may have passed or become less intense, allowing the client to gain a sense of control over the next choices she makes.

Exercise has been reported as helpful, as well. In a case study of "Ms. A," a 26-year-old female with a 13-year history of NSSI, the clinicians incorporated an exercise intervention where Ms. A was provided with a 60-minute workout video (Wallenstein & Nock, 2007). She was asked to exercise three times per week and also in response to NSSI urges. During a 5-week time frame, the client went from self-injuring 2.25 times per week to .37 times per week. Once the client discontinued the exercise she increased her NSSI to 2.33 times per week. However, once exercise was reintroduced, NSSI was extinguished for the remainder of the study. It was believed that the engagement in exercise helped to increase the client's mood, which in turn reduced her urge to self-injure. Therefore, asking clients to incorporate physical activity or exercise into their weekly routine, or at minimum when they may be experiencing urges to self-injure, may be helpful in decreasing the desire to engage in NSSI behaviors to regulate emotions.

Alternatives to Self-Injury or Distraction Methods

In order to gain tolerance to distress, and delay engagement in NSSI, alternatives to self-injury have been suggested by clinicians, researchers, and individuals who self-harm as being effective in minimizing and decreasing NSSI (Wester & Trepal, 2005). Providing alternatives is not a solution to NSSI but an intervention that can assist in delaying time between urges and actual engagement in NSSI so the client can gain more control over his behavior or have time to be put into place more effective, adaptive coping strategies. In order to determine the appropriate alternative to suggest, an initial assessment of NSSI needs to occur, including assessing for the reasons or functions of self-injury and the client's stopping point in their episodes of NSSI. It is important to have an understanding of the functions and stopping point of NSSI to know how to match up possible alternative behaviors. Realistically, most clients do not always come in fully aware of the functions and stopping points of their NSSI behaviors. When asked, "What is the reason you cut?" most clients respond, "I don't know." Therefore, to gain this information a behavioral or functional assessment may need to be conducted. Discussion of assessment of NSSI is provided in Chapter 4.

What is important is the matching of the alternative behavior to the function or the stopping point. For example, if the function of self-injury is to alleviate intense emotion, specifically anger and aggression, then the alternative method needs to be one that will help in alleviating anger and aggression. While this may seem simple, it may not necessarily be so for a client. For example, anger and aggression can be alleviated in a variety of ways; however, if the person feels angry and tends to take a razor blade and slash angry lines into her arm, then the alternative may need to mimic this experience of anger and slashing movements. This experience may be something such as taking a paper and slashing it or ripping it up with aggression, thus seeing or hearing the same slashing sensation in one's hands, while also seeing jagged edges in the paper. If a client tends to self-harm when he is angry, but what truly calms him down is the sensation of burning on his skin, then he may need to match up the sensation of burning (rather than the function of anger) with putting ice on his skin to gain the same sensation and alleviate anger without tissue damage; therefore, matching combination of function (e.g., social, affective: restlessness, anger) and stopping points (e.g., seeing blood, experiencing a sensation). While not an exhaustive list, some possible alternatives matched to the function of NSSI are provided in Table 8.1.

TABLE 8.1. Examples of Alternatives to NSSI

Alternatives to Functions for NSSI

Aggression or Anger	Restlessness or Anxiety	Regulation of Emotion or Sad/Depressed
▪ **Create and destroy with Play-Doh or modeling clay** ▪ **Throw things (e.g., ice cubes at brick wall, eggs in shower)** ▪ **Smash fruit with sledgehammer** ▪ **Punch pillows or punching bag** ▪ **Rip apart things (e.g., newspaper, stuffed animal, old cassette tape)** ▪ **Throw darts at a picture** ▪ **Finger paint aggressively on large sheets of paper on wall**	▪ Run or walk, exercise ▪ Get fingers or hands busy (e.g., cook, type on computer, mold clay) ▪ Do karate, rollerblade, or other activities ▪ Scream or yell ▪ Clean or organize ▪ Text on phone or electronic device ▪ Play video game ▪ Draw or journal ▪ Sit and bounce on an exercise ball ▪ Do collage work (e.g., tearing up or cutting out pictures, picking colors, pasting) ▪ Make a positive list of things you like about self	▪ Deep breathing exercises ▪ Mindfulness to focus and experience emotion nonjudgmentally ▪ Repetitive counting or writing of sentences or words ▪ Creating locked box (described below) to gain control ▪ Relaxation techniques ▪ Yoga ▪ Free associate through talking or journaling ▪ Visualize one's feelings, then visualize calming those feelings

(*Continued*)

TABLE 8.1. (Continued)

Alternatives for Stopping Points for NSSI

Visual	Sensations	Feeling Grounded
▪ **Draw red lines with paint or markers on skin** ▪ **Paint areas where usually expect to see visuals** ▪ **Slowly put non-toxic paint in the bathtub or water to see the spread of red (simulation for blood)** ▪ **Draw slash lines in paper** ▪ **Look at and focus on other pictures (e.g., artwork or photos), ensuring the pictures are not triggering** ▪ **Tattoo skin with washable ink with image or picture of the NSSI visual**	▪ Take a cold or hot shower, but careful not to scald skin ▪ Hold ice cubes on specific area of skin ▪ Rub Vicks or Bengay ointment on skin ▪ Snap rubber band on wrist or other area of body ▪ Brush skin with toothbrush ▪ Wrap clay or Play-Doh around part of skin ▪ Pull on or rub woolly cloth on skin ▪ Bite into a hot pepper ▪ Slap floor or table hard	▪ Walk barefoot and be mindful of sensations on feet ▪ Put lotion on and rub into skin slowly and in a repeated motion ▪ Sing along with a song and pay attention to each word ▪ Breathe deeply and use relaxation techniques ▪ Focus on the surroundings in the room, paying attention to how near or far they are from self ▪ Pay attention to all five senses, taking in what things smell like, look like, sound like, feel like, and taste like (when appropriate)

It needs to be stressed that alternatives to NSSI are *not* solutions; they are simply a stop-gap that may decrease the amount of tissue damage caused by NSSI while allowing time between urges and actual engagement in self-injury. Additionally, alternatives should not be prescribed or suggested without oversight, as clients who may not have a desire to stop self-injuring can find ways to turn these alternatives into new methods to self-harm (e.g., adding salt to the ice cube or putting salt on the skin before applying the ice cube, which causes a burn mark). Therefore, before providing alternatives to NSSI it is important to assess a client's motivation to stop self-injury (as suggested above in the TTM and MI section).

While typically it has been found to be most helpful to connect alternatives or distraction methods to the functions of self-injury or the reasons an individual stops self-harming in the moment, other distraction methods have been suggested or used simply for the purpose of delaying NSSI from occurring in the moment, with hopes that this delay will serve at least one of many purposes. The purpose of this delay includes: (1) decreasing the severity of the self-harm behavior due to a decrease in intensity of emotion or urge to self-injure; (2) not engaging in NSSI at all due to delaying the desire to self-harm long enough that the urge has dissipated; or (3) finding a new adaptive method to cope, due to allowing other strategies to be used during the distraction period. Therefore, the goal of general distraction methods is to delay actual engagement in self-injury so that urges to self-harm decrease or new coping methods are incorporated that help the individual feel grounded, regulate emotions, or communicate to others without hurting oneself physically.

These distraction methods include, but are not limited to:

- *Physical activity*. Engaging in various forms of physical activity in which the individual engages in movement of some kind. This can include exercising, ripping up papers, throwing pillows or a ball at a wall, sports, or dancing. The movement can lead to distraction but also entails releasing energy that feels pent up that can be connected to anxiety, ruminating thoughts, or intense emotions.
- *Communicating*. This typically includes talking out one's feelings, frustrations, or concerns with another person who is trusted. Keep in mind, talking it out with a peer who self-injures may or may not be the best approach, as this has at times been found to increase NSSI behaviors. However, it is important to consider someone who will not judge the person or the behavior but ultimately will help by listening and possibly offering suggestions. Communicating may also include writing letters or creating drawings to show others how one feels, or the cause of the emotion. Some clients prefer to communicate with others online. Of course the client can determine how willing he is to actually give this to the other individual, but just getting the thoughts and feelings out may be helpful and may feel less overwhelming. Most commonly we think communication is sharing or

dialoguing with others, which is one method of communication; however, communicating also can be to oneself. Typically the individual may not be very clear, or may feel like their feelings or thoughts are muddy, or may be moving too fast, and, therefore, takes a moment to write a list or letter to the self, to journal, or to draw a picture that they can later interpret. The goal of doing this may be to just purge and get out the emotion and thoughts so that they can begin to see or decipher what they have written down. Consider free association in this process.

- *Being creative.* This may include anything from expressive arts, such as drawing and painting; writing, in terms of journaling, free association; playing instruments or listening to music; and more. The goal here is occupying one's time and mind, which results in focusing on something other than the desire to self-harm. Therefore, just momentarily it may put self-injuring out of their mind while they focus intently on something else.

There are many more methods of distraction, including things that may comfort oneself (e.g., bath, shower, warm blankets), getting out of the area where one wants to self-injure (e.g., getting away from methods of self-harm, the stimulus that led to desire to self-harm), or working or being productive (e.g., taking care of someone else, cleaning). The Royal College of Psychiatrists in London has provided an entire printable document for distraction methods for NSSI. On this document, they provide permission for others to print and photocopy in order to use in practice or hand to clients. http://www.rcpsych.ac.uk/pdf/self-harm%20distractions%20and%20alternatives%20final.pdf.

One of the goals of alternatives and distraction methods is to allow enough time that the individual might incorporate a new adaptive coping strategy that works. Adaptive, problem focused coping seems to be key in decreasing or extinguishing NSSI behaviors. In a case study of eight clients, Wester, Downs, and Trepal (2016) found that problem focused coping was the only thing that differentiated clients in outpatient treatment who decreased or extinguished their NSSI behaviors versus increased self-harm. More specifically, those who decreased or stopped self-injuring by the time they terminated therapy had increased the degree to which they used problem focused coping strategies and decreased avoidant coping strategies, while the clients that increased their frequency or number of methods used to self-harm by termination of counseling had maintained their usage of avoidant coping strategies, with very little use of problem focused coping. So what does this mean? This means a few things: first, while distraction methods can be helpful in the short-term, ultimately it relies on avoidant coping methods, and therefore it should be a short term intervention that is used to simply delay the time where someone has the urge to self-injure and the actual engagement to self-injure. Secondly, during this delay, it is imperative that more adaptive problem focused coping strategies are incorporated.

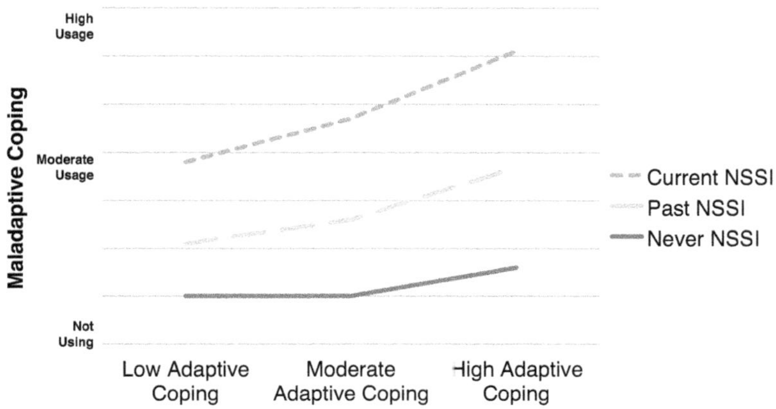

Image recreated from Trepal et al., 2016

FIGURE 8.2. Adaptive and Maladaptive Coping Usage by NSSI Engagement

While this sounds simple, it may not be. As can be seen in Figure 8.2, individuals who reported currently engaging in NSSI behaviors reported using *both* high levels of maladaptive and adaptive coping strategies. This means that these clients tended to not only self-injure, but potentially use substances, engage in denial, or avoid the problems altogether, while *also* journaling, actively attempting to problem solve, talking to others, and asking others for help. The first author has had clients sit across from her and say, "When I get angry, or feel like I want to cut, but instead I go for walks, journal, or listen to music." Originally these statements were acceptable and felt as if this was progress being made by the client, yet the cutting never stopped, nor did it decrease. Eventually it was determined that while this client was attempting to engage in what might be considered adaptive, problem focused coping, these strategies were either not the best coping strategies for this person, or she did not know how to engage in the coping method effectively. Since self-injury is typically selected due to lack of other effective, adaptive coping methods, it is important to slow down when working with a client who self-injures and consider walking them through, step by step, the process of coping using other methods. For example, talking with a client about using walking or exercising to help cope or alleviate distress, you might say something such as: "When anxious or angry, you might consider going for a walk." Once the client agrees that this is possible or they are willing to engage in this particular coping method, help them proceed through what they should be doing during this walk. Such as, "When you are walking consider paying attention to your surroundings, being mindful of what you see, smell, and hear. Take deep breaths, and imagine some of the emotion you are feeling being released out into the air." Consider taking a walk during the therapy session if this is feasible. This is just an example, but by trying out various coping methods during the therapy session you can see how individuals are engaging in the various coping behaviors, therefore better understanding what they are doing effectively versus what they need some coaching on to implement better. Yet they may not truly understand the most effective ways to implement successfully.

Guided Imagery

Guided imagery has been used in a variety of ways when working with clients who NSSI. More specifically, many decades ago in one of the first reports of using relaxation with patients who self-injured, Malon and Berardi (1987) discussed nine patient case studies in which their use of hypnotic relaxation strategies worked to help clients feel relaxed and in control. Guided imagery is an intervention in which the person engages in a process of mental visualization that typically can result in a sense of relaxation. It has been suggested that while relaxation is one of the primary goals of guided imagery, it can also simultaneously distract from the desire to self-injure (Kress, Adamson, DeMarco, Paylo, & Zoldan, 2013).

Guided imagery can be led many different ways. One of the most frequently used methods of guided imagery is for individuals to imagine being in a relaxing, safe place. Once they can imagine themselves in this location, they are usually instructed to experience or imagine what they see, hear, feel, or smell. This imagined place might be the beach or ocean, a mountain scene, a room in one's house, or a specific chair. It is helpful to allow a client to select the location of the guided imagery. While this is one of the more common forms of guided imagery used to help clients relax, other forms of guided imagery can include future-oriented images or thinking, as well as developing alternative solutions. For example, one form of guided imagery might include asking a client to consider an alternative solution to a previous event, thus not selecting self-injury to regulate their emotions or solve their problem, but instead imagining they have selected something else. What might that solution have been, what might it have looked like, what would the result be with that alternative? This can include just visualizing the self and the situation but may include how other consequences may have been altered or how others may have interacted or reacted with the client. Guided imagery can also include future orientation, for example, asking the client to think ahead a few years or even ten years; what might they have accomplished, what might they be doing, is self-injury a part of this visualization or not, and if not, what happened for them to stop harming themselves. This may help clients get at possible solutions to ending the self-harm now, pulling on internal strengths they already have but may not fully be in conscious awareness.

There are recommended steps for guided imagery that have been compiled from our experiences as well as a variety of other recommendations (see Table 8.2). Some ways of helping clients relax include teaching them breathing exercises, breath counting, or helping them learn how to tune in to their body and be mindful. Relaxation may be something that you and your client need to explore together about what will work for him or her. Also once guided imagery is completed, it

TABLE 8.2. Guided Imagery Process

Recommended Guided Imagery Process
1. Assess that guided imagery is appropriate for the client, checking their grounding with reality, stress level over guided imagery. This should include educating the client on what guided imagery is, as well.
2. Assist with the development of and learning of relaxation strategies.
3. Determine type of guided imagery. If visualizing a calming safe place, then have the client fully develop the imagery scene that promotes security, safety, and calming sensations. If you are doing guided imagery on a past event, then determine that specific event and make sure there is a grounding aspect (such as your voice or the room or the feel of the chair or a specific noise) that will help bring the client back into the room mindfully if he experiences intense emotions by visualizing a stress-producing event. Finally, if it is a future-oriented imagery, then determine the time frame that is most appropriate to visualize.
4. Help the client begin to get into the guided imagery by using your voice or music, as determined by you and the client. You, as the therapist, should not be absent during this process, but should serve as a facilitator.
5. During the guided imagery, present the area of need through a task or question. For example, “After that event happened, what did you do differently other than self-injury? How did you solve it this time? How did you cope?” or “Now that you are fully immersed in the surroundings, take a moment and wiggle your toes, feel the anxiety/anger/other emotion just wiggle out of them, seeping out of your pores and into the sand. Once it feels like all of the tension/emotion is out of your toes, take a moment while lying on the beach, listening to the waves, to experience the same emotion/feelings/tension slowly leave your feet.” This facilitation and guidance should occur until the goal (determined by you and the client) of relaxation is complete.
6. While still in the guided imagery, support the client in visualizing herself as empowered and successful. This may be by saying something like, “Now imagine that this new strategy you implemented worked, and was successful. What was it? What did it feel like? What does that success feel like? Who found out about it or recognized your success?”
7. Then slowly bring the guided imagery back up to the surface, to the room in which you and your client are present. It should not be an abrupt departure, but one that backs slowly out of the imagery, entering back into reality.

is helpful to process the experience with your client. This includes asking your client what that felt like or how she experienced it, did the relaxation portion work for her, was there anything that felt like a barrier or that inhibited fully experiencing the guided imagery, and does she notice any changes in her body, thoughts, feelings, or overall sensations.

Rewriting Narratives

An external locus of control is typically the lens in which individuals who self-injure see their circumstances. What this means is that they may not often feel in control of their self, emotions, thoughts, or even situations but, instead, feel like that control is external to them (e.g., parent, peers, significant other). Therefore, mental health professionals may consider using techniques that emphasize the development of a strong internal locus of control. Some of these methods are the tried and true methods of restating sentences using "I language" (e.g., instead of "She totally screwed me over" to "I did not like what she did"; instead of "He made me feel sad" to "I feel sad because I didn't like what he said"), decision lists (e.g., making a list of all of the possible decisions a client had in that specific moment, or in a future moment, that he could have selected), and the well known cognitive behavioral analysis process, which was discussed in the previous chapter.

Another way of helping clients develop an internal locus of control is to help the client rewrite their narrative. This is a technique that may be more common to Narrative Therapy but can be used as an intervention in other theoretical orientations and connected to cognitive, emotive, and other goals. Individuals who self-injure tend to have magical thinking, defined as "pre-symbolic language that lacks differentiation between the real and the symbolic signifier and signified" (Gregory & Mustata, 2012, p. 1047). More specifically, individuals who self-injure tend to see their behavior (i.e., cutting, burning) as a magical substitute for emotion regulation, and externalize the control of their feelings and thoughts onto the self-injury itself. So what you frequently might hear is, "It calmed me down" or "I can't function without it" or "It helped me control my thoughts/feel grounded" or even "It gained me the attention that I needed." What is occurring here is the attribution of control of social situations, cognitive control, and emotion regulation onto self-injury itself, therefore externalizing the behavioral and emotional control onto the behavior or "object" of NSSI. By placing control on NSSI, the individual does not believe or experience control internally. When this occurs, using narrative techniques to rewrite a personal narrative or story around herself and NSSI can help an individual change her language and relationship with NSSI and with other individuals (DiMaggio, Salvatore, Azzara, & Catania, 2003) from more externally focused to more internally focused loci of control. You can help the client use the rewriting process to add strength (e.g., give more strength to the emotion versus the blood in self-injury), to separate the self from a problem (e.g., remove the label of self-injurer from the person), and to assist the self in gaining control over the NSSI. Consider the following process in rewriting narratives or storylines (Table 8.3).

TABLE 8.3. Process of Rewriting Narratives

1. **Find the problem or trouble spot**	You and the client should step back from the situation and look at it with an objective eye. First, if the client is labeling himself as a "self-injurer," thus self-injury and self being one and the same, then consider externalizing the problem and labeling the self-injury itself to remove this from the person. Then consider other potential trouble spots, such as negative outcomes, actual use of self-injury, emotions that feel intense or overwhelming, when a client gets stuck or shuts down, when he feels the need for attention, or isolation.
2. **Title the trouble spot**	Consider what the potential aspect or belief is that leads to this trouble spot, or negative outcome. Taking a moment and naming this belief can be therapeutic and informative. For example, if the client tends to get angry, and the anger feels out of control, resulting in self-injury, have her name and title the anger (e.g., a big red dragon). This title provides you as the clinician with information on the intensity (e.g., "a big red dragon" can provide you with a different picture than "a hot mug"). Also, what is the belief behind the anger, when the big red dragon appears? For example, is it that they were left out, that someone did it to them on purpose (i.e., this externalizes the locus of control, something that eventually needs to shift within the client to internal locus but not yet), or something else. But understanding that can help the client better understand when their anger (or dragon) appears.
3. **Understand the weak spots**	Take a moment and explore with the client when this trouble spot, in this case the "big red dragon," knows when she is weak to it, when she is vulnerable to the anger, when she needs it and, thus, understanding the various times when it can "take over," in some regard. This can also be done with self-injury itself, when self-injury (or whatever title or name the client gives to it) knows it is needed, knows when it can help, but also knows when the client is vulnerable and it can swoop in and take over.
4. **Find the inner strength**	Now it is time to help the client pull on inner strengths and resources, and gain some internal locus of control. During this phase of rewriting one's narrative, the client decides when she has the strength to keep self-injury, or anger (i.e., red dragon), at bay. When she has the strength to say no, to make the decision that now is not the time. This process can also include what else she would like to use or do instead.
5. **Find support for the new story**	Finding support can be varied. This can be writing a fuller narrative, including previous and future events that might put the client at risk of self-injury or anger (red dragon). But it can also be finding others who may support this new story, a story of the client finding strength to combat the problem or trouble narrative and finding a new restorative, strength-based narrative.

Emotive and Relational Based Intervention

Feeling Identification Activities

It is typical for individuals who self-injure to have a difficult time identifying and labeling their feelings. Usually they know they feel an intense, overwhelming emotion but are unclear on what the emotion is. If asked what they felt before they self-injured, most clients will say, "I don't know." Or even prompted to think about emotions and feelings, most clients who self-harm have a difficulty identifying any emotions or may overuse one emotion label, such as anger or sadness. The second author once had a client early in treatment ask, "Why do you always want me to talk about feelings? I don't even know what that means." Sometimes, clients may grow up in families where the identification and expression of feelings is not valued or encouraged. For example, if a young child falls down off their bike and skins their knee, they may start to cry. Parents or caregivers react in different ways. One parent might hug the child, acknowledge their painful feelings, help fix up the injury, and encourage them to self-soothe by keeping their leg up and watching TV. Another parent might tell the child that tears mean weakness and to "suck it up," get back on their bike, and keep going. In either of the scenarios above, the child learns a message of how feelings are to be dealt with in the family. When an individual tends to overuse one emotional label (e.g., anger), rarely is the overused identified emotion their actual emotion, or at minimum it may not be the true underlying emotion. For example, when Kallie's friend walks down the hallway holding the hand of Kallie's boyfriend, Kallie feels angry. While anger may be a true and valid emotion, potentially under this emotion is hurt or jealousy, a sense of distrust for her friend or even a feeling of insecurity.

Individuals who self-injure have been identified most frequently as having alexithymia, which is the inability to identify and describe emotions being experienced or previously felt. Alexithymia results from lack of emotional awareness and labels, along with other things such as interpersonal connections. Focusing solely on the emotional identification side of things, it can be helpful to provide clients with feeling language, which may take the form of a feeling face chart that can help clients identify a face that feels like they do on the inside.

It can also be helpful for the client to become connected to their body, to become mindful. Where do they feel emotions, and what does it feel like (e.g., red-hot pan, fluttering butterflies, tension, dizzy, like something wants to run)? And how does this progression of emotions feel in their body, in terms of physical sensations and intensity? A picture of a body (see Figure 8.3), which clients can use to identify the locations of their feelings in their body, can be helpful. Consider allowing clients to use various colors, shapes, or ways of identifying and representing their emotions in their physical body. Combining this physical body shape with a feeling faces chart can help clients increase their ability to identify, label, and describe their emotive states that may lead to self-injury. This is important not only to decrease self-injury but also to assist in selecting appropriate coping strategies to

Where do you feel your feelings in your body?

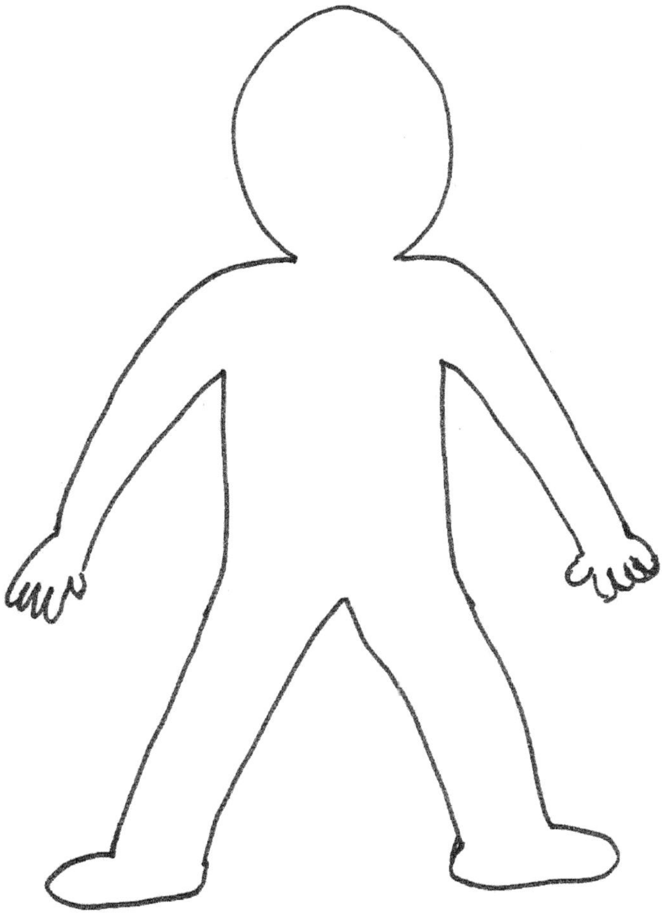

FIGURE 8.3. Physical location of feelings

regulate emotions, as different coping strategies may be more effective for different feelings. For instance, running may be a great way to relieve stress, anger, or anxiety but may not work as well to alleviate sadness.

Reflective Mask Intervention

Expressive arts are one way to help clients create space or distance from feelings or concerns in order to reflect on them and create solutions. This is somewhat similar to the externalizing process in rewriting one's narrative, not in the sense that you talk about or label concerns, problems, or self-injury, but more so with the idea that expressing oneself artistically can sometimes help a client communicate or gain insight in ways that talking cannot achieve. Masks have been used in therapy and discussed as a possible intervention even back into the 1980s. More than likely, various mask activities had been used prior to that time point, but this is one of the first time points that the use of masks in therapy is documented. Landy (1986) noted four ways a mask can be used in therapy: (1) to represent two sides of a conflict or decision, (2) to express one's identity to a group, family, or therapist, (3) to explore dreams or imagery, or (4) to express a social role.

In therapy the mask should be considered an image of the person, an extension or representation of the self. It should be noted though that there are two sides of the mask, the outside, or the front of the face, and the inside, or the underbelly of the mask. Frequently the outside of the mask is used to represent what others know or see, what we show to other people, while the inside or underbelly of the mask is used to represent internal thoughts, emotions, or desires (e.g., see Figure 8.4). These can be things that might not be as obvious to others, or what the client may keep hidden from others. For example, a client could be asked to use the mask to indicate a role in the family, with the perceived role on the outside of the mask (the front, what people see) and the desired role on the inside of the mask (the internal thoughts, perceptions, or desires). In regards to self-injury, most individuals keep self-injury to themselves. It is a hidden behavior, something that most people in their lives do not know. Even if friends, family members, or significant others do know that an individual self-harms, they frequently do not know or understand the internal experiences of the person. Layer this onto the possibility that individuals

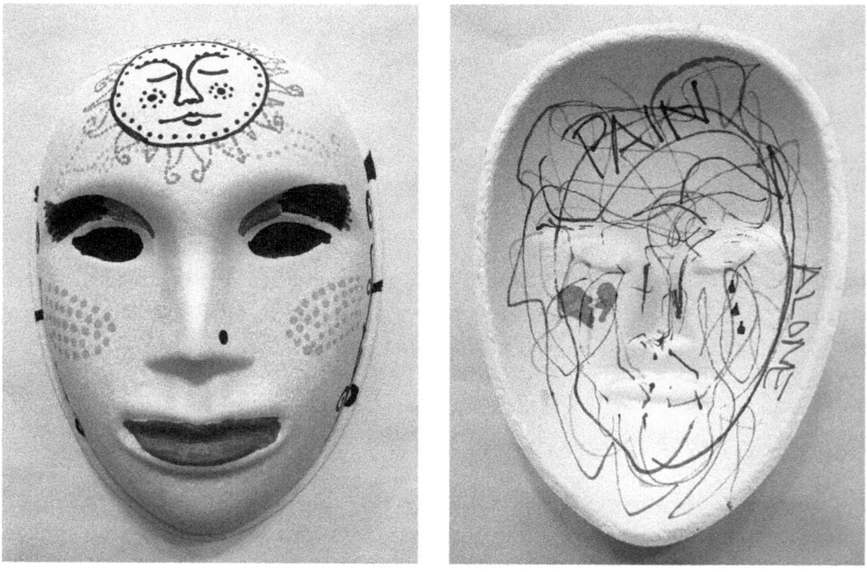

FIGURE 8.4. Example of front and inside of a mask

who NSSI typically have difficulty identifying or describing their feelings, communicating feelings or needs to others, or may be unclear to the true reason they self-injure; using expressive arts, particularly the mask intervention, can be helpful in gaining insight (for both the clinician and the client himself) and helping others understand. It can also clarify what goals may be needed in regards to emotion regulation, feeling grounded, ruminating thoughts, and more.

In setting up the activity, consider the mask intervention as a projective technique, one in which the client gets to project herself onto the mask. She can project self-injury onto the mask, but more than likely it is helpful to get at the underlying reasons for self-injury and thus think of the client more holistically. When handing the mask to the client, the clinician should provide many mediums for the client to use to decorate the mask. This may include, but is not limited to, paint, markers, crayons, glue, glitter, feathers, buttons, paper, and tissue paper. Clients are instructed to "construct (decorate, make, develop, create) the outside or front of your mask in a way that represents what you show to others, what you present to others, or what you let them know about you." Once the client has created the outside of her mask, it is helpful to ask process questions to the client, including "how did it feel to create the mask?" "Anything new you realized as you were drawing the mask about what you allow others to see, about what you present to the outside world?" "How does it feel to wear this mask?"

Once the client has processed the outside of the mask, she is then instructed to "Create (develop, make) the inside of the mask in a way that represents what you do not show others, what occurs inside of you, what you carry around but others may not know." Again, once the inside is created, it is important to process this much the same way, including asking "Did you realize anything as you were making the inside?" "What was creating the inside of the mask like for you?" It is also helpful in some cases, as in the case of one client (Trepal-Wollenzier & Wester, 2002), to have clients have the inside of the mask talk to or dialogue with the outside of the mask, and vice versa. More specifically, consider having the client write a letter from one side of the mask to the other. They can answer questions such as (a) how has the outside of the mask helped the inside of the mask, (b) how has it created a barrier or gotten in the way of what is on the inside, (c) what does the outside/inside of the mask need from the other side, or need in general, and (d) what is needed now, what does each side need now? How long ago was the mask created? An example of the mask is provided in Figure 8.4.

Locked Box Activity

For those who self-injure, frequently emotions or thoughts feel out of control and overwhelming. This can be due to not having adequate coping skills, the inability to identify and label emotions, and engaging in self-injury (as well as other maladaptive coping strategies), which only temporarily relieves the intensity of the current situation, albeit never resolving the originating concern. Therefore,

Box 8.3 Locked Box Activity Steps

1. First provide your client (or ask them to bring) a small box. This box can be a small trinket box, cardboard box, shoe box. Most craft stores provide small wooden or cardboard boxes for less than $1. Regardless of the box, it should have a lid or way to close the box.
2. Make sure you have an abundance of craft material, including, but not limited to, markers, paint, pipe cleaners, paper, tissue paper, feathers, buttons, glue, and beads.

   Instruct your client to take a moment and consider what they feel they don't have control over. This can be internal (e.g., emotions, thoughts, behaviors) or external (e.g., school bully, mother-in-law). *"Take a moment and consider the things we have been talking about, ______. This may not be an exhaustive list, but I would like you to write down a list of things that you feel may be beyond your control, or at times feel out of control."*
3. Once the client has an idea of the thing or things that they feel they don't have control over, that tends to lead to self-injury or causes anxiety or stress, have them create with the crafts provided something that represents each internal and external aspect they would like control over. This creation should be whatever best represents the objects for the client and may include metaphorical objects, drawings, sculptures, or could be a word or sentence written on a piece of paper. (At this moment you should also provide the box to the client so that he or she understands the size of the box. However, you should not instruct the client to make sure they design objects to fit in the box, as they can decide if that is what they need to do or not.) Your instructions for the client may be something like this: *"Now that you have your list, I want you to take a moment and use these objects in front of you to design or create objects or words that best represent these things that you would like more control over in your life. After you create these items, I am going to have you place them in this box. If you feel something is missing from the supplies here, please do not hesitate to tell me."*
4. After the client has created all of his or her objects, instruct them to now take a moment to look at and design the box. They can paint, draw, glue, as needed. Something you might say to your client at this point is, *"The next step today is going to be placing all of what you have created into the box provided. Before placing the items in, consider what you want your box to look like. Some boxes have locks, some do not, and some have words, while others have pictures. Please consider what you feel like your box needs for your items and concerns to be stored safely inside."*

5. Once your client has designed the outside of the box, have him or her place all of their objects inside of the box and close the box (securing it if necessary). The following questions can be used to process the experience:

    a. *What was this experience like for you? Was anything surprising or helpful in this process?*
    b. *Are you surprised that all of your items did/did not fit inside of your box?*
    c. *Please tell me about each item you created, and consider the texture, size, and object you used to represent it. Does the size or texture say anything about your experience of ___?*
    d. *Do you feel like your box needs anything else? Do you feel that each object can be contained in the box and kept there until you decide to open the box?*
    e. *Where do you feel is the safest place to store your box? Is there a location at home, does it need to stay here in the counseling room?*

6. At this point, the box can continue to be used in counseling or as homework at home—depending on where the client decided to store the box. Where the client decides to store the box may depend on how much control he/she feels they have, their coping abilities, or what is in the box itself. If the client decides that the box can stay at home, on a shelf, in a closet, under a stack of books, or anywhere else, the goal will be to have the client determine when he or she has the strength, energy, and resources to take time to deal with one or more objects that are in the box. They can choose to take only one object out at a time (recommended) and work through or cope with some portion of it (e.g., if a client's internal emotion that feels out of control is anger, when might she be able to take this anger out of the box at a time when she feels calm, in control, and has time to focus. Can she list or consider other reactions she can have to different situations during this time, and can she consider where in her body she feels the onset of anger and list potential physical stages that anger goes through in her body before it becomes out of control [e.g., see *feeling identification activities* discussed earlier in this chapter]). If the object that feels out of control is external (e.g., situation with a friend, or sister-in-law), when the client does not feel emotionally distraught or wrapped up in emotion or frustration, can he open the box and take out the object that represents this external person or thing. Then consider the best way to approach this person or thing, what might he say or do, or how he might be able to react in the future that might be more beneficial to him.

FIGURE 8.5. Example of the outside and inside of a locked box activity with a client

tension, stress, emotions, and thoughts tend to continue to build up with added situations, and the original events or problems still exist. This can feel overwhelming and impossible to deal with. The locked box activity can provide some sense of control, at times. More specifically, at times, the locked box activity can help a client gain the perception that they have some control over their choices or decisions. See how to conduct the locked box activity in Box 8.3 and an example picture of the locked box in Figure 8.5.

Communication Activities

Individuals who self-injure tend to have poor communication abilities, due to low self-awareness, alexithymia, or poor social skills. Frequently, in working with clients, most clients feel like they have communicated to parents or significant others the stressors that led to NSSI. However, when asking others, most individuals felt like nothing was ever communicated. Other clients rarely seek anyone out to talk about self-injury or other concerns due to a fear of being judged. This can lead to increased usage of NSSI or even the use of self-injury in order to communicate what the individual feels like is a dire situation. Therefore, working on communication can be helpful and sometimes imperative in working with clients who self-injure. Communication and social skills are incorporated in other evidence-based treatments, such as problem solving therapy (PST) and dialectical behavior therapy (DBT). What one needs to consider is working with clients from a skills perspective and training them how to communicate verbally and nonverbally.

While it may seem basic, starting with communication 101 strategies can be helpful. This includes communicating only when they have calmed down and they can collect their thoughts. Thus, training in relaxation techniques or guided imagery is needed to help the client gain control over thoughts and emotions before they begin to communicate. This may include teaching a client to walk away if they are not calm and re-approach the person at a later time, if possible. It may include also teaching clients to write down what they want to say, using bullet points or an outline, or even, for some clients, a script. The use of I-statements becomes important in learning communication skills. Also important is taking it beyond communication 101 and teaching clients the use of nonverbal communication, as well, that the use of their body to convey feelings and statements is important, along with what words they may be saying. Practicing this in session with you can be important. Using role-play, clinician–client dialogue, and empty chair techniques can be helpful.

Psychopharmacological Intervention

While very few researchers have explored evidence-based treatments for NSSI (as noted in Chapter 7), even less research has been conducted to explore the effectiveness or impact of psychopharmacology or various drugs in reducing NSSI behaviors. The evidence has been somewhat mixed, with some researchers suggesting that medication has no impact, while other medication did seem to have an impact, albeit a small one (Hawton et al., 1998). Few studies have had the internal controls necessary to determine whether the medications truly were the result of decreases or abstinence from NSSI or something else (Turner et al., 2014). Turner and colleagues did mention that five different drug classes have been explored, including SSRIs (e.g., fluoxetine), antipsychotics (e.g., ziprasidone), SNRIs (e.g., venlafaxine), opioids (e.g., buprenorphine), and opioid antagonists (e.g., naltrexone). In summing all of the studies, each drug class did seem to have an impact on decreasing NSSI behaviors, with some studies having stronger controls (i.e., randomized clinical trials) than others.

What needs to be noted here is that there is no medication that will innately decrease NSSI behaviors. What needs to be assessed is the underlying cause or reason for NSSI behaviors (e.g., depression, anxiety, dissociation). If prescribed medication, the pharmacotherapy should be directed towards that underlying reason or diagnosis, rather than the self-injury itself. No researchers have pieced apart the impact of the medication on the mental health symptoms or diagnosis outside that of NSSI behaviors. Stated another way, no researcher has provided results on how the pharmacological treatment has impacted the actual depressive symptoms (or anxiety, dissociation, etc.), which in turn might ultimately impact NSSI behaviors, or whether NSSI decreases prior to other mental health symptoms. More research needs to be done with pharmacological treatments before clinicians can truly determine the impact of medication on NSSI.

Social Contagion, a Treatment Consideration

Another difficulty that arises in various settings where individuals are in groups (e.g., K–12 settings, college campuses in dorms and social groups, inpatient group treatment settings) is social contagion. Social contagion is defined as the spread of affect or behavior from one person to another or to a larger group. The goal in any setting would be how to prevent social contagion, but also how to manage it once it occurs. Contagion, or the spread of NSSI behaviors, has been found to be rampant in residential and inpatient facilities. Many authors, researchers, and clinicians have reported NSSI as occurring in significant clusters of youth and adult residential patients (e.g., Richardson et al., 2012; Walsh & Doerfler, 2009). Individuals who are residing in residential or inpatient care have been found to increase NSSI behaviors. More specifically, 33% of individuals who had never self-harmed prior to being admitted began self-harming within two months, and 39% of individuals who had a history of NSSI also continued to self-injure (Boxer, 2010). This suggests that residential care tends to expose individuals to NSSI, as well as increase the exposures. Therefore, Richardson and colleagues (2012) ask mental health professionals to consider whether the benefits of residential and inpatient care are worth the risks inherent in this setting for NSSI for each individual client.

One typical method that has been tried to prevent social contagion of NSSI, which is not that effective, is to keep things quiet, both generally as well as once it occurs. For example, the school counselor becomes aware of a student in middle school who self-injures. In order to make sure that the behavior does not spread or become more problematic, she decides to not say anything to anyone, other than the student's family. Keeping completely silent, though, is not necessarily the answer. First, individuals are hearing about self-injury from many different places, including friends, social media, movies, magazines, television shows, and books. One person even indicated they learned about self-injury from their health class (Adler & Adler, 2007). So remaining quiet is not the answer, as this may also decrease the degree to which students seek out school personnel or mental health professionals to talk about self-injury, for fear that they will be judged. A request to not remain silent about self-injury also does not mean that it is talked about constantly or necessarily directly to individuals at large in a setting, as this may increase the prevalence of self-injury too.

Consider the possibility of doing outreach, classroom guidance, or even school assemblies on a related issue; for example, coping behaviors. Talk to individuals about coping behaviors, including both adaptive coping methods and maladaptive coping methods, the latter of which can include self-injury. Talk about how these strategies work (or not) in regulating emotions, helping one feel better, and resolving existing problems. Give students example cases such as someone fighting with a boyfriend or friend, another person coming to school angry about something that was said, and walk them through how these various coping strategies may work or not work, or how something like NSSI may feel like it works temporarily but ultimately the problem still exists. So work on preventing NSSI, as well as the contagion of NSSI, by talking to individuals or students about coping behavior, with NSSI being one possible method of coping that may not ultimately be effective.

Conclusion

This chapter provided information on interventions other than those within manualized or evidenced-based practices that have been found to be helpful in working with clients who self-injure. Emotion regulation strategies, creative and expressive interventions, and psychopharmacological treatment were reviewed. It is important that mental health professionals remember that each client who self-injures is unique. Thus, a one-size-fits-all approach to NSSI treatment will not work. Clinicians are encouraged to honor their clients' strengths and interests when choosing interventions, as well as to match the interventions with treatment goals.

References

Adler, P. A., & Adler, P. (2007). The demedicalization of self-injury: From psychopathology to sociological deviance. *Journal of Contemporary Ethnography, 36*, 537–570.

Boxer, P. (2010). Variations in risk and treatment factors among adolescents engaging in different types of deliberate self-harm in an inpatient sample. *Journal of Clinical Child and Adolescent Psychology, 39*(4), 470–480.

DiMaggio, G., Salvatore, G., Azzara, C., & Catania, C. (2003). Rewriting self-narratives: The therapeutic process. *Journal of Constructivist Psychology, 16*, 155–181.

Gregory, R. J., & Mustata, G. T. (2012). Magical thinking in narratives of adolescent cutters. *Journal of Adolescence, 35*, 1045–1051.

Hawton, K., Arensman, E., Townsend, E., Bremner, S., Feldman, E., Goldney, R., Gunnell, D., Hazell, P., van Heeringen, K., House, A., Owns, D., Sakinofsky, I., & Traskman-Bendz, L. (1998). Deliberate self-harm: Systematic review of efficacy of psychosocial and pharmacological treatments in preventing repetition. *British Medical Journal, 317*, 441–446.

Hoffman, R. M., & Kress, V. E. (2010). Adolescent nonsuicidal self-injury: Minimizing client and counselor risk and enhancing client care. *Journal of Mental Health Counseling, 32*, 342–347.

Klonsky, E. D., & Glenn, C. R. (2008). Resisting urges to self-injure. *Behavioural and Cognitive Psychotherapy, 36*, 211–220.

Kress, V. E., Adamson, N., DeMarco, C., Paylo, J., & Zoldan, C. A. (2013). The use of guided imagery as an intervention in addressing nonsuicidal self-injury. *Journal of Creativity in Mental Health, 8*, 35–47.

Kress, V. E., & Hoffman, R. M. (2008). Non-suicidal self-injury and motivational interviewing: Enhancing readiness for change. *Journal of Mental Health Counseling, 30*, 311–329.

Landy, R. J. (1986). The image of the mask: Implications for theatre and therapy. *Journal of Mental Imagery, 9*, 43–56.

Long, M., Manktelow, R., & Tracey, A. (2015). The healing journey: Help seeking for self-injury among a community population. *Qualitative Health Research, 25*, 932–944.

Malon, D. W., & Berardi, D. (1987). Hypnosis with self-cutters. *American Journal of Psychotherapy, 41*, 531–541.

Miller, W. R., & Rollnick, S. (2002). *Motivational interviewing: Preparing people for change* (2nd edition). New York: Guilford Press.

Muehlenkamp, J. J. (2006). Empirically supported treatments and general therapy guidelines for non-suicidal self-injury. *Journal of Mental Health Counseling, 28*, 166–185.

Prochaska, J. O., & Norcross, J. C. (2001). Stages of change. *Psychotherapy, 38*, 443–448.

Richardson, B. G., Surmitis, K. A., & Hyldahl, R. S. (2012). Minimizing social contagion in adolescents who self-injure: Considerations for group work, residential treatment, and the internet. *Journal of Mental Health Counseling, 34*, 121-132.

Trepal-Wollenzier, H. C., & Wester, K. L. (2002). The use of masks in counseling. *Journal of Clinical Activities, Assignments and Handouts in Psychotherapy Practice, 2*, 123–130.

Turner, B. J., Austin, S. B., & Chapman, A. L. (2014). Treating nonsuicidal self-injury: A systematic review of psychological and pharmacological interventions. *Canadian Journal of Psychiatry, 59*, 576–585.

Wallenstein, M. B., & Nock, M. K. (2007). Physical exercise as a treatment for non-suicidal self-injury: Evidence from a single-case study. *The American Journal of Psychiatry, 164*, 350–351.

Walsh, B., & Doerfler, L. A. (2009). Residential treatment of self-injury. In M. K. Nock (Ed.), *Understanding non-suicidal self-injury: Origins, assessment, and treatment* (pp. 271–290). Washington, DC: American Psychological Association.

Wester, K. L., Downs, H., & Trepal, H. C. (2016). Counseling outcomes of non-suicidal self-injury for eight clients in outpatient treatment: A retrospective case study. *Counseling Outcome Research and Evaluation, 5*, 1–18.

Wester, K. L., & McKibben, W. B. (2016). Participants' experiences of nonsuicidal self-injury: Supporting existing theory and emerging conceptual pathways. *Journal of Mental Health Counseling, 38*, 12–27.

Wester, K. L., & Trepal, H. C. (2005). Working with clients who self-injure: Providing alternatives. *Journal of College Counseling, 8*, 180–189.

Section IV
Education and Advocacy

nine
NSSI and the Family

I am working with a family that has a child who self-injures. However, there seems to be a dearth of information for the client's loved ones, those that are trying to maintain a healthy home environment. Can anyone recommend any books or articles that deal with the parents' or loved ones' perspective on NSSI?

The quote above was taken from an online listserv for mental health professionals. Although we know a lot of information about NSSI—where it comes from, how to assess the behaviors, and which treatments are helpful—there is little information available for the family members of those who self-injure. Mental health clinicians have important considerations regarding families when working with individuals who self-injure. For example, what aspects of family dynamics leads into an individual selecting NSSI, should families be in treatment, what information and support do families need when they have a child or family member who self-injures?

Consider the case study in Box 9.1 as if you were the parent. What type of information would you want or need? How might your reactions and internal feelings about your daughter self-injuring impact how you might react to the NSSI but also to Brenna? Now take a moment and consider that you are working with Brenna as a clinician. What do you need to consider in terms of confidentiality, what you talk with Brenna's mom about in terms of Brenna's behavior, what education or information Brenna's mom may need about NSSI, as well as what support she may need and what referrals may need to be made?

Box 9.1 Case Study: Brenna

You are a parent of a 13-year-old girl named Brenna. Your daughter is in middle school and you have noticed that over the past year or so she is becoming increasingly moody and more interested in spending time with her peers (in real life or online) than with her family. Recently, you have discovered that she has been cutting herself. Your feelings are intense. Not only are you dealing with the transition from elementary to middle school, you are also feeling disconnected from your child, and guilty and concerned about her behaviors. You are separated from your spouse and are living apart. You have not shared your feelings about the NSSI with him.

Family Context and NSSI Dynamics

As covered in Chapter 5 (Diagnostic Considerations), there are many possible mental health conditions with which NSSI has been associated. These include, but are not limited to, eating disorders, anxiety, substance abuse, impulse control, and post-traumatic stress. While this doesn't explain all cases of self-injury, individuals who self-injure tend to come from homes where physical abuse, sexual abuse, or neglect has occurred (Walsh & Rosen, 1988) or from families where there is high conflict or violence (Conterio, Lader, & Bloom, 1998). Other events that have occurred in families where an individual self-injures include parental divorce and loss, such as death of a loved one (Suyemoto, 1998). While violence, abuse, and loss is not an exhaustive list of what may occur within a family, it is important to remember that the NSSI may be a symptom of an issue within the family. However, it is also paramount to know that the presence of any of these aforementioned dynamics does not always result in self-injury.

It is important to explore family dynamics, as it plays a role. Individuals who engage in NSSI have reported higher levels of families with invalidating environments (Martin, Bureau, Cloutier, & Lafontaine, 2011). These environments are disconnecting, and because children's experiences are not validated, they tend to not be bonded to their parents in a way where they can rely on them for emotional support. The second author once worked with a college student who described her home environment in this way. Her father was prone to yelling. He would get home from work every day and seem irritated at everyone (including the client, her mother, her sister, and even the family dog). Her mother struggled with hoarding and was very consumed with collecting things around the house. Thus, neither parent was connected with the family system and everyone avoided each other when they were at home together. The client could not remember a time when the family did anything together, nor did she report that she felt connected with her parents emotionally. When the letter arrived stating that she had been accepted to college, she hid it in her room for a month because she didn't know how her parents would react. She herself was very excited about being accepted and also felt scared and unsure about the move and the increased academic demands that college would bring. When she finally decided to tell them that she had been accepted, her dad yelled at her for not telling them earlier and her mom had no response (positive or negative). The client's feelings about the acceptance remained unacknowledged and unaddressed.

Families Participating in Treatment

According to Klonsky, Muehlenkamp, Lewis, and Walsh (2011), integrating family therapy into NSSI treatment has been proven useful. It has been recommended that clinicians assist family members with understanding NSSI (Hoffman, Hinkle, & Kress, 2010; Trepal, Wester, & MacDonald, 2006). Family members can be very valuable in terms of managing the client's home environment and helping them to cope with change. However, as mentioned earlier, the family may also be a primary source of the client's stress or tension. They may even be significant sources of the client's trauma history. So, careful assessment needs to be considered when talking to individuals about causes and triggers of their NSSI behaviors.

Families may be involved in treatment in myriad formats and levels. In operating from a strengths-based perspective, Selekman (2009) assumes "all self-harming clients and/or their couple partners and families have the strengths and resources to change; they are the experts" (p. 96). Families are often an important aspect of NSSI treatment, and they are the experts on their own system. Thus, it is important to prepare them to be successful in their loved one's treatment. The following sections outline some ways in which families may be involved in NSSI treatment and what they might expect.

What Family Members May Experience During NSSI Treatment

Ethics—Informed Consent and Confidentiality

Although common ethical issues associated with NSSI were covered in Chapter 6, all family members involved in a client's treatment will likely participate in a discussion about informed consent and confidentiality with a mental health professional. Throughout the process of informed consent, clinicians will outline what families can expect in treatment. However, how clinicians react, their limits to confidentiality, and information provided to a parent, partner, or family member may differ based on setting (e.g., school, outpatient, inpatient), along with other considerations such as the age of the client, couple or family situation, crisis or severity level, and other contextual factors and behavior (e.g., impulsivity, substance abuse). For example, some mental health clinicians will mainly see the child or youth client. These clinicians will discuss the parameters of treatment with the family and seek their consent, and may ask for weekly or periodic session times (say 10 minutes at the beginning or end of the session) to catch up with the parents. However, most of the session time will only involve the child. Other mental health providers will practice from a family therapy modality. In this type of treatment, the child client will be the "identified patient," but the entire family will participate in most of the sessions. Other times, adult clients may participate in couples counseling when one partner self-injures. The client who self-injures may participate in individual sessions and the partner may occasionally join in. It is important that families ask treatment providers questions during the process of informed consent. If they are unsure of the parameters of treatment, or of expectations for themselves or the clinician, they do have the right to ask. Families and clinicians may be at odds when the expectations for treatment are not clear (e.g., the family expects the NSSI behaviors to stop at a quicker rate than is possible or probable; Selekman, 2009).

So when does a clinician inform parents or legal guardians of NSSI behaviors reported by a minor? This is a tricky question. Let's take some cases into consideration. First let's consider Amanda, a 14-year-old female who self-injures by pulling her hair out on her arms and her eyelashes. Her mom has not yet noticed this behavior, but has noticed fidgeting behavior. Her mom is concerned about her, so she brought her into therapy. Amanda does not directly talk about NSSI, but you noticed it and address it with her. Amanda mentions she tends to pull her hair, as it helps her to alleviate anxiety, which she frequently feels when uncomfortable or when in high-pressure situations. She mentions this occurs frequently when talking with her mom, due to her mom's high expectations. Given the case of Amanda, is informing her mother necessary? Would it increase or decrease Amanda's NSSI behavior? More than likely, her mom would become concerned and anxious about her behavior, and potentially put more pressure on Amanda to stop the NSSI, which, in turn, would probably increase the NSSI. Currently Amanda's behavior is not life-threatening, so it may be acceptable to keep this behavior confidential at the moment, regardless of setting (e.g., outpatient mental health services, school setting, college setting), unless it begins to increase in severity. However, a clinician needs to be knowledgeable about her organization's policies. Some school policies may state that any form of self-harm needs to be immediately reported to a parent or legal guardian, while in an outpatient setting, there may be more leeway.

Let's consider a second case. Mark is a 16-year-old male who indicates he has self-harmed for 6 years. He reports having a container of razors, and even one scalpel, that he uses to self-harm. When assessing his self-harm behavior you come to understand that Mark frequently reports entering into a blind rage, of which only NSSI helps to ground him. When experiencing this blind rage, Mark reports not really knowing what he is doing until he feels pain from cutting. Sometimes he has cut deeper than he wanted, mostly due to him not being fully aware in the moment. While there is still more information you need from Mark about his

NSSI to determine adequate treatment, this case is an example of where, even though Mark may have no intention of killing himself when he self-injures, he may accidentally do so due to dissociating in his moments of anger. Therefore, informing his parents would be important in this situation, regardless of therapeutic setting, so they are clear about the potential danger.

These are just two cases, which may feel more clear-cut than most client cases that clinicians counsel. Therefore, it is important for clinicians to determine the limits to confidentiality they are comfortable with, and indicate this in the first session with the minor client (assent), as well as the parent and legal guardian (consent). The limits spelled out in agency policy (e.g., school setting) or during the informed consent for outpatient or inpatient treatment should include when NSSI will be reported to a parent and when it will not be. Mental health professionals need to consider if this is based on the type of method, the frequency of NSSI engagement, the severity of wounds, or the context in which one self-harms. It may include a combination of all of the above, yet this needs to be clearly understood by the parent, as well as the youth, so that trust can be built and confidentiality can be maintained. For some mental health professionals, this boundary may be that every form and case of NSSI discussed will be reported. Other clinicians may have a wider boundary where only what is deemed as high-risk behavior or behaviors that may result in accidental death are discussed with parents. Regardless of the boundaries each practitioner has, this needs to be determined ahead of time and put into an informed consent document for clients.

Confidentiality, or keeping private the information between the client and clinician, may be a concern when families participate in treatment. With the client's permission, the mental health professional may also share information about their treatment with family members. However, as discussed in Chapter 6, parents and guardians of minor children ultimately hold the right to access information about their minor child. This can be problematic when the child is not a willing participant in treatment or when family dynamics are such that information is not freely shared between parties (e.g., families where keeping secrets is common practice). In addition, adult clients and those who are part of couple relationships may also each have confidentiality rights to consider, depending on the treatment setting. Some mental health professionals may choose to work with the member of the couple who self-injures separately and only see the other party occasionally in joint sessions. Some clinicians will want to work with the couple together most of the time or may even want to hold individual sessions with the party who does not self-injure.

Finally, although risk assessment has been covered in other chapters, it is always important that families have a thorough understanding of the need to keep clients safe. Confidentiality may be broken when the potential for self-harm in the form of suicide or extensive NSSI exists. Mental health professionals often try to practice where the client is treated in the least restrictive setting (Berg, Hendricks, & Bradley, 2009). For example, if a client is expressing suicidal ideation but does not have an identified plan or means, the clinician will most probably continue to assess the situation rather than attempt to hospitalize them. As this relates to NSSI, counselors may identify behaviors (e.g., not practicing safe wound care) that are high risk; however, they will continue to assess and monitor the situation rather than overreacting or changing the client's level of care. Clinicians are ethically bound to be judicious about the confidential information that they do disclose related to client safety (Berg and colleagues, 2009).

Assessment

Given some of the potential underlying family correlates for NSSI (e.g., abuse, neglect, high conflict), it is likely that a mental health practitioner will want family members to participate in an initial assessment that includes safety concerns (Teague-Palmieri & Gutierrez, 2016). Families may be asked to participate in various forms of assessment, including, but certainly not limited to, developing a genogram (a pictorial map of family members and functioning) or being involved in rounds of circular questioning where each family member's perspective on the NSSI can be heard. Family members will likely have various perspectives on the client's NSSI (Trepal et al, 2006), and it will be important that the clinician gathers this information. Given what is known about NSSI family treatment, clinicians may also assess parent–child relationships and communication (Byrne et al., 2008).

Psychoeducation

Families come in all shapes and sizes. Family therapists will often liken families to the mobiles that hang over a baby's crib. Each arm of the mobile is important, and when one arm wobbles, the rest of the mobile tries to right itself and stabilize its overall position. Families operate in the same way. If one member of the unit is "wobbling," or struggling with an issue like NSSI, the rest of the members react in ways that try to stabilize the family system. This can mean different things for different families. Both assessment and psychoeducation can help the system to stabilize.

Teague-Palmieri and Gutierrez (2016) maintain that psychoeducation about NSSI is a very important component of family treatment. Counselors may also try to assess how much the client's family knows about their self-injury. Important distinctions, such as the relationship between NSSI and suicide need to be understood by all family members (Teague-Palmieri & Gutierrez, 2016). When families misinterpret NSSI behaviors as suicidal in intent, they may mistakenly overreact (Selekman, 2009), which may in turn worsen the situation, familial relationships, or increase severity in NSSI.

In educating families about NSSI behaviors in general, Yip (2006) stresses that it is important for families to understand the meaningfulness of NSSI and the client's feelings behind the behaviors. If family members listen with empathy and

Box 9.2 Sample Respectful Curiosity Questions for Family Members

Curiosity Questions

- What does self-injury do for you? How does it help or not help?
- What are some reasons it might be hard for you to stop?
- When do you most need self-injury?
- How do you view yourself when you succeed at not self-injuring?
- Is there anything missing in our relationship, that if present, would make a difference?

Making I-Statements

- I am sorry I feel uncomfortable. It is hard for me to know that you hurt.
- I am glad we are talking about this. I have felt worried about it for a while.
- I don't always know what to say, but I am trying to understand.
- If you don't want to talk to me now, I understand. I just want you to know I am here when you decide it is okay to talk.
- Is it okay if I check in or would you prefer to come to me?

Sample questions and statements were adapted and summarized from suggestions provided by Whitlock and Purington (2013b, p.2).

care, clients are more likely to feel understood and supported. As parents or partners want to know more about their loved one's NSSI, they will naturally want to ask them questions. They are advised to approach this discussion in a way that displays respect and empathy for their child/partner and their NSSI. Caroline Kettlewell (2000) calls these types of questions *respectful curiosity*. Whitlock and Purington (2013) also suggest that parents use *I-statements* during these discussions in order to promote non-threatening or non-blaming communication.

Mental health professionals may also try to assess communication patterns within the family (Yip, 2005). This assessment should include general communication patterns, but also communication around NSSI specifically. As stated earlier, NSSI may have originated due to violent or invalidating environments. Family members may not have identified or communicated their feelings, or may have been punished for doing so (e.g., a child being spanked for crying). Thus the communication patterns may have been such that children learned not to communicate feelings, or that it was not safe to do so, leading to a possibility of using self-injury to cope or alleviate the feelings and thoughts building up internally. Additionally, consider communication patterns around NSSI. Given the stress associated with NSSI, common communication concerns involve power struggles and reactions to NSSI episodes. If family members are unprepared for their reactions or for their loved one's inevitable return to NSSI episodes during treatment, they may overreact or act in extreme ways that they feel will protect their child from further self-harm (Selekman, 2009). For example, parents might threaten their teen with hospitalization, they might admonish them with over-the-top consequences for self-injuring, or they might retreat emotionally (Selekman, 2009). One member of a couple may threaten to leave the other if they do not stop self-injuring. These reactions should be explored in treatment.

How Families Can Deal with NSSI Episodes

Selekman reminds parents not to "play detective" (p. 113) and constantly ask their child how often they feel like self-harming, or repeatedly check on their injury sites. This type of watchdog behavior can put the youth on edge, possibly leading to further desire to self-harm. It can also lead parents to feel as though they have to be behavioral enforcers. This can be a heavy burden, as parents will feel responsible for the NSSI.

It is important to avoid placing the parent/family members into roles where they are the client's behavioral enforcers or punishers. See the case in Box 9.3.

In Taylor's case, her mom has the best of intentions. She wants to be helpful and means well. However, what might happen the next time Taylor is feeling stressed and tries to locate her razor blades? What potential family dynamics might be created by her mother becoming a behavioral enforcer?

In the case above, when her mom became a behavioral enforcer, Taylor found another way to self-injure. She also reacted to her mom's increased control and consequences, placing the two in a power struggle. Whitlock and Purington (2013a)

Box 9.3 Case of Taylor

Taylor has been in ongoing treatment for NSSI. She has been cutting herself in times of stress for the past two years and has the goal of reducing the behaviors. Taylor has been working on developing alternative coping methods when faced with stress or the desire to self-injure.

Taylor's mom is also participating in her treatment. She has come to several counseling sessions and is well aware of Taylor's goals for reducing the NSSI and developing different coping methods. Taylor's mom, while well-intentioned, has decided that she is going to hide all of Taylor's razor blades from now on. She feels that if she can just remove the temptation of the implements then Taylor will have one less thing to worry about. When she is stressed and can't find her usual razors, Taylor's mom assumes that Taylor will be forced to try other more healthy coping methods.

Box 9.4 Case of Taylor, continued

The next time Taylor is triggered, she can't find her razors. She rages at her mom. Feeling responsible for Taylor's safety and not liking her back talking, Taylor's mom takes away her phone and grounds her for a week for being disrespectful. Taylor retreats into her room and isolates. She finds an alternative way to self-injure by burning herself with her curling iron. Taylor tells her mom that she will continue to engage in NSSI until she gives her the phone back. Her mom is left feeling hopeless and in a struggle for power and control.

Box 9.5 Case of Taylor, continued

Taylor continues to work on her goals of simultaneously reducing her NSSI and enhancing her range of alternative coping skills. Her mom is also participating in Taylor's treatment. During one session, Taylor and her mom decide to partner together to work on her goals. Her mom has agreed not to hide Taylor's implements and Taylor has agreed to obey the house rules on back talking. They brainstorm concrete ways that they can accomplish her goals with her mom in a supportive role. One idea Taylor has is that when she is feeling triggered, she and her mom could go together on a walk or watch an episode of reality television (one of their favorite things to do together) until the urge to self-injure passes. She has found that it usually takes between 30 minutes and one hour until the urge subsides or she finds alternative ways to manage. Either of these activities seems to fit within that time frame. Taylor's mom agrees to become a partner in helping her to achieve her goals without judgment or punishment. They both agree to begin practicing this partnership this week and evaluate the outcome together.

outline specific strategies for dealing with power struggles (when a child refuses to listen to a parent or obey a known rule). Strategies include: disengaging from the struggle early, creating win-win situations, collaboration, patience and persistence, and gratitude. See the case example below for an example of collaboration.

While in Box 9.5 Taylor and her mom come to an agreement around house rules and mom's watchdog behavior, families can also suggest developing family policies around NSSI, if warranted (Purington & Whitlock, 2013; Selekman, 2009). Selekman calls these "constructive parental management strategies" (p. 114). He suggests that, when parents are disempowered by their child's chronic NSSI, they create a "policy" around what they will no longer tolerate (e.g., threats, suicidal gestures) and what they will commit to, as well (e.g., stop yelling, remain calm) in order to regain a sense of control. This type of intervention should be done when the youth is not in a heightened emotional state and should be supervised by a mental health professional. In addition, once responsibility for behaviors is maintained, the youth should be recognized for their role in positive family changes (Selekman, 2009).

Familial Reactions to NSSI

Another aspect of family NSSI treatment may include a focus on assessing and working with family reactions to NSSI. There may be a great deal of worry and tension in the home about a family member's self-injury, or there may be a general avoidance of discussing the NSSI. As mentioned earlier, all families function as systems where changes in behaviors in one person or persons usually impact the others in various ways. For example, two parents may react to NSSI behaviors in the teen in different ways. One parent might try to talk to the teen and get them to stop the behaviors (over-engagement) while the other parent might withdraw and avoid the teen completely (under-engagement). Both of these parents might then be in conflict with one another over their approach (under- or over-engagement) with their teen. To further complicate matters, siblings will also have their own responses to the situation. The teen that self-injures will also have their own reactions to each family member. The non-self-injuring member of a couple may become hyper-vigilant around the partner who self-injures. So, as you can see, family dynamics can be really complex.

Box 9.6 What Parents May Be Feeling About NSSI (Byrne & Colleagues)

- Stigma about NSSI behaviors
- Guilt
- Blame
- Anger
- Frustration
- Questioning parenting skills
    - *What do I do now?*
    - *How do I set limits and if I do, what would/do I set?*
    - *How do I maintain boundaries?*
    - *How do we have a healthy relationship moving forward?*
- That the child who self-injures, or the NSSI, has become the focus of family life

According to some studies, there are more and less helpful ways of reacting to NSSI. The following strategies are adapted from various resources (Chapman & Dixon-Gordon, 2007; Levenkron, 1998; Lifesigns Parent Fact Sheet, 2008; Toprak, Cetin, Guven, Can, & Demircan, 2011; Yip, Ngan, & Lam, 2003).

Non-Helpful Responses

- Taking away, or threatening to take away, items used to self-injure (e.g., razors) in an attempt to control the behavior. This is akin to removing a life preserver when someone is drowning.
- Showing feelings such as disgust or negative emotions
- Blaming your child for the behaviors
- Ignoring the behaviors
- Role reversing (child becomes parentified)
- Not providing safety or security for your child
- Asking to see wounds (unless you are concerned for medical reasons)
- Blaming your spouse or other family members for the NSSI or their reactions to the behaviors

In addition, there has also been some evidence that supportive families can be protective against self-injury (Chapman & Dixon-Gordon, 2007; Toprak et al., 2011; Yip et al., 2003).

Helpful Responses

- Talking with your child about their problems or concerns and worries
- Talking with your child about the NSSI
- Listening to your child without judging
- Practicing patience with your child's feelings
- Supporting your child with practical assistance (e.g., dealing with scars)
- Supporting your spouse in relation to approaching the NSSI
- Being a positive role model for conflict resolution and dealing with feelings
- Assisting your child in resolving interpersonal conflicts appropriately (e.g., with teachers, siblings, peers, partners, parents)
- Going with your child to counseling or to their doctor
- Educating yourself about NSSI
- Constructively processing your own feelings about NSSI
- Building a support system for your child and family

Education about Treatment

In addition to learning about NSSI, families may also be provided with information about treatment. This may include information about various treatment settings (e.g., outpatient therapy, family therapy, inpatient therapy) or other approaches (e.g., art therapy, DBT, CBT, PST). This may also include important information about the use of alternative behaviors that help in distracting an individual from the urge to NSSI. Chapters 7 and 8 provide information about various theoretical and practical approaches to treating NSSI. The format of information may differ based on the setting the clinician is in. For example, in a school setting the clinician may be providing this information in terms of possible referral sources for longer-term treatment; however, in an outpatient setting the mental health practitioner may be indicating what type of treatment they will be providing.

Regardless, once in treatment, families will need to be given information about which specific approach the mental health professional is using and what will be expected of them. For example, the second author was working with a 13-year-old female client who self-injured and her mother in family treatment. She described her approach to working with the NSSI behaviors (cutting on the arms) as cognitive-behavioral. CBT was described—particularly with respect to the role of thoughts influencing behaviors, and a plan for treatment was outlined early on in sessions. With the client's permission, she included the mother in a functional behavioral analysis of the NSSI. In addition, the mother was included in weekly homework assignments regarding developing positive coping skills, when appropriate. There is a sample family treatment preparation form (Box 9.7) that

Box 9.7 Questions and Reflections for Family Prior to First Therapy Appointment

1. Seek support from a licensed professional who specializes in non-suicidal self-injury (NSSI)
2. Your child's behaviors may get worse before they get better, even when in mental health treatment
3. Do not shame child for relapse in NSSI
4. Have support lined up for yourself (parent/caregiver)
5. Each individual's reasons for self-injuring, including your child's, are different, and motivations for self-injury are not always the same
6. Your child's self-injury may not be a suicide attempt
7. Do not punish or put ultimatums on NSSI behavior for your child; this has the potential to increase the frequency, severity, or secrecy of the behavior
8. Your loved one may use temporary alternatives to NSSI to stimulate a similar pain or visual response without causing bodily harm
9. Treating self-injury seems to be most effective when clients can improve their attachment security with you or someone
10. Your child will continue to feel a variety of desirable and undesirable emotions

Adapted from Teague-Palmieri and Gutierrez (2016)

includes questions and reflections that family members can use prior to their first appointment with a mental health professional. This may be a form that a clinician provides (faxes, emails, mails) to families who are requesting an appointment for a youth who self-injures.

As part of treatment, and education, mental health professionals should facilitate communication between parents and children to address the following: both of their feelings about NSSI, changes and events in the family, and individual rights and responsibilities related to treatment (Yip and colleagues, 2003). This can be helpful in working with families due to the potential that communication was problematic to begin with, as well as the intense emotions or feelings of fear or inadequacy that parents may experience about their child self-injuring. According to Rissanen, Kylm, and Laukkanen (2008), some parents feel even closer to and report positive feelings in being able to discuss NSSI with their adolescents.

Postvention

Postvention has historically been described as actions employed after a crisis, such as a suicide or suicide attempt, that may include intervention and education (Shneidman, 1981). Although postvention is a procedure commonly employed after suicide attempts, Trepal et al. (2006) adapted postvention procedures for families coping with NSSI. Postvention is not meant to be a clinical technique or treatment for NSSI. Rather, it is a series of interventions and assessments aimed at helping to increase understanding and make appropriate referrals. Thus, families may encounter postvention actions at crisis times in NSSI treatment (e.g., when NSSI is first discovered, working within the school system, during a crisis). Trepal and colleagues (2006) recommend family postvention with self-injury to include the following components: (a) information and education, (b) assessment of family system, and (c) support, referrals, and resources. A sample postvention intervention case, adapted from Trepal and colleagues, is provided below:

Postvention Intervention Case

Brenna Hageman is 13 years old. Her parents have been separated for approximately 6 months and are currently living apart. Brenna is in the 7th grade at Raymond Middle School. Brenna's mom recently discovered that she is engaging in NSSI when she walked in on her in the bathroom cutting herself with a razor blade over the sink. When mom walked in, Brenna ran out of the room and slammed her door, crying. She has refused to talk to her mom about the incident. Brenna's mom has made an appointment with her school counselor. The school counselor employs the following NSSI postvention actions with Ms. Hageman:

I. **Information and Education:** The school counselor asks Ms. Hageman, "Tell me what you know about self-injury?" Ms. Hageman replies that she does not know much, but she has always thought that it means that people are "crazy" and "suicidal" when they harm themselves. The school counselor employs recommended educational aspects about NSSI such as facts about age of onset, treatment, and prognosis. The school counselor also takes care to employ a no-blame approach where the behaviors are externalized so that neither Brenna nor Ms. Hageman is "the problem." The school counselor attends to Ms. Hageman's feelings about the NSSI (processing her guilt, disconnection, and concern). The school counselor also dispels NSSI myths (e.g., that NSSI and suicide are synonymous).

II. **Assessment of Family System:** The school counselor briefly assesses the family system. She learns that Brenna is an only child and that her parents have recently separated. In fact, Brenna's father moved into his own apartment approximately 6 months ago, and she has recently been spending every other weekend with him there. The school counselor asks Ms. Hageman about her relationship and communication with Mr. Hageman and learns that, prior to the separation, they had not had a happy marriage for quite some time. Ms. Hageman reports that the relationship is strained but not overtly conflictual. The school counselor takes steps to assist Ms. Hageman in talking to Mr. Hageman about Brenna's NSSI. In addition to exploring the family system, the school counselor may want to consider exploring the communication patterns of the family. For example, if the marital relationship was strained, how was communication prior to separation? Was Brenna involved in the communication, and what might she be informed of regarding the separation at this point? While Brenna refuses to talk with mom about the NSSI, how has mom attempted to approach her, if at all (e.g., from an authoritarian position, one of power, or avoidance) regarding the NSSI specifically? Has the presence of NSSI altered the family dynamics and individual relationships, and if so, how?

III. **Support, Referrals, and Resources:** The school counselor lets Ms. Hageman know that she is not alone and that they have a number of children and families in the school currently engaged in treatment for their NSSI. They provide Ms. Hageman with a list of individual and family mental health professionals in the local community who they have referred families to before. The school counselor takes care to instill hope and promises to follow up with both Brenna (at school the next day) and Ms. Hageman (at the end of the week to confirm that she was able to connect with the referrals and make an appointment).

Support and Resources for Families

Another important aspect of family treatment for NSSI is the enhancement and development of support and resources. While families may feel alone in their concerns about their child who is self-injuring, there are some sources of support out there, and it is important that families know how to access them easily.

It is also very important that family members take care of themselves. Have you ever been on a plane when the flight attendants are describing the safety procedures?

Box 9.8 Sources of Support for Families

Call the school counselor
Gain resources to take your child to a mental health professional
Seek support for yourself from a mental health professional
Call your child's pediatrician
Contact your primary care physician
Call a friend or partner to process your feelings

They always say, put the oxygen mask on yourself before putting one on your child. The same is true in this situation. Families will be better equipped to help their family members if they take care of themselves. There are resources available for families, particularly parents and legal guardians, about NSSI. These include, but are not limited to:

Books

Some of these books may be triggering to read for those who self-injure. However, they are easily accessible for family members.

Alderman, T. (1997). *The scarred soul: Understanding & ending self-inflicted violence.* Oakland: New Harbinger.
Gratz, K. L., & Chapman, A. L. (2009). *Freedom from self-harm: Overcoming self-injury with skills from DBT and other treatments.* Oakland: New Harbinger.
Hollander, M. (2008). *Helping teens who cut: Understanding and ending self-injury.* New York: The Guilford Press (*This is a book specifically for parents).
Khemlani-Patel, S., McVey-Noble, M., & Neziroglu, F. (2006). *When your child is cutting: A parent's guide to helping children overcome self-injury.* Oakland, CA: New Harbinger Publications.
Martin, G., Hasking, P., Swannell, S., & McAllister, M. (2013). *Seeking solutions to self-injury: A guide for parents and families.* Brisbane, Australia: Child and Adolescent Psychiatry, The University of Queensland.
Strong, M. (1998). *A bright red scream: Self-mutilation and the language of pain.* New York: Penguin.

Fiction Books

Levenkron, S. (1997). *The luckiest girl in the world.* New York: Penguin.
McCormick, P. (2002). *Cut.* New York: Scholastic.

Websites

Moyer, Haberstroh, and Marbach (2008) report that information related to NSSI is rampantly found online and that adolescents are fierce consumers of these websites and online forums. They recommend that websites be reviewed in their entirety for content, authorship/support, and for potentially triggering material. In addition, Haberstroh and Moyer (2012) report that some clients seek online support as a supplement to mental health treatment. Thus, it is recommended that parents also monitor their children's Internet use related to NSSI.

Non-Suicidal Self-Injury: When the Solution Becomes the Problem
http://www.nssiresource.com/#!parents/c66t
This site contains information on NSSI and its effects as presented on various forms of social media.

The Cornell Research Program on Self-Injury and Recovery
http://www.selfinjury.bctr.cornell.edu/resources.html
The website provides extensive resources for parents and other caregivers, friends, mental health service providers, and other professionals. There is information and resources on NSSI in the schools, treatments, dispelling myths, and helpful websites, videos, and books. The site also contains an excellent section where specific resources regarding parenting strategies are offered.

Self-Injury Outreach and Support—Parent's Page
http://www.sioutreach.org/learn/parents
This non-profit outreach group provides information and resources. This parent's page contains information on treatments, approaches to discussing self-injury, and recommended readings and other resources.

S.A.F.E. ALTERNATIVES
http://www.selfinjury.com
The website presents information about treatment approaches, professional networks, and other educational resources to help people end self-injurious behavior.

Adolescent Self-Injury Foundation
http://www.adolescentselfinjuryfoundation.com/page7
This non-profit organization aims to offer hope in the recovery process for adolescents and young adults who self-injure and their families. The site has facts and information about self-injury, including misconceptions and warning signs, as well as information for parents and friends of those who self-injure.

Conclusion

In summary, family support can be a very important part of NSSI treatment. However, families may experience a lack of information regarding both NSSI and what to expect in treatment. It is important to remember that those who self-injure should not be reduced to labels, nor should NSSI be the sole focus of the family. These clients still need to be supported in their growth and development of other life domains and tasks (friendship, love, education, spirituality, family, career) (Yip, 2006). The information presented in this chapter hopes to alleviate some of these concerns and better prepare families for the treatment journey.

References

Berg, R., Hendricks, B., & Bradley, L. (2009). Counseling suicidal adolescents within family systems: Ethical issues. *The Family Journal: Counseling and Therapy for Couples and Families, 17*(1), 64–68. doi: 10.1177/1066480708328601

Byrne, S., Morgan, S., Fitzpatrick, C., Boylan, C., Crowley, S., Gahan, H., Howley, J., Staunton, D., & Guerin, S. (2008). Deliberate self-harm in children and adolescents: A qualitative study exploring the needs of parents and carers. *Clinical Child Psychology and Psychiatry, 13*(4), 493–504. doi: 10.1177/1359104508096765

Chapman, A. L., & Dixon-Gordon, K. L. (2007). Emotional antecedents and consequences of deliberate self harm and suicide attempts. *Suicide and Life-Threatening Behavior, 37*, 543–552.

Conterio, K., Lader, W., & Bloom, J. K. (1998). *Bodily harm: The break-through healing program for self-injurers*. New York: Hyperion.

Haberstroh, S., & Moyer, M. (2012). Exploring an online self-injury support group: Perspectives from group members. *The Journal for Specialists in Group Work, 37*(2), 113–132. doi: 10.1080/01933922.2011.646088

Hoffman, R. M., Hinkle, M. G., & Kress, V. E. (2010). The use of letter writing in family therapy for adolescent non-suicidal self-injurious behavior. *The Family Journal, 18*, 24–30.

Kettlewell, C. (2000). *Skin game: A memoir*. New York: St. Martin's Press.

Klonsky, E. D., Muehlenkamp, J. J., Lewis, S. P., & Walsh, B. (2011). *Nonsuicidal self-injury: Advances in psychotherapy evidence-based practice*. Cambridge, MA: Hogrefe.

Levenkron, S. (1998). *Cutting: Understanding and over-coming self-mutilation*. New York, NY: W. W. Norton & Company.

Lifesigns Parent Fact Sheet (2008). Retrieved from http://www.berkeley87.org/vimages/shared/vnews/stories/5395b9884ba4c/Self%20Injury%20factsheet-parents-v4.pdf

Martin, J., Bureau, J., Cloutier, P., & Lafontaine, M. (2011). A comparison of invalidating family environment characteristics between university students engaging in self-injurious thoughts & actions and non-self-injuring university students. *Journal of Youth Adolescence, 40*, 1477–1488.

Moyer, M., Haberstroh, S., & Marbach, C. (2008). Self-injurious behaviors on the net: A survey of resources for school counselors. *Professional School Counseling, 11*(5), 277–284.

Purington, M., & Whitlock, J. (2013). *Family policies: Safety concerns and contracts*. The Practical Matters series, Cornell Research Program on Self-Injury and Recovery. Ithaca, NY: Cornell University.

Rissanen, M. L., Kylm, J. P. O., & Laukkanen, E. R. (2008). Parental conceptions of self-mutilation among Finnish adolescents. *Journal of Psychiatric & Mental Health Nursing, 15*(3), 212–218. doi: 10.1111/j.1365-2850.2007.01214.x

Selekman, M. D. (2009). *The adolescent & young adult self-harming treatment manual: A collaborative strengths-based brief therapy approach*. New York: W. W. Norton & Company.

Shneidman, E. S. (1981). Postvention: The care of the bereaved. *Suicide and Life-Threatening Behavior, 11*, 349–359.

Suyemoto, K. L. (1998). The functions of self-mutilation. *Clinical Psychology Review, 18*(5), 531–554.

Teague-Palmieri, E. B., & Gutierrez, D. (2016). Healing together: Family therapy resources and strategies for increasing attachment security in individuals engaging in nonsuicidal self-injury. *The Family Journal: Counseling and Therapy for Couples and Families, 24*(2), 157–163. doi: 10.1177/1066480716628629

Toprak, S., Cetin, I., Guven, T., Can, G., & Demircan, C. (2011). Self-harm, suicidal ideation and suicide attempts among college students. *Psychiatry Research, 187*(1–2), 140–144.

Trepal, H., Wester, K., & MacDonald, C. (2006). Self-injury and postvention: Responding to the family in crisis. *The Family Journal: Counseling and Therapy for Couples and Families, 14*, 342–348.

Walsh, B. W., & Rosen, P. M. (1988). *Self-mutilation: Theory, research, and treatment*. New York: Guilford.

Whitlock, J., & Purington, M. (2013a). *Dealing with power struggles*. The Practical Matters series, Cornell Research Program on Self-Injury and Recovery. Ithaca, NY: Cornell University.

Whitlock, J., & Purington, M. (2013b). *Respectful curiosity*. The Practical Matters series, Cornell Research Program on Self-Injury and Recovery. Ithaca, NY: Cornell University.

Yip, K. (2005). A multi-dimensional perspective of adolescents' self-cutting. *Child and Adolescent Mental Health, 10*, 80–86.

Yip, K. (2006). A strengths perspective in working with an adolescent with self-cutting behaviors. *Child and Adolescent Social Work Journal, 23*(2), 134–146. doi: 10.1007/s10560-005-0043-4

Yip, K., Ngan, M., & Lam, I. (2003). A qualitative study of parental influence on and response to adolescents' self-cutting in Hong Kong. *Families in Society, 84*(3), 405–416.

ten
Supervision Issues

The supervision of mental health professionals working with clients who self-injure is integral to supporting both clinician development and client care. In this chapter, supervision will be described and recommendations and guidelines for supervisors who work with supervisees counseling clients who engage in NSSI will be outlined.

Supervisees are mental health professionals who are considered to be "in training" for independent practice. These clinicians can include students in training programs who see clients as a part of their practicum or internship requirements or pre-licensed counselors who are obtaining supervised clinical hours towards their independent licensure. While there are important developmental differences between a pre- and post-degree clinician-in-training, a stable component is the active presence of a clinical supervisor. This person, while supervising at the pre- or post-degree level, maintains the ultimate responsibility for the welfare of the clients who are under the clinician-in-training's care. Thus, it is paramount that supervisors have a clear understanding of specific issues related to clients who self-injure in order to best supervise and guide their supervisees in their work.

Imagine this: You are a clinical supervisor who works in a large community mental health center. You have a number of new supervisees who lack experience working with actual clients; particularly those with challenging concerns such as NSSI. Given the high rates of self-injury, it is very likely that your supervisees will be on the front lines of working with clients who engage in these behaviors. How will you approach this issue? What developmental, clinical, ethical, and legal concerns will you consider? How will you best prepare your supervisees for this work?

What Is *Supervision*?

Supervision is "an intervention provided by a more senior member of a profession to a more junior colleague or colleagues who typically (but not always) are members of the same profession. This relationship is evaluative and hierarchical, extends over time, and has the simultaneous purposes of enhancing the professional functioning of the more junior person(s); monitoring the quality of professional services offered to the clients that she, he, or they see; and serving as a gatekeeper for the profession the supervisee seeks to enter" (Bernard & Goodyear, 2014, p. 9). Thus, supervision has clinical, administrative, and evaluative functions.

Supervisors have different approaches to supervision, and these often include developmental, theoretical, and role-based components (Bernard & Goodyear, 2014). As you can see in Figure 10.1, supervisors are charged with a lot of responsibility. They have to manage all of this while keeping in mind the counselor's stage of development and, of course, paying acute attention to monitoring client care. The circle represents the supervisor's core foci (attending to client care, facilitating counselor development, managing administrative functions, and counselor evaluation). These core components rotate in the manner in which they are prioritized from day to day in supervision. While all are important, the supervisor must prioritize and focus on one area or another at different times.

FIGURE 10.1. Simultaneous roles and functions of supervision

Recommendations for Supervisors

The following sections contain specific recommendations for supervisors, adapted from the supervision literature (e.g., Bernard & Goodyear, 2014; Boie & Lopez, 2011; Hoffman & Kress, 2008), who work with supervisees counseling clients who self-injure across treatment settings. These recommendations include: 1) supervisor competence with NSSI, 2) utilizing a model of supervision, 3) supervisee NSSI education, 3) risk management, 4) differences in counseling settings, and 5) managing personal reactions. Each will be considered below.

Supervisor NSSI Competence

It has been recommended that in order for supervisors to work with supervisees who are working with clients who self-injure, they must first assess their own competence and comfort with NSSI (Hoffman & Kress, 2008). Box 10.1 provides some

Box 10.1 Reflecting Back: Supervisor Reflection Questions About NSSI Competence

If you are currently a supervisor, think back to your time spent as a supervisee. Ask yourself the following:

- What strengths did your supervisor possess that helped you to become an effective clinician?
- What do you model after your supervisor/s and what do you do differently and why?

Now, think about your experience with clients who self-injure . . .

- Do you remember your first client who self-injured? If you've never worked with a client who self-injured, consider another client who engaged in a behavior that you were uncertain of, or unfamiliar with.
- How did you learn to work with these behaviors?
- Was experience your best teacher?
- Did you seek supervision or continuing education? What was helpful about each?
- What is your comfort level in working with clients who self-injure?

Make an accurate assessment of your preparation to work with supervisees around NSSI.

initial reflection questions that supervisors can use to determine their own experience, competence, preparation, and comfort with NSSI. If there are concerns about any area, supervisors should seek out their own supervision, peer consultation, or refer supervisees to a more appropriate supervisor (Hoffman & Kress, 2008).

Utilizing a Model of Supervision

As stated earlier, supervisors are called on to attend to many moving parts in supervision, including both supervisee development and client care. When approaching any type of supervision relationship, it is important for supervisors to practice from a model that helps them structure supervision goals and outcomes. Supervisors also utilize models to help them assess their supervisees' needs as well as appropriate supervision responses. Much like counseling theories, there are many models and approaches to clinical supervision. Various models focus on supervisee development, specific theoretical approaches, or roles that the supervisor may operate from. One supervision model, the Discrimination Model (a process model; Bernard, 1979) will be explored in detail below. This model was chosen for its practical utility and framework for demonstrating supervision aspects related to NSSI.

The Discrimination Model

Bernard (1979) developed the Discrimination Model to provide a template for supervisors to organize their choices in supervision. The model is fairly simple to use. It contains 3 roles (*Teacher, Counselor, Consultant*) and 3 foci for supervision (Intervention, Conceptualization, Personalization). The *Teacher* role is assumed for giving specific instruction, feedback, or modeling, The *Counselor* role is utilized when the supervisor wants to focus on the supervisee's internal processing and encourage reflective processing. Finally, the *Consultant* role is used to move into more of a peer-like stance where the supervisor encourages the supervisee to come up with their own solutions (Bernard & Goodyear, 2014, p. 52). The three foci include the following focus areas that supervisors can use to narrow their sessions to a particular focus area. Specifically, the Intervention focus includes the supervisee's actual skills observed in counseling sessions. The Conceptualization focus includes the way the supervisee conceptualizes cases or the interventions they have chosen. Finally, the Personalization focus includes the supervisee's balance between objectivity and viewing the client through their own lens of their experiences and interpretations. Thus, at any time during a supervision session, the supervisor might choose to respond in one of 9 ways. Table 10.1 provides an illustration of the model in practice (adapted from Bernard & Goodyear, 2014).

Supervisors who use the Discrimination Model can assess particular areas where their supervisees are struggling (such as conducting an NSSI assessment

TABLE 10.1. Discrimination Model in Supervision Practice

Focus of Supervision	Teacher	Counselor	Consultant
Intervention	Supervisor teaches the supervisee specifics about NSSI assessment using DBT's chain analysis and models this in session	Supervisor works with supervisee to practice challenging clients so that supervisee is comfortable with this skill	Supervisor helps to brainstorm new techniques to use with a client
Conceptualization	Supervisor watches a video of supervisee doing an NSSI assessment with a client and provides feedback	Supervisor works with supervisee to process conflicting feelings about referring a client	Supervisor helps to generate treatment referral options
Personalization	Supervisor teaches the supervisee to self-identify feelings that come up for them in session with a particular client	Supervisor helps to process the supervisee's strong interpersonal reactions to their client	Supervisor discusses potential solutions for strong interpersonal reactions to clients

Adapted from Bernard and Goodyear (2014)

or having a strong reaction to a client). Then, the supervisor can decide which approach they want to take based on the focus needed in session. For example, if the supervisee is uncertain how to conduct an NSSI assessment, the supervisor would take a Teaching role with a focus on intervention to help the supervisee select an appropriate NSSI assessment tool, learn how to ask the questions, and understand how to implement the assessment. However, if the supervisee had a strong personal reaction of disgust to the client, shocked that his client would engage in such self-harm behavior, then the supervisor may take a Counselor role that starts with a personalization focus to explore the supervisee's personal reactions to NSSI and to his client, but then may also shift to a Consultant or Teacher role with a conceptualization focus to work with the supervisee to better understand the purpose of motives behind NSSI for the client.

The Discrimination Model is particularly useful for newer supervisors who have trouble shifting from the counseling role to the supervisor stance. It provides a very concrete map for making decisions in supervision sessions. Keep in mind that there are more supervision models to help supervisors work with clinicians other than the Discrimination Model; however, the Discrimination Model is a widely used and known model for supervision.

Supervisee Education on NSSI

Regardless of the supervision model utilized, education is always an important aspect of supervision. In a review of studies on the topic, McHale and Felton (2010) found that the lack of education and training on NSSI was directly related to negative attitudes towards these behaviors. It is suggested that specific education on the topic of NSSI plays a role in effective clinical work (Zila & Kiselica, 2001). Further, De Stefano, Atkins, Nelson Noble, and Heath (2012) interviewed counselors in training who had worked with at least one client who self-injured. The counselors reported that they found NSSI behaviors to be challenging, including provoking strong reactions in themselves, increasing their concerns about ethical and legal issues, and questioning their own competence to work with clients who engaged in self-injury. These same counselors constructed internal models of NSSI, including how best to conceptualize and treat these behaviors. They felt mixed support from their supervisors in terms of learning how to manage their own emotions, truly understanding these behaviors, and navigating the best ways to work with clients who self-injure (DeStefano et al., 2012).

Thus, training and education are important precursors for both supervisees and supervisors who work with clients who self-injure. DeStefano and colleagues (2012) found that most of the counselors in their study fell back on the relationship when working with clients (i.e., they used empathy—or tried to understand and relate to their clients, providing a safe space to voice concerns) rather than using specific skills, techniques, or strategies when working with clients who self-injured. Basic knowledge of NSSI can include theories of the development and maintenance of the behaviors, as well as assessment issues, types of NSSI, and specific types of treatments that have been shown to be effective.

Given that the client's cultural background can also play an important role related to NSSI (Wester & Trepal, 2015), supervisors are encouraged to explore this topic, as well. For example, supervisors could encourage supervisees to learn about various cultural strengths (e.g., close family and community relationships) and concerns (e.g., keloid scarring) related to a teenage African American client.

Box 10.2 Supervisor Strategies for NSSI Education

- Role-plays where supervisors model and demonstrate NSSI assessment
- Guest speakers
- Viewing of social media sites related to NSSI and other media (movies, videos)
- Workshops on suicide assessment, diagnosis, and specific treatment modalities (e.g., DBT)
- Consider the role of the client's cultural background in case conceptualization and treatment planning

Supervisors should directly bring up NSSI issues in supervision as well as encourage supervisees to conduct their own research on the topic (Hoffman & Kress, 2008).

Distinguishing Between NSSI and Suicide

Hoffman and Kress (2008) stress that one important distinction related to assessment that supervisors must make sure that their supervisees are aware of is that between NSSI behaviors and suicide. Because the relationship between these two behaviors is complex, supervisors are encouraged to monitor their supervisees' abilities and skills with suicide assessment. Understandably, new clinicians are often insecure about what they would do if a client presents with suicidal ideation; and with limited knowledge about NSSI, new clinicians may make the mistake of assuming NSSI is suicidal behavior. Mental health professional training programs typically cover general information about suicide assessment; however, Juhnke (1994) proposes that training supervisees in suicide assessment should include education and practice in the assessment of risk factors, the ability to develop a clear and comprehensive case conceptualization to present for consultative purposes, and the capacity to propose next step interventions to minimize client safety risks. Of course, risk factors for suicide have been found to include NSSI behaviors; yet NSSI is not a typical topic in training programs at this point.

Finally, it is important to mention continuing education related to new and evolving NSSI assessment and treatment methods. As codes of ethics and standards of practice evolve, both supervisors and supervisees need to stay abreast of current developments in the field. Consider that even 10 years ago the definition of NSSI was still mixed with behaviors such as substance abuse, overdosing, and parasuicide. Additionally, NSSI was not even under consideration for its own diagnostic category, but was simply a symptom within the diagnostic criteria for Borderline Personality Disorder. Therefore, knowledge of NSSI (along with other clinical symptoms) can change fast, resulting in a need for supervisors and clinicians to stay abreast of the research.

Box 10.3 Strategies for Risk Assessment

- Role-play both suicide and risk assessments
- Give supervisees a quiz on mandatory questions to be asked during risk assessments
- Have supervisees write out protocols for risk assessment to verify understanding
- Have supervisees write out the proper emergency contact procedure for the setting in which they work
- Live observation of supervisees doing risk assessment, if possible

Risk Management

Risk management is an important consideration for supervisors. For example, as discussed in Chapter 5, diagnostic issues involving NSSI are complex. Supervisors are ultimately responsible for the clients that their supervisees are seeing; thus, it is important that they maintain an appropriate level of oversight regarding assessment and risk management issues as they relate to clients who self-injure. Hoffman and Kress (2008) suggest that supervisors keep a close eye on supervisees' assessment skills related to NSSI. High-risk behaviors may include safety concerns about the actual self-injury (e.g., the client typically self-injures while they are incapacitated due to substance use or rage) or more practical concerns about self-injury methods (e.g., the client reuses razor blades through multiple episodes of self-injury without cleaning them or shares instruments with others who also self-injure). Supervisors need to help supervisees (or new clinicians) understand NSSI behaviors that are considered high risk or cause major tissue damage, that could result in accidental death or harm to self, versus NSSI behaviors that are considered more minor or low risk, as these assessments and determinations can impact when confidentiality needs to be breached (see more information on this in Chapter 6).

Another important area of risk management is wound care. Clients who do not practice adequate wound care, or those who self-injure repeatedly without allowing wounds to heal, may be at higher risk for primary and secondary infections, thus requiring direct medical intervention.

Supervisors should prepare supervisees to do a thoughtful and detailed risk assessment (see Chapter 4 for more information on intake and NSSI assessments), including gathering pertinent information on NSSI methods used, frequency, duration, and accompanying thoughts. This is where approaching a supervision session with a supervisee from the Teacher role to provide education on NSSI assessments and guide supervisees through this process is important, as supervisees run the risk of developing an underreactive (e.g., resulting in the possibility of increased suicide risk or potential for medical concerns related to NSSI) or overreactive stance (e.g., rushing clients to the hospital for an evaluation prior to thorough assessment; Hoffman & Kress, 2008). It may also be advisable to co-construct a plan for supervisees that provides structure for the risk assessment (Hoffman & Kress, 2008). The plan would obviously change based on setting but could include such items as 1) supervisee's making note of their immediate reactions to the client's NSSI, 2) concrete choices for what to do next in the session (e.g., immediately contact the supervisor to assist in risk assessment, follow a certain assessment protocol), and 3) specific choices based on the assessment (e.g., who to contact regarding hospitalization, what to do if the client is a minor) (Hoffman & Kress, 2008).

Since supervisors are simultaneously responsible for monitoring their supervisees' clinical development and client care, it is recommended that they gather as much direct data about their supervisees' work with clients as possible (Hoffman

& Kress, 2008). The most common data that supervisors receive from supervisees is what is termed "self-report." Self-report typically equates to a supervisee simply describing to the supervisor what happened. This type of data is not the most reliable, as it is filtered through the supervisee's lens, resulting in deliberately or inadvertently leaving out important information. For example, the clinician may have asked a question such as "Have you ever wanted to harm yourself?" to which the client says "yes." The clinician appropriately follows up with a question regarding the recency of the behavior, such as "When was the last time you wanted to harm yourself?" And the client indicates "four months ago." At this point in the session, the clinician deems that self-harm, or NSSI, is no longer a concern for the client and moves on with the rest of the typical intake. Therefore, since she felt that she conducted this assessment appropriately, she may not report this to her supervisor, when, in fact, more questions need to be asked about actual intentions of the behavior, consequences of the behavior, and follow-through of thoughts of wanting to self-harm. Thus, reliance on self-report is not always the most adequate method in supervision, particularly to assist the supervisor in understanding and walking supervisees through risk assessment.

In addition, due to their inexperience, supervisees may miss pertinent items or misinterpret their clients' actions or words in a session. An example of this may be that a client, who is maintaining eye contact with a clinician throughout an intake, leans back, looks away, and mumbles "no" to the suicide or self-harm question. The discrepancy between the client's verbal response and nonverbal behaviors would be an important aspect to follow up on, yet it might be missed by a neophyte clinician, who would inadvertently not report it in supervision. Thus, supervisors are reminded to gather additional data that comes in the form of direct observation of counseling sessions, review of case notes and treatment plans, and regular review of transcripts and recordings of sessions.

A final important aspect of risk management is documentation. As mentioned in Chapter 6, documentation, such as case notes, is extremely important for tracking client progress and monitoring care. Supervision notes function in much the same manner. Supervisors document their sessions with their supervisees and record information on both counselor development and client care recommendations. Following the risk management recommendations detailed above, supervisors are cautioned to document risk management education as well as supervisee directives and their resulting actions in supervision session notes.

Counseling Setting

Another important supervision consideration is the setting within which the supervisee's counseling is taking place. For example, given the statistics on NSSI behaviors, clinicians who work in schools at all levels (elementary, middle, and high school) should all have specific and general knowledge of NSSI related to developmental issues. In addition, clinicians-in-training who work in college settings are also likely to encounter clients who engage in these behaviors. Finally, clinicians-in-training who work in residential treatment and hospital settings are also likely to work with clients who self-injure, while these clients will also exhibit a myriad of other severe comorbid symptoms and diagnoses, as well. Each of these treatment settings has specific parameters (including ethical and procedural implications for intervening and/or working with students and clients who self-injure). Thus, it is paramount that clinical supervisors be aware of these parameters. Finally, supervisors are encouraged to verify that their supervisees are aware of the crisis procedures of their particular setting—well in advance of the first session—because you can't always plan for a crisis in the settings in which they work. Supervisors are encouraged to role-play potential crisis situations (Hoffman & Kress, 2008), an example of entering the supervision session from a Teacher role.

Managing Personal Reactions

As mentioned earlier, supervisors and supervisees may both have strong personal reactions to clients who self-injure. It has been observed that other health professionals, such as nurses, have reactions to NSSI that include guilt, anxiety, helplessness, frustration, and confusion about professional boundaries (Rayner, Allen, & Johnson, 2005). A recent study of counselors-in-training at the predegree level found that they indeed had negative reactions to clients who self-injured (DeStefano et al., 2012). The way that supervisees react to their clients who self-injure may also influence their clinical decision making in positive or negative ways. For example, consider a supervisee who experiences feeling angry with their client who self-injures because they interpret the behavior as manipulative. The supervisee may then demonstrate a lack of empathy for the client and their concerns. These feelings may also influence how the supervisee proceeds in the session (e.g., what dynamics they pay attention to). On the other hand, consider a supervisee who feels helpless with a particular client who self-injures. These feelings may undermine the supervisee's confidence with assessment and/or treatment interventions.

Now consider that a supervisor has a strong reaction to NSSI behaviors. This can result in teaching or modeling for the supervisee "appropriate" (or really inappropriate) behaviors that they may in turn take back into session when working with a client. Thus, managing personal reactions with clients who self-injure is very important, and supervisors can help model this aspect (Hoffman & Kress, 2008). The supervisory alliance, or the working relationship between the supervisor and supervisee, is an especially critical component of supervision. The strength of this alliance can support supervisee exploration of conflicting feelings (e.g., empathy and shock/judgment) regarding NSSI. So, just as the therapeutic relationship is one of the most important factors in client outcomes, this is similar at the supervision level, as well.

Interpersonal Process Recall

Interpersonal Process Recall (IPR; Kagan, 1980) is one effective method for encouraging meta-cognitive processing of internal reactions in counseling sessions. This type of supervision intervention can help supervisees to explore their personal reactions carefully. IPR is conducted by bringing in a video- or an audio-recorded counseling session to supervision, and supervisors and supervisees watch/listen to various portions of the recording. In IPR, supervisors take on the consultant role and supervisees get to re-experience the session in a supportive context. Ideally, supervisors should review the recorded session for segments that are interpersonal (i.e., something might be happening in the supervisee's mind) or they can ask the supervisee to choose the segment to be viewed. When watching/listening to the session, the supervisor asks specific questions for the supervisee to reflect on and consider. Note the following example:

> Supervisee and supervisor watch a portion of a recorded counseling session with a client who has recently disclosed that they are engaging in NSSI behaviors. The supervisor chooses to stop the recording after the client's initial disclosure, and the following occurs:
>
> *Supervisor:* So, can you tell me a little bit about what was going on in your mind when the client disclosed their self-injury?
>
> *Supervisee:* I don't know! All I can remember is that my mind was racing, racing, racing. I kept jumping ahead to thinking about things like risk assessment and what questions I might need to ask her. I also wondered how long she had been self-injuring and if she had told anyone else about it. I was also curious about where she was self-injuring and even how she was self-injuring.
>
> *Supervisor:* How do you think she would have reacted if you said that?
>
> *Supervisee:* I'm not sure. I didn't want to come across as prying or too interested because I didn't want to shut her down after such an important disclosure.
>
> *Supervisor:* What do you think she wanted from you?
>
> *Supervisee:* Probably, she just wanted to tell someone and not have to worry about their reaction.
>
> *Supervisor:* What do you wish you had said to her?
>
> *Supervisee:* I wish that I had shared how I felt that she had taken the risk to share the fact that she was self-injuring with me. It was an important disclosure.

In the excerpt above, the supervisee is provided with a place to face their fears about the client's self-disclosure related to NSSI behaviors. The supervisor is careful to stick with questions that are close to the topic and avoids veering into a teaching role related to NSSI assessment (which might have been very easy or tempting to do!). IPR can be a powerful tool to help supervisees understand their internal process (i.e., reactions, thoughts, feelings), but should obviously not be used as the sole method of supervision. For example, in this case, the supervisor probably does at some later point need to enter the teaching role of supervision and assess their supervisee's knowledge and skills related to NSSI assessment and risk management. However, IPR may serve as a useful tool to explore interpersonal dynamics in the session that the supervisee may not have been aware of.

In the next example, the supervisee has decided to stop the recording that they are viewing:

Supervisee: In that moment *[on the recording]*, after she told me about the first time that she burned her stomach with the iron, I was really sweating.
Supervisor: Did it remind you of anything?
Supervisee: It reminded me of a time when I burned myself on a stove and how painful that was. Although it was unintentional, I can still remember the sting.
Supervisor: How did that make you feel about her?
Supervisee: It made me feel sorry for her. The feeling was one of pity, I guess.

Again, the supervisor's stance is more reflective and facilitative than educational or corrective. The supervisee had the opportunity to reflect on a portion of the counseling session that they had a reaction to, as well. This IPR exchange activity is one example of a way in which supervisors can encourage supervisees to explore their own feelings and reactions and then how those might be impacting their relationships with their clients in session.

Self-Care

An important yet often neglected concept is that of self-care. All too often new supervisees feel pressured to take on more clients, or increasingly difficult cases,

Box 10.4 Supervision Strategies for Managing Interpersonal Reactions

- Utilize Interpersonal Process Recall (IPR)
- Explore supervisee-client boundary issues
- Encourage supervisees to reflect on personal reactions to NSSI through journaling

without the corresponding time being made to engage in self-care. Clinician burnout, compassion fatigue, and impairment are all too real dangers of the profession (Lawson & Venart, 2005). Clinicians report that clients who self-injure are among some of their most stressful cases, so supervisors should take note of the need to emphasize self-care. As described in detail in the introductory section of this book, wellness has been conceptualized across models in a holistic manner to include the following 6 domains: a) Cognition, b) Emotion and Coping, c) Physical, d) Social, e) Cultural and Occupational Context, and f) Spiritual (Granello, 2012; Hettler, 1980; Myers & Sweeney, 2005; Witmer & Sweeney, 1991). When there is a positive change in wellness, in any one of these domains, it has been proposed that overall wellness increases (Myers, Sweeney, & Witmer, 2000). Thus, helping supervisees to specifically focus on one wellness domain at a time can lead to both a decrease in the potential for burnout and an increase in their overall wellness and fortitude when working with clients (Lenz & Smith, 2010).

Supervisors are wise to help facilitate the exploration of cognitive, physical, emotional, and spiritual self-care strategies in supervision. Lenz and Smith (2010) suggest that supervisors intentionally include wellness as a construct in supervision. They offer a 4-phase model called the Wellness Model of Supervision (WELMS). This model includes *wellness education*, *assessment*, *planning*, and *evaluation* that can continuously be applied in supervision as new goals are set and reached (Lenz & Smith, 2010). According to their model, supervisors should make the enhancement of wellness a priority in supervision. Supervisees can be encouraged to learn about all aspects and domains of wellness (wellness education). They can then be guided through an appraisal (assessment) of their personal wellness using either formal or informal tools. Supervisees can research each of the wellness domains identified above and define how they personally interpret them to be relevant to their lives. Once supervisees identify areas for growth and develop personal wellness goals (planning), the supervisor can assist them in constructing a developmental plan. The following worksheet, 10.A, can be adapted to help supervisees who work with NSSI to focus on wellness goals in supervision. You can use Worksheet 10.A in supervision with a supervisee. Box 10.5 provides an example of how it might be completed. For example, if a supervisee identifies that they are dissatisfied with their cultural identity, or have a lack of feeling connected to their culture, they could work on a wellness plan to find concrete ways to increase their satisfaction (e.g., attend cultural events, talk with family members about their cultural background, read books by an author from their cultural background). If supervisees are able to incrementally achieve these goals, they may feel a greater sense of understanding and connection to their clients' cultural concerns (Lenz & Smith, 2010, p. 236). Finally, supervisors and supervisees can continuously co-evaluate the wellness plan as goals are achieved, revisited, or when new situations emerge.

SAMPLE DEVELOPMENTAL WELLNESS PLAN

(adapted from Lenz & Smith, 2010)

1. **Emotions and coping:** (please indicate your current experience of stress and emotion, including how you may be regulating your stress and emotion)

2. **Satisfaction:** (list one or more of the emotions, stress, and/or coping mechanisms used in the question above)

Current satisfaction with: ________________

Not satisfied at all									Very satisfied
1	2	3	4	5	6	7	8	9	10

Current satisfaction with: ________________

Not satisfied at all									Very satisfied
1	2	3	4	5	6	7	8	9	10

3. **Changing this may effect self and work with my clients in the following ways:** (please indicate what will occur if you alter anything related to emotion, stress, and coping listed above).

4. **Intervention:** (please indicate what you will do to alter what you are not satisfied with above)

   Objective:
   Strategies:

5. **I will know when I have made some progress when:**

Box 10.5 Sample Developmental Wellness Plan

(adapted from Lenz & Smith, 2010)

1. **Emotions and coping:** (please indicate your current experience of stress and emotion, including how you may be regulating your stress and emotion)

I am feeling overwhelmed and stressed. Lack knowledge in NSSI. NSSI is disgusting and freaks me out. I have talked with my supervisor about it, and have made sure to decompress after the session with my client.

2. **Satisfaction:** (list one or more of the emotions, stress, and/or coping mechanisms used in the question above)

Current satisfaction with: _disgust_

Not satisfied at all									Very satisfied
1	2X	3	4	5	6	7	8	9	10

Current satisfaction with: _coping attempts_

Not satisfied at all									Very satisfied
1	2	3	4	5X	6	7	8	9	10

3. **Changing any of the above may affect self and work with my clients in the following ways:** (please indicate what will occur if you alter anything related to emotion, stress, and coping listed above).

   a. *I will have an increased awareness of positive stress-relieving behaviors (more options available to me in times of stress)*
   b. *I will be more able to remain present with my clients, in a nonjudgmental fashion, in session*
   c. *I will have an increased awareness and appreciation of my client's experiences of stress and coping behaviors*
   d. *I will be better able to manage my time instead of being constantly worried and getting behind*

4. **Intervention:** (please indicate what you will do to alter what you are not satisfied with above)

Objective: Increase knowledge about and experience with positive stress-relieving behaviors; increase in knowledge about NSSI behaviors

Strategies:

a. *Research and practice deep-breathing techniques*
b. *Try a new yoga class at the gym*
c. *Spend time with a friend at least once a week*
d. *Write in my journal when I am feeling stressed*
e. *Read information and research about NSSI*

5. I will know I have made some progress when:

My rating on the satisfaction scale will have increased from a 2 to a 6 (disgust) and a 5 to a 7 (coping attempts); I will have completed at least 3 of my strategies listed above.

A Final Note about Ethics

Supervisors are responsible for both clinician development and client care. In this service, they are also responsible for making sure that their supervisees are following ethical guidelines. For more information on NSSI and ethical codes, see Chapter 6. Part of our ethical obligation as clinicians is to recognize our need for self-care, resulting in an ethical responsibility for supervisors to follow through on this with supervisees. Supervisors should not assume that supervisees can clearly identify an ethical dilemma, so supervisors are reminded to check in with their supervisees often in order to gauge their understanding of ethical concerns.

In summary, supervision is an extremely important activity for client safety and well-being. It is also paramount for the personal and professional development of clinicians-in-training when working with clients who self-injure. Supervisors are encouraged to pay close attention to NSSI and its resulting dynamics and to monitor their supervisees' clinical work closely. In addition, supervisors are also encouraged to continue to monitor their own personal and professional development related to NSSI.

References

Bernard, J. M. (1979). Supervisor training: A discrimination model. *Counselor Education & Supervision, 19*, 60–68.

Bernard, J. M., & Goodyear, R. K. (2014). *Fundamentals of clinical supervision* (5th edition). Boston: Allyn and Bacon.

Boie, I., & Lopez, A. (2011). Supervision of counselors working with eating disorders: Utilizing the integrated developmental model. *The Clinical Supervisor, 30*, 215–234. doi: 10.1080/07325223.2011.607744

De Stefano, J., Atkins, S., Nelson Noble, R., & Heath, N. (2012). Am I competent enough to be doing this? A qualitative study of trainees' experiences working with clients who self-injure. *Counselling Psychology Quarterly, 25*(3), 289–305. doi: 10.1080/09515070.2012.698981

Granello, P. F. (2012). *Wellness counseling.* Upper Saddle River, NJ: Pearson.

Hettler, B. (1980). Wellness promotion on a university campus. *Family and Community Health, 3*, 77–79.

Hoffman, R. M., & Kress, V. E. (2008). Client non-suicidal self-injurious behavior: Considerations for clinical supervisors. *The Clinical Supervisor, 27*(1), 97–110. doi: 10.1080/07325220802221561

Juhnke, G. A. (1994). Teaching suicide risk assessment to counselor education students. *Counselor Education and Supervision, 34*, 52–57.

Kagan, N. (1980). *Interpersonal process recall.* East Lansing, MI: Author.

Lawson, G., & Venart, B. (2005). *Preventing counselor impairment: Vulnerability, wellness, and resilience.* Retrieved from http://www.counseling.org/wellness_taskforce/index.htm

Lenz, A. S., & Smith, R. L. (2010). Integrating wellness concepts within a clinical supervision model. *The Clinical Supervisor, 29*, 228–245. doi: 10.1080/07325223.2010.518511

McHale, J., & Felton, A. (2010). Self-harm: What's the problem? A literature review of the factors affecting attitudes towards self-harm. *Journal of Psychiatric and Mental Health Nursing, 17*, 732–740.

Myers, J. E., & Sweeney, T. J. (2005). The indivisible self: An evidence-based model of wellness (reprint). *Journal of Individual Psychology, 61*, 269–279.

Myers, J. E., Sweeney, T. J., & Witmer, J. M. (2000). The wheel of wellness: A holistic model for treatment planning. *Journal of Counseling & Development, 78*, 251–266.

Rayner, G. C., Allen, S. L., & Johnson, M. (2005). Countertransference and self-injury: A cognitive behavioral cycle. *Journal of Advanced Nursing, 50*, 12–19.

Wester, K., & Trepal, H. (2015). Non-suicidal self-injury: Exploring the connection among race, ethnic identity, and ethnic belonging. *Journal of College Student Development, 56*(2), 127–139.

Witmer, M. J., & Sweeney, T. J. (1991). A holistic model for wellness and prevention over the lifespan. *Journal of Counseling & Development, 71*, 140–148.

Zila, L. M., & Kiselica, M. S. (2001). Understanding and counseling self-mutilation in female adolescents and young adults. *Journal of Counseling & Development, 79*, 46–52.

eleven
NSSI Advocacy and Prevention

Although not new to the mental health professions, prevention and advocacy are relatively new areas in the world of NSSI. This chapter will explore topics including wellness, prevention, and advocacy. In addition, various example NSSI advocacy efforts will be presented.

Some mental health professionals practice from different models. The medical model proposes that mental health concerns are rooted in psychopathology. Mental health practitioners who practice from this orientation focus on a diagnosis and treatment path. While all clinicians understandably need to be aware of these concepts (e.g., diagnosis, treatment planning, psychotropic medications and their usage), some mental health professionals closely adhere to a wellness and developmental approach. This means that they always consider client concerns within developmental parameters. It also means that they take the term "human growth and development" quite seriously—meaning that they believe in client wellness instead of pathology.

In the introduction, wellness was defined as having emotional, spiritual, and social, among other, components. Wellness is all-encompassing of clients' lives and can impact an individual greatly. Clinicians believe that wellness is important, and this can definitely become one of the primary goals in the therapeutic relationship. Achieving enhanced wellness or improved lifestyle work–life integration can be the key to preventing many mental health concerns (Myers & Sweeney, 2008). The concepts of advocacy and prevention can be rooted in the wellness approach. Each will be considered below.

Advocacy

Advocacy in the mental health professions can include actions taken with or on behalf of clients. An advocate is someone who publically supports something that they believe in. Given the stigma of most mental health concerns, including NSSI, considering oneself an advocate can be a daunting prospect. In fact, some mental health professionals, such as counselors and social workers, consider advocacy one of their ethical obligations.

The American Counseling Association (ACA) endorsed the ACA Advocacy Competencies (Lewis, Arnold, House, & Toporek, 2003). These serve as guidelines for clinicians to be aware of the advocacy domains in which they are responsible for practicing. The competencies remind clinicians of important concepts such as empowerment (clinician acts with the client) or advocacy (clinician acts on behalf of the client). The competencies also address various levels of advocacy intervention (client/student, school/community, and public). Finally, these competencies also include client/student and system change at both the micro and macro levels. For example, micro level client advocacy related to NSSI could include such things as empowering a teen client to have a discussion with their parent about wanting

Box 11.1 Mental Health Professional Ethical Codes Related to Advocacy

American Counseling Association Code of Ethics (2014)

A.7.a. Advocacy

When appropriate, counselors advocate at individual, group, institutional, and societal levels to address potential barriers and obstacles that inhibit access and/or the growth and development of clients.

National Association of Social Workers (2008) Code of Ethics

6.04 Social and Political Action

(a) Social workers should engage in social and political action that seeks to ensure that all people have equal access to the resources, employment, services, and opportunities they require to meet their basic human needs and to develop fully.

to wear a long sleeve T-shirt while swimming. Large-scale, systemic advocacy could include participation in legislative efforts that center on ameliorating discrimination and removing barriers to access of mental health services. Thus, there exist many possibilities to become an NSSI advocate. Clinicians are charged with advocating in these efforts both with and on behalf of their clients and the communities they serve.

Sample Advocacy Activities

Because advocacy efforts related to NSSI are a relatively new topic, there are limited resources regarding these efforts. However, many organizations exist to raise awareness, educate the public and professionals, and improve access to treatment, support research, and advocate for the NSSI community at different levels. The activities below represent current advocacy efforts as well as other programs that could be adapted to focus on NSSI.

Organized or Group Advocacy Activities

Self-Injury Awareness Day (SIAD, March 1)

Many organizations representing various mental health concerns (e.g., domestic violence, suicide) have formally organized awareness days to highlight these issues. Self-Injury Awareness Day is recognized annually on March 1st. On this day, various events are held around the world to raise awareness of NSSI. There are orange or orange and purple colored ribbons and wristbands that can be worn by those who self-injure or worn in solidarity with those who do. There are also multiple websites (see http://www.lifesigns.org.uk/siad/ as an example) where you can get involved or encourage others to get involved with NSSI advocacy. Possible activities include: printing out a SIAD poster and putting it up, handing out NSSI fact sheets, wearing ribbons/wristbands, educating others about NSSI myths (e.g., only teen girls self-injure), making Public Service Announcements (PSAs) on your local media stations, sharing information about NSSI via social media, helping to create policies about NSSI in your school, club, or organization, or joining NSSI advocacy organizations and donating your time or money to the cause (Lifesigns, n.d.).

NSSI Awareness and Advocacy Conference

Organizations such as OCD Texas, an affiliate of the International Obsessive Compulsive Disorder Foundation (http://www.ocdtexas.org/), hold annual regional conferences in order to raise awareness and promote advocacy around these concerns and their treatment. Clinicians could partner with clients, their families, and other allies to put on a local conference related to NSSI. Sample events include sessions for family members of those who self-injure and sessions specific to certain groups of those who self-injure (under 10, teens, young adults, older adults, women, men, etc.). Conference offerings could also include speakers or panelists who have either provided treatment to those who self-injure or include those who have successfully gone through this treatment. Other components could include a mentoring program (survivor and someone in treatment; family-to-family mentoring) or consultations with local medical and mental health providers. Finally, fundraising could be an important component of such an event. Considerations such as planning time and event space would mean that considerable financial resources would be needed. Raising awareness of NSSI may also entail raising donations and funds to continue to pursue this important advocacy work.

Legislative Advocacy

Some organizations that advocate and support those who suffer from various mental health disorders (such as NEDA—the National Eating Disorders Association—www.nationaleatingdisorders.org) maintain active legislative advocacy programs. NEDA developed the Solutions Through Advocacy and Reform (STAR) program. According to their website, the purpose of the program is to "legislatively advocate for awareness, education, early intervention and prevention programs, funding for research, and improved access for the treatment of eating disorders" (NEDA, n.d.). This program has supported both state and federal efforts to advocate for early eating disorder screening, access to mental health services, concerns related to accurate advertising and media, and resolutions related to eating disorder awareness. They maintain an active website where members and interested parties can take action in these efforts. A similar program could be developed related to NSSI. For example, a program might be developed for school mental health professionals to engage in early screening and provide referrals for individuals and families for mental health services. Clinicians could provide outreach and advertising in their local communities and college campuses through public service announcements and op-ed pieces in their local newspapers about NSSI. These forms of outreach provide education and resources for individuals and families about where to receive help, as well as public awareness that NSSI does not equate "crazy."

Stigma Free Campaign

The National Alliance on Mental Illness (NAMI) (http://www.nami.org/) has a current campaign related to pledging to end stigma regarding mental illness. This type of campaign could be adapted, as there often exists stigma around these behaviors and those who struggle with NSSI. Various campaign components include: an actual electronic pledge that people can sign indicating their commitment to be stigma free, a social media campaign, and a call to action related to mental health issues (for more information see: https://www.nami.org/stigmafree#whatisstigmafree).

Research

The International Society for the Study of Self-injury (ISSS) (http://www.itriples.org) was founded in 2006. According to their website, the mission of the organization is to "advance scientific understanding of non-suicidal self-injury; influence and enhance non-suicidal self-injury assessment, treatment, prevention, education, and policy; and to foster collaboration among individuals dedicated to these aims" (n.d.). For those who are interested in collaborating, the organization holds an annual meeting.

Media Literacy Programs

There are high rates of information about NSSI currently available on the Internet, both in popular and social media. Given the pervasiveness of the media and its potential to influence these behaviors into everyday culture, it may play a role in the spread of NSSI, called contagion (Purington & Whitlock, 2010, p. 11). If youth are media consumers, then the information that they are digesting about NSSI has the potential to normalize, glamorize, or even promote these behaviors. While access and information that clients receive online needs to be assessed and monitored, there may also be positive aspects to the increased attention paid to NSSI in the media, such as raising awareness and increasing help-seeking (Purington & Whitlock, 2010). Purington and Whitlock (2010) suggest that it is possible to utilize a media literacy intervention both at school and in the home in order to encourage people to become critical consumers of media information about NSSI. In order to encourage crucial reflection on media messages, it is recommended that questions for reflection include such topics as who developed the media message and who was the message intended for, what is being conveyed, what is the message about (values, implications), how the message might be interpreted from different points of view, and how might the person want to respond, among others (Project Look Sharp, 2016). For more information about media literacy approaches and sample handouts that could be adapted, visit Project Look Sharp (www.projectlooksharp.org).

Individual Advocacy Activities

If you do not want to participate in an organized NSSI advocacy activity, there are still ways that you can be involved in advocacy efforts.

Wristbands and Ribbons

Sometimes, people want to wear a symbol of the cause that they are advocating for. By making or purchasing a wristband or ribbon, you are able to support NSSI organizations as well as advertise the cause. When people ask about the ribbon or wristband, you have a great opportunity to raise awareness about NSSI. Wristbands for NSSI awareness and advocacy are available for purchase on several of the websites mentioned later in this chapter.

Advertising

Other options that have the potential for high advocacy impact include providing information about NSSI through various channels such as social media (e.g., Twitter, Facebook, Snapchat, Periscope), printing off or creating a poster about NSSI facts, or writing letters to local politicians or organizations to highlight NSSI. Sample handouts, fact sheets, and posters are freely available on several of the websites mentioned in this chapter.

Becoming a Spokesperson

Another option for advocacy is to consider becoming a spokesperson for NSSI. If you have struggled with NSSI in the past, sharing your story can be a powerful way to advocate for others who are not as far along in their journey. You can give personal examples and testimony about the obstacles that you have faced in your recovery. Many organizations such as schools, universities, and conferences have the need to recruit speakers on various topics for different events.

Prevention

Prevention is also an important concept and can be integral to the support of wellness. Whereas sometimes some mental health professionals are primarily focused on secondary and tertiary prevention and intervention efforts, such as diagnosis, treatment, and remediation of concerns, other times they are invested in preventing these concerns from arising in the first place. This may mean that part of a mental health practitioner's work must focus on prevention efforts such as enhancing client parenting practices, leading groups on healthy relationship development with middle school students, or spending time working on developing mindfulness practices with older adults. These preventative efforts are thought to serve as buffers against developing or worsening mental health concerns.

Prevention can include primary efforts: those aimed at preventing NSSI before it begins, as well as secondary efforts that are aimed at decreasing the severity of NSSI once an individual is already engaging in these behaviors. According to Levine and Smolak (2006) prevention efforts are multifaceted and can include universal, selected, and targeted types. Universal prevention efforts are aimed at a larger institution or organization, or are designed to address larger societal norms. This may include forms of outreach such as public service announcements or posting information on social media outlets. An example may be a college or university providing outreach or education about NSSI for the entire student body, or a larger organization, such as the Cornell Research Program on Self-Injury and Recovery, providing resources to the general public for free access on their website. Selected intervention/prevention is typically aimed at individuals who do not have a specific issue or do not currently engage in NSSI. The goal of these efforts is to decrease the possibility that these individuals will engage in NSSI, as well as help to educate them about the behavior. An example of selected prevention is to provide education or workshops to train others on what NSSI is, or for school mental health professionals to provide classroom guidance to a particular group or grade level prior to the onset of NSSI. Finally, targeted prevention is aimed at those who are at risk for NSSI engagement. These are individuals who may be engaging in behaviors, or showing signs, that are indicators of factors related to NSSI. These include, but are not limited to, individuals exhibiting symptoms of depression or anxiety, those who have poor coping skills or already engage in other maladaptive or avoidant coping methods, and those who have difficulty communicating with others, including peers, family members, or professionals.

As we learned in Chapter 2, a variety of NSSI models purport that self-injuring behaviors arise from familial and biological factors, along with lack of coping or communication skills. Prevention may focus on targeting the risk factors for NSSI. Thus, prevention efforts specific to NSSI may include helping children and their parents to learn the early identification and expression of feelings and emotions. Efforts may also focus on developing a repertoire of healthy coping strategies aimed at different goals, such as emotion focused or active coping. Further, prevention efforts may take on cultural components such as helping facilitate connections and belonging within various client communities. An advocacy option is to develop a prevention program targeting some aspect of NSSI. The program could be directed towards clinicians, parents/families, or students/peers. The Cornell Research Program on Self-Injury website (http://www.selfinjury.bctr.cornell.edu/about-self-injury.html#tab13) contains recommendations for NSSI prevention efforts, including enhancing coping skills and social connection, targeting educational efforts at both professionals and peers, deconstructing media's influence, and reducing stigma around help-seeking. Developing a prevention program can take time and effort, and the results may not be immediately noticeable. However, this is an important area of future research related to NSSI.

Sample Prevention Programs

Similar to NSSI advocacy efforts, prevention programming is also a relatively new topic, so resources and research regarding these efforts are also limited. The programs and examples below represent prevention ideas related to NSSI that could be adapted. These efforts and activities have been suggested by organizations, authors, or have been conducted and implemented by the authors or other clinicians.

Student/Peer Programs

One aspect to consider on a more universal or targeted level is organized advocacy on school campuses (Trusty & Brown, 2005). For example, the first author was contacted by a middle school that requested her to come and talk to 7th and 8th grade students about self-injury. However, as mentioned throughout the treatment and interventions (Chapters 7 and 8), providing specifics about NSSI can be problematic. It can lead to increases in self-injury due to triggering individuals who currently engage in NSSI, providing ideas or creating a social contagion where students or individuals in the group setting talk about the behavior on a larger scale. So when this middle school requested an assembly talking about NSSI specifically, the first author compromised and indicated she would talk about coping and problem solving skills, of which NSSI would be one potential option individuals use to cope. Therefore, assemblies were provided separately for both grade levels in which various coping methods (both adaptive and maladaptive) were discussed. Specifically, coping methods were tied to actors, actresses, and artists whom teenagers would be familiar with in pop culture. Adolescent students were able to identify with these famous individuals and were able to indicate how they typically coped (e.g., punching other people, drinking, self-injury, or in more adaptive problem solving methods). Throughout the assembly, with hundreds of students, we talked about how these methods were helpful to the person or not helpful to the person, and if not helpful, what other problem solving strategies might be better implemented. During this presentation, the first author invited two students to open up the party prank "snake in a nut can," where springs pop out of a nut can when it is opened. The purpose of this activity was to demonstrate coping strategies. So while the conversation of problem solving was occurring in the assembly, the students were asked to put the "snakes" back in their cans. The person who had coped adaptively only had to put one "snake" back into the can, while the individual who had coped maladaptively had to put multiple snakes back in the can. The latter proved to be difficult, and the student usually had to ask other students for help. This helped to visually drive the point home that when an individual copes adaptively, it is easier to "put the lid back on" after a crisis or situation occurs; but when coping maladaptively (such as using NSSI), the problems never resolve, and thus it becomes more difficult to cope or alleviate the stress.

One study examined what adolescents believed that their peers (both online and in real life) could do to support someone who self-injured. The researchers discovered that the teens had specific suggestions involving listening, ending NSSI stigma, and reaching out to adults for help (Berger, Hasking, & Martin, 2014). A possible prevention advocacy option would be to develop a middle school class presentation program based on these suggestions. In addition to the presentation on topics including what NSSI is, where it comes from, and what to do about it, a handout could be developed to include the following specific suggestions for students:

Box 11.2 Peer Handout or Sign About NSSI

What should I do when my friends tell me they self-injure?

- Talk and listen—be a friend
- Tell an adult—teachers and parents want to assist
- Talk to someone at school—school counselors and teachers can help
- Don't judge them—let's end the stigma
- Work to raise awareness of self-injury at the school

Adapted from Berger and colleagues (2014)

Parent/Family Prevention Programs

Trusty and Brown (2005) remind school counselors and other mental health professionals that family advocacy and empowerment are key components of their professional responsibility. Developing family prevention programs involving NSSI can be crucial to support youths' well-being both at home and at school. Clinicians could consider partnering with the school's PTA or local community organizations or places of worship to offer such programming. Mental health professionals should also consider the level of prevention programming (primary or secondary).

Berge, Loth, Hanson, Croll-Lampert, and Neumark-Sztainer (2011) recommend that prevention programs be developed to support families during life cycle transitions such as those associated with changes in schooling, a major illness or hospitalization, the death of someone close, relationship changes, or abuse in order to buffer against the development of eating disorders (ED). Given the comorbidity of these behaviors, NSSI prevention programs targeting parents can include topics such as helping children and families to deal with stressful family dynamics associated with transitions (e.g., divorce) or abuse (physical, emotional, sexual).

In another study, those currently engaged in eating disorder treatment recommended that parents and families discuss both the role of managing feelings and coping mechanisms, as the inability to handle strong feelings or cope played an initial role in the development of their eating disorder (Loth, Neumark-Sztainer, & Croll, 2009). With this in mind, NSSI primary prevention efforts could also be aimed at parents of young children to assist caregivers with teaching their children to identify and express their emotions. Helping parents empower their children to develop a range of coping mechanisms could address some of the underlying NSSI dynamics later on.

Secondary prevention (aimed at decreasing the severity of behaviors once someone is already engaged) efforts could focus on supporting families and parents during their child's NSSI treatment. Programs could focus on ways to increase positive parent–child communication. The first author created and implemented a family information and support session about NSSI. Specifically, families were able to sign up and come to a 2-hour session where they were provided information about NSSI, how to communicate with their child, what behaviors may increase or cause the behavior to increase in frequency or severity, as well as time for each family member to ask questions and connect to each other in a form of support. Mental health professionals could conduct this type of informational session across various settings

Prevention/Education Programs for Other Professionals

Prevention programs may also target other professionals who work with those who self-injure and/or their families. Both authors have consulted with many school districts and presented at school counselor trainings regarding NSSI related to different school-age student populations and best practices for the school setting. In addition, the second author has spoken to other mental health professionals at a local eating disorder treatment center related to NSSI and its comorbidity with eating disorders/disordered-eating behaviors.

White, Trepal-Wollenzier, and Nolan (2002) provide recommendations for NSSI prevention on college campuses that include educational outreach to student life staff and resident assistants, mental health service referral information for faculty, and information about NSSI reactions in order to decrease stigma. College counselors can also provide NSSI awareness and prevention information on bulletin boards in the dorms and by linking helpful websites to the one for the counseling center (White et al., 2002). Wester and Trepal (2015) recommend that college counselors advocate and inform university first responders (university police, residence life staff, etc.) who may initially encounter a student who self-injures on campus. It has also been recommended that mental health professionals serve as advocates for students who self-injure on college campuses. At times, residence life or judicial affairs/student conduct staff may not fully understand these often stigmatized behaviors (White et al., 2002). In addition, many college campuses have policies related to mandatory withdrawal or time spent on leave from school related to various mental health concerns (e.g., NSSI discovered in the dorm setting, suicide attempts). Mental health professionals can advocate for students in these situations in order to increase the understanding of the university community. These are only a sample of the many opportunities that exist for mental health professionals to advocate for and prevent NSSI.

Protocols and Policies

Different K–12 schools, universities, and inpatient mental health facilities typically have protocols on how to intervene in various situations. This usually includes suicide or violent situations. Less often has this included protocols specific to NSSI. The difficulty with not having NSSI-specific protocols is that when secondary intervention is necessary, it is either unclear what steps to take, or NSSI is treated in a similar manner to suicidal behaviors. Given that in school or university settings, mental health professionals are not likely to be the first person to become aware of NSSI (e.g., first responders, campus police, teachers, peers), a protocol can be helpful in managing the situation effectively. Suggestions for NSSI protocols have been made for K–12 school systems, with less focus on college campuses or inpatient settings. However, the latter two settings may be able to alter the below-stated protocol to best fit their needs and setting.

Many different organizations and authors provide information about how schools need to create a school policy that separates NSSI from suicidal behaviors, such as the Cornell Research Program on Self-Injury and Recovery, and Toste and Heath (2010). The Cornell Research Program offers the majority of their resources for free online, including how schools can develop and implement a school protocol. Suggestions of what to include in a school protocol for NSSI are:

- Definitions and what NSSI actually includes
- How to identify NSSI, including student behavioral identifications (e.g., warm clothes for season, constant bracelets or watches in same location on body) as well as questions to ask students
- The chain of command for NSSI cases. More specifically, who to contact when NSSI is recognized, who to refer the student to, and if that person is not currently in the building, who the second person is that should be informed
- Who should become involved, such as should the school nurse always be informed, should teachers be notified or not, and if and when school administrators need to be informed

- When and if parents should be contacted. Most schools may have a policy that parents should always be contacted about youth high-risk behavior; however, keep in mind that sometimes it may be the parents or family that could increase the NSSI behaviors. Regardless of the decision, in order to take the guesswork out, a school NSSI policy should include if and when parents and legal guardians are contacted and what is provided to the parents (e.g., should parents be contacted when a student is dragging a safety pin across their skin versus when cutting with a razor blade)
- Who the main liaison is between student, school, and parents. This consistency can help the school staff members know who should be talking to the parent, and increases the uniformity of information provided to others
- When mental health referrals should be made or provided to student and parent for follow up services
- How frequently or when follow up should occur for students who have self-injured and/or their parents; and what this follow up might look like for low- versus high-risk cases of NSSI behaviors

School protocols are important so that all personnel in the school building understand what to do in the case of self-injury. This protocol, along with general treatment and information about NSSI behaviors, should be provided in training to all school personnel.

Box 11.3 Online Resources for NSSI

Below are some sample websites for organizations that highlight NSSI awareness. A brief description of each website is included.

Lifesigns

http://www.lifesigns.org.uk/

Lifesigns calls itself a self-injury guidance and support network. They maintain an active website with a plethora of resources related to NSSI advocacy, including a blog, a variety of informative fact sheets (for parents, males, general information, to create school policies), myth awareness, and social media links. They also maintain confidential support forums as well as selling NSSI awareness wristbands and engaging in fundraising. Lifesigns has a ton of great information for Self-Injury Awareness Day advocacy activities.

To Write Love on Her Arms

https://twloha.com/

To Write Love on Her Arms (TWLOHA) is a non-profit organization dedicated to providing hope and outreach to those struggling with self-injury, depression, addiction, and suicide. This group maintains a website and active blog, raises funds, and tries to bridge traditional links to services by holding music festivals or tours on college campuses. They also sell merchandise, such as their signature t-shirts, which also raise awareness of these issues.

Conclusion

There are many different things that mental health professionals can do to advocate for individuals who self-injure. This includes educating other professionals, including teachers and medical and mental health providers for individuals who may engage in NSSI. Advocacy can also include educating family members and providing a variety of resources; however, it does also include prevention efforts and the development of awareness.

References

American Counseling Association. (2014). *ACA code of ethics*. Alexandria, VA: Author.

Berge, J. M., Loth, K., Hanson, C., Croll-Lampert, J., & Neumark-Sztainer, D. (2011). Family life cycle transitions and the onset of eating disorders: A retrospective grounded theory approach. *Journal of Clinical Nursing, 21*, 1355–1363, doi: 10.1111/j.1365-2702.2011.03762.x

Berger, E., Hasking, P., & Martin, G. (2014). Adolescents' perspectives of youth non-suicidal self-injury prevention. *Youth & Society*, 1–20. doi: 10.1177/0044118X13520561

ISSS (n.d.). Retrieved from http://www.itriples.org

Levine, M. P., & Smolak, L. (2006). *The prevention of eating problems and eating disorders: Theory, research, and practice*. Mahwah, NJ: Lawrence Erlbaum.

Lewis, J., Arnold, M. S., House, R., & Toporek, R. L. (2003). *Advocacy competencies: American counseling association task force on advocacy competencies*. Retrieved from http://www.counseling.org/Resources/Competencies/Advocacy_Competencies.pdf

Lifesigns (n.d.). Retrieved from http://www.lifesigns.org.uk/siad/

Loth, K., Neumark-Sztainer, D., & Croll, J. K. (2009). Informing family approaches to eating disorder prevention: Perspectives of those who have been there. *International Journal of Eating Disorders, 42*, 146–152.

Myers, J. E., & Sweeney, T. J. (2008). Wellness counseling: The evidence base for practice. *Journal of Counseling & Development, 86*, 482–493.

National Association of Social Workers (NASW). (2008). *Code of ethics of the national association of social workers*. Washington, DC: Author.

NEDA (n.d.). Retrieved from http://www.nationaleatingdisorders.org/

Project Look Sharp. (2016). *Key questions to ask when analyzing media messages*. Retrieved March 11, 2016 from http://www.projectlooksharp.org/?action=medialithandouts

Purington, A., & Whitlock, J. (2010). Non-suicidal self-injury in the media. *The Prevention Researcher, 17*(1), 11–13.

Toste, J. R., & Heath, N. L. (2010). School response to non-suicidal self-injury. *The Prevention Researcher, 17*, 14–17.

Trusty, J., & Brown, D. (2005). Advocacy competencies for professional school counselors. *Professional School Counseling, 8*, 259–265.

Wester, K., & Trepal, H. (2015). Non-suicidal self-injury: Exploring the connection among race, ethnic identity, and ethnic belonging. *Journal of College Student Development, 56*(2), 127–139.

White, V. E., Trepal-Wollenzier, H., & Nolan, J. (2002). College students and self-injury: Intervention strategies for counselors. *Journal of College Counseling, 5*, 105–113.

Index

For Product Safety Concerns and Information please contact our EU representative GPSR@taylorandfrancis.com
Taylor & Francis Verlag GmbH, Kaufingerstraße 24, 80331 München, Germany

www.ingramcontent.com/pod-product-compliance
Ingram Content Group UK Ltd.
Pitfield, Milton Keynes, MK11 3LW, UK
UKHW021305260926
475702UK00048B/685
9781138780354